Russian

A ROUGH GUIDE
PHRASEBOOK

Compiled
by Lexus

Credits

Compiled by Lexus with Irina and Alistair MacLean

Lexus Series Editor:	Sally Davies
Rough Guides Phrasebook Editor:	Jonathan Buckley
Rough Guides Series Editor:	Mark Ellingham

This first edition published in 1997 by Rough Guides Ltd, 1 Mercer Street, London WC2H 9QJ.

Distributed by the Penguin Group.

Penguin Books Ltd, 27 Wrights Lane, London W8 5TZ
Penguin Books USA Inc., 375 Hudson Street, New York 10014, USA
Penguin Books Australia Ltd, 487 Maroondah Highway, PO Box 257,
     Ringwood, Victoria 3134, Australia
Penguin Books Canada Ltd, Alcorn Avenue, Toronto, Ontario, Canada
     M4V 1E4
Penguin Books (NZ) Ltd, 182-190 Wairau Road, Auckland 10, New Zealand

Typeset in Rough Serif and Rough Sans with Minion Cyrillic Regular to an
     original design by Henry Iles.
Printed by Cox & Wyman Ltd, Reading.

British Library Cataloguing in Publication Data
A catalogue for this book is available from the British Library.

ISBN 1-85828-251-9

CONTENTS

INTRODUCTION

The Rough Guide Russian phrasebook is a highly practical introduction to the contemporary language. Laid out in clear A-Z style, it uses key-word referencing to lead you straight to the words and phrases you want – so if you need to book a room, just look up 'room'. The Rough Guide gets straight to the point in every situation, in bars and shops, on trains and buses, and in hotels and banks.

The main part of the Rough Guide is a double dictionary: English-Russian then Russian-English. Before that, there's a section called **The Basics**, which sets out the fundamental rules of the language and its pronunciation, with plenty of practical examples. You'll also find here other essentials like numbers, dates, telling the time and basic phrases.

Forming the heart of the guide, the **English-Russian** section gives easy-to-use transliterations of the Russian words, and to get you involved quickly in two-way communication, the Rough Guide includes dialogues featuring typical responses on key topics – such as renting a car and asking directions. Feature boxes fill you in on cultural pitfalls as well as the simple mechanics of how to make a phone call, what to do in an emergency, where to change money and more. Throughout this section, cross-references enable you to pinpoint key facts and phrases, while asterisked words indicate where further information can be found in The Basics.

In the **Russian-English** dictionary, we've given not just the phrases you're likely to hear (starting with a selection of slang and colloquialisms), but also all the signs, labels, instructions and other basic words you might come across in print or in public places.

Finally the Rough Guide rounds off with an extensive **Menu Reader**. Consisting of food and drink sections (each starting with a list of essential terms), it's indispensable whether you're eating out, stopping for a quick drink or browsing through a local food market.

счастливого пути!
sh-chasl**ee**vava poot**ee**!
have a good trip!

The Basics

PRONUNCIATION

Throughout this book Russian words have been transliterated into romanized form (see the Cyrillic Alphabet on pages 4–5) so that they can be read as though they were English bearing in mind the notes on pronunciation given below:

a	as in **a**t	iy	i as in bit followed by
ay	as in m**ay**		y as in **y**es
e	as in m**e**t	J	like the s in
g	hard g as in **g**et		measure
H	a guttural ch as in the	o	as in n**o**t
	Scottish word lo**ch**	s	as in mi**ss**
i	as in b**i**t	y	as in **y**es
I	i sound as in **I** or **eye**	ye	as in **ye**s

Letters given in bold type indicate the part of the word to be stressed.

ABBREVIATIONS

acc	accusative case	m	masculine
adj	adjective	n	neuter
dat	dative case	nom	nominative case
f	feminine	pl	plural
fam	familiar	pol	polite
gen	genitive case	prep	prepositional case
instr	instrumental case	sing	singular

NOTES

When two forms of the verb are given in the dictionary sections, the first form is the imperfective aspect and the second is the perfective aspect (see The Basics page 23 for further information).

THE CYRILLIC ALPHABET

Set out below is the Cyrillic alphabet, the names of the letters and the system of transliteration used in this book:

А, а	ah	a as in **a**t
Б, б	beh	b
В, в	veh	v
Г, г	geh	g as in **g**et or v
Д, д	deh	d
Е, е	yeh	ye as in **ye**s
Ё, ё	yo	yo as in **yo**nder
Ж, ж	Jeh	J: pronounced like the s in mea**s**ure
З, з	zeh	z
И, и	ee	ee
Й, й	ee kratka-yeh	sometimes y as in bo**y**, but usually silent
К, к	ka	k
Л, л	el	l
М, м	em	m
Н, н	en	n
О, о	o	when stressed, o as in n**o**t; when unstressed, a as in **a**t
П, п	peh	p
Р, р	er	r
С, с	es	s
Т, т	teh	t
У, у	oo	oo as in b**oo**t
Ф, ф	ef	f
Х, х	Ha	H: a guttural ch as in the Scottish word lo**ch**
Ц, ц	tseh	ts as in ha**ts**
Ч, ч	cheh	ch as in **ch**urch
Ш, ш	sha	sh as in **sh**ip
Щ, щ	sh-cha	sh-ch
Ъ, ъ	tvyordi znak	hard sign: no sound, but indicates hardening of preceding consonant
Ы, ы	iy	i as in b**i**t followed by y as in **y**es
Ь, ь	myaHkee znak	soft sign: no sound but softens preceding letter

Э, э	eh	e as in **e**nd
Ю, ю	yoo	yoo
Я, я	ya	ya as in **ya**m

б, в, г, д and з may be pronounced p, f, k, t and s respectively, usually when they occur at the end of a word or when preceding certain consonants. For example:

выход [víyнat] exit   **вход** [fнot] entrance

Combinations and Diphthongs

АЙ, ай	I:	i sound as in **I** or **eye**; ee if unstressed
ЕЙ, ей	yay	
ИЙ, ий	ee	
ОЙ, ой	oy	as in **boy**; I: i sound as in **I** or **eye** if unstressed
ЫЙ, ый	i	as in b**i**t

RUSSIAN HANDWRITING

Handwritten Russian does not always resemble the printed characters. The letters below are examples of actual Russian handwriting:

А, а	К, к	Х, х
Б, б	Л, л	Ц, ц
В, в	М, м	Ч, ч
Г, г	Н, н	Ш, ш
Д, д	О, о	Щ, щ
Е, е	П, п	Ъ, ъ
Ё, ё	Р, р	Ы, ы
Ж, ж	С, с	Ь, ь
З, з	Т, т	Э, э
И, и	У, у	Ю, ю
Й, й	Ф, ф	Я, я

ARTICLES

There are no articles (a, an, the) in Russian:

окно
akn**o**
window/a window/the window

полотенце
palat**ye**ntseh
towel/a towel/the towel

Context clarifies the equivalent English article:

вы не возражаете, если я открою окно ...?
viy nyeh vazra**J**a-yetyeh, **ye**slee ya atkr**o**-yoo akn**o**?
do you mind if I open the window?

дайте мне, пожалуйста, полотенце
d**I**tyeh mnyeh pa**J**a**l**sta, palat**ye**nseh
can I have a towel?

NOUNS AND CASES

Nouns

Russian nouns have one of three genders — masculine, feminine or neuter. The gender is determined by the noun ending. Most nouns ending in a consonant are masculine:

вагон	отец	дом
vag**on**	at**ye**ts	dom
carriage	father	house

Nouns ending in -й are also masculine:

музей	трамвай
mooz**yay**	tramv**I**
museum	tram

Most nouns ending in -a or -я are feminine:

машина	сестра
mash**iy**na	syestr**a**
car	sister

учительница
ooch**ee**tyelneetsa
teacher (woman)

тётя	спальня
t**yo**tya	sp**a**lnya
aunt	bedroom

гостья
g**o**stya
guest (woman)

Most nouns ending in a soft sign -ь are feminine, but some are masculine (indicated by (f) or (m) in the English-Russian section of this book):

мелочь (f)	дверь (f)
m**ye**lach	dvyer
small change	door

кровать (f)
krav**a**t
bed

рубль (m)	день (m)
roobl	dyen
rouble	day

картофель (m)
kart**o**fyel
potato

Most nouns ending in **-o** or **-e** are neuter:

блюдо	пиво	вино
bl**yoo**da	p**ee**va	veen**o**
dish	beer	wine

море	отделение
m**o**ryeh	od-dyel**ye**nee-yeh
sea	department

Nouns ending in **-мя** are neuter:

время	имя
vr**ye**mya	**ee**mya
time	first name

Some nouns ending in **-a** or **-я** that refer to males are masculine:

мужчина	дядя
moosh-ch**ee**na	d**ya**-dya
man	uncle

Cases

Russian has six cases: nominative, accusative, genitive, dative, instrumental and prepositional. Noun endings change depending on the case. The case endings used depend on the following factors:

- whether the noun is masculine inanimate (objects), masculine

animate (people or animals), feminine or neuter

- whether the noun is singular or plural

- whether the noun stem ends in г, к, х, ч, щ, ж or ш, in which case и is used instead of ы in the ending

Nominative Case

The nominative is the case of the subject of a sentence. In the following examples, 'shop' and 'he' are in the nominative:

магазин открыт
magaz**ee**n atkr**i**yt
the shop is open

он сегодня приехал
on syev**o**dnya pree-**ye**Hal
he arrived today

Accusative Case

The object of most verbs takes the accusative. In the following examples the objects (the sights, stamps and pen) are in the accusative:

мы хотим осмотреть
    достопримечательности
miy Hat**ee**m asmatr**ye**t
dastapreemyech**a**tyelnastee
we want to see the sights

вы продаёте марки?
viy prada-**yo**tyeh m**a**rkee?
do you sell stamps?

вы не одолжите ручку?
viy nyeh adal.J**i**tyeh **roo**chkoo?
may I borrow your pen?

Some prepositions indicating motion or direction towards something are followed by the accusative:

в
v
to; into

на
na
to; onto

через
ch**ye**ryes
through

в Москву
vmaskv**oo**
to Moscow

мы едем на вокзал
miy **ye**dyem na vakz**a**l
we're going to the station

я пройду через парк
ya prid**oo** ch**ye**ryes park
I'll walk through the park

Genitive Case

The genitive is used to indicate possession:

машина Кати
mash**i**yna k**a**tee
Katya's car

There is no word for 'of' in Russian. The genitive is used to translate 'of':

бутылка водки
boot**i**ylka v**o**tkee
a bottle of vodka

плитка шоколада
pl**ee**tka shakal**a**da
a bar of chocolate

The genitive is also used after some prepositions, for example:

до
do
until; to

у
oo
by; at

около
okala
near, by; beside; about

до Москвы
da maskv**iy**
to Moscow

у Саши
oo s**a**shi
at Sasha's house

около гостиницы
okala gast**ee**neetsi
beside the hotel

Dative Case

The dative is used for indirect objects with verbs like 'to give' and 'to send'. It often corresponds to 'to' (as in 'to me') in English:

дайте мне ..., пожалуйста
d**i**tyeh mnyeh ..., pa**l**alsta
please give me ...

я дал ему это
ya dal yem**oo** **e**ta
I gave it to him

See the forms of personal pronouns on pages 21–22.

The dative is also used after some prepositions, for example:

к
k
to, towards

по
pa
on; along

к вокзалу
k vakz**a**loo
to the station

по улице
pa **oo**leetseh
along the street

Instrumental Case

The instrumental is used to show by whom or by what means an action is carried out. It is used to translate 'by' when referring to means of transport:

мы приехали поездом
miy pree-**ye**Halee p**o**-yezdam
we came by train

авиапочтой
avee-a-p**o**chtI
by airmail

The instrumental is also used with some prepositions:

под
pot
under

перед
p**ye**ryet
before; in front of

с
s
with

под столом
pat stal**o**m
under the table

перед обедом
p**ye**ryed ab**ye**dam
before lunch

я пью чай с лимоном
ya pyoo chI sleem**o**nam
I take tea with lemon

Prepositional Case

The prepositional is used with most prepositions which indicate the position or location of something:

на
na
at; on

в
v
at; in

на самолёте	в городе
na samal**yo**tyeh	vg**o**ratyeh
on the plane	in the town

на улице	на вокзале
na **oo**leetseh	na vakz**a**lyeh
on the street	at the station

It is also used with the preposition:

о
o
about

они говорили о фильме
anee gavar**ee**lee a f**ee**lmyeh
they were talking about the film

Numbers and Cases

Numbers in Russian also determine the case of the noun. 1 and all numbers ending in 1 (eg 21, 31 and so on) are followed by a noun in the nominative singular; 2, 3, and 4 and all numbers ending in 2, 3, and 4 (except for 11, 12, 13 and 14) take the genitive singular; all other numbers (including 11, 12, 13 and 14) take the genitive plural:

одна бутылка	две бутылки
adn**a** boot**iy**lka	dvyeh boot**iy**lkee
one bottle	two bottles

три женщины
tree Jensh-cheeni
three women

двадцать одна женщина
dv**a**tsat adn**a** Jensh-cheena
21 women

один час	семь часов
ad**ee**n chas	syem chas**of**
one hour	seven hours

двадцать четыре часа
dv**a**tsat chyet**iy**ryeh chas**a**
24 hours

See Numbers on pages 32–33.

Noun Cases

In the following tables, when the noun stem ends in г, ж, к, х, ч, ш or щ, и is used instead of ы in the noun endings, for example:

язык/языки [yaz**iy**k/yaz**iy**kee]
language/languages

марка/марки [m**a**rka/m**a**rkee]
stamp/stamps

masculine singular inanimate

	carriage	museum	rouble
nom	**вагон**	**музей**	**рубль**
	vag**o**n	mooz**yay**	roobl
acc	**вагон**	**музей**	**рубль**
	vag**o**n	mooz**yay**	roobl
gen	**вагона**	**музея**	**рубля**
	vag**o**na	mooz**yeh**-ya	roobl**ya**
dat	**вагону**	**музею**	**рублю**
	vag**o**noo	mooz**yeh**-yoo	roobl**yoo**
instr	**вагоном**	**музеем**	**рублем**
	vag**o**nam	mooz**yeh**-yem	roobl**yo**m
prep	**вагоне**	**музее**	**рубле**
	vag**o**nyeh	mooz**yeh**-yeh	roobl**yeh**

masculine singular animate

	artist	driver
nom	**художник**	**водитель**
	Hood**o**Jneek	vad**ee**tyel
acc	**художника**	**водителя**
	Hood**o**Jneeka	vad**ee**tyelya
gen	**художника**	**водителя**
	Hood**o**Jneeka	vad**ee**tyelya
dat	**художнику**	**водителю**
	Hood**o**Jneekoo	vad**ee**tyelyoo
instr	**художником**	**водителем**
	Hood**o**Jneekam	vad**ee**tyelyem
prep	**художнике**	**водителе**
	Hood**o**Jneekyeh	vad**ee**tyelyeh

feminine singular

	car	aunt	door
nom	**машина**	**тётя**	**дверь**
	mash**iy**na	t**yo**tya	dvyer
acc	**машину**	**тётю**	**дверь**
	mash**iy**noo	t**yo**tyoo	dvyer
gen	**машины**	**тёти**	**двери**
	mash**iy**ni	t**yo**tee	dvy**e**ree

	car	aunt	door
	машине	**тёте**	**двери**
	mash**iy**nyeh	**tyo**tyeh	dv**ye**ree
instr	**машиной**	**тётей**	**дверью**
	mash**iy**nı	**tyo**tyay	dv**ye**ryoo
prep	**машине**	**тёте**	**двери**
	mash**iy**nyeh	**tyo**tyeh	dv**ye**ree

dat

neuter singular

	dish	sea	first name	department
nom	**блюдо**	**море**	**имя**	**отделение**
	bl**yoo**da	**mo**ryeh	**ee**mya	ad-dyel**ye**nee-yeh
acc	**блюдо**	**море**	**имя**	**отделение**
	bl**yoo**da	**mo**ryeh	**ee**mya	ad-dyel**ye**nee-yeh
gen	**блюда**	**моря**	**имени**	**отделения**
	bl**yoo**da	**mo**rya	**ee**myenee	ad-dyel**ye**nee-ya
dat	**блюду**	**морю**	**имени**	**отделению**
	bl**yoo**doo	**mo**ryoo	**ee**myenee	ad-dyel**ye**nee-yoo
instr	**блюдом**	**морем**	**именем**	**отделением**
	bl**yoo**dam	**mo**ryem	**ee**myenyem	ad-dyel**ye**nee-yem
prep	**блюде**	**море**	**имени**	**отделении**
	bl**yoo**dyeh	**mo**ryeh	**ee**myenee	ad-dyel**ye**nee-ee

masculine plural inanimate

	carriage	museum	rouble
nom	**вагоны**	**музеи**	**рубли**
	vag**o**ni	mooz**yeh**-ee	roobl**ee**
acc	**вагоны**	**музеи**	**рубли**
	vag**o**ni	mooz**yeh**-ee	roobl**ee**
gen	**вагонов**	**музеев**	**рублей**
	vag**o**naf	mooz**yeh**-yef	roobl**yay**
dat	**вагонам**	**музеям**	**рублям**
	vag**o**nam	mooz**yeh**-yam	roobl**ya**m
instr	**вагонами**	**музеями**	**рублями**
	vag**o**namee	mooz**yeh**-yamee	roobl**ya**mee
prep	**вагонах**	**музеях**	**рублях**
	vag**o**naн	mooz**yeh**-yaн	roobl**ya**н

masculine plural animate

	artist	driver
nom	**художники**	**водители**
	ноod**o**Jneekee	vad**ee**tyelee
acc	**художников**	**водителей**
	ноod**o**Jneekaf	vad**ee**tyelyay
gen	**художников**	**водителей**
	ноod**o**Jneekaf	vad**ee**tyelyay
dat	**художникам**	**водителям**
	ноod**o**Jneekam	vad**ee**tyelyam
instr	**художниками**	**водителями**
	ноod**o**Jneekamee	vad**ee**tyelyamee
prep	**художниках**	**водителях**
	ноod**o**JneekaH	vad**ee**tyelyaH

feminine plural

	car	aunt	door
nom	**машины**	**тёти**	**двери**
	mash**i**yni	t**yo**tee	dv**ye**ree
acc	**машины**	**тётей**	**двери**
	mash**i**yni	t**yo**tyay	dv**ye**ree
gen	**машин**	**тётей**	**дверей**
	mash**i**yn	t**yo**tyay	dvyer**yay**
dat	**машинам**	**тётям**	**дверям**
	mash**i**ynam	t**yo**tyam	dvyer**yam**
instr	**машинами**	**тётями**	**дверями**
	mash**i**ynamee	t**yo**tyamee	dvyer**ya**mee
prep	**машинах**	**тётях**	**дверях**
	mash**i**ynaH	t**yo**tyaH	dvyer**ya**H

neuter plural

	dish	sea	first name	department
nom	**блюда**	**моря**	**имена**	**отделения**
	bl**yoo**da	mar**ya**	eemyen**a**	ad-dyel**ye**nee-ya
acc	**блюда**	**моря**	**имена**	**отделения**
	bl**yoo**da	mar**ya**	eemyen**a**	ad-dyel**ye**nee-ya
gen	**блюд**	**морей**	**имён**	**отделений**
	bl**yoo**t	mar**yay**	eem**yo**n	ad-dyel**ye**nee

	dish	sea	first name	department
dat	блюдам	морям	именам	отделениям
	blyoodam	maryam	eemyenam	ad-dyelyenee-yam
instr	блюдами	морями	именами	отделениями
	blyoodamee	maryamee	eemyenamee	ad-dyelyenee-yamee
prep	блюдах	морях	именах	отделениях
	blyoodaн	maryaн	eemyenaн	ad-dyelyenee-yaн

Irregular Plurals

Several common nouns have irregular plurals:

дом/дома	[dom/dama]	house/houses
поезд/поезда	[poyest/payezda]	train/trains
город/города	[gorat/garada]	town/towns
номер/номера	[nomyer/namyera]	room/rooms; number/numbers
сестра/сёстры	[syestra/syostri]	sister/sisters
брат/братья	[brat/bratya]	brother/brothers
мать/матери	[mat/matyeree]	mother/mothers
сын/сыновья	[siyn/sinavya]	son/sons
дочь/дочери	[doch/dochyeree]	daughter/daughters
друг/друзья	[drook/droozya]	friend/friends

Some common Russian nouns do not change in the plural or according to case and are known as indeclinable nouns:

кафе	[kafeh]	cafe
кино	[keeno]	cinema
кофе	[kofyeh]	coffee
метро	[myetro]	underground, (US) subway
пальто	[palto]	overcoat
такси	[taksee]	taxi
фойе	[fi-yeh]	foyer

Prepositions

The following are some common prepositions and the cases they take (see also pages 8–10):

без [byes] (+ gen) without
в [v] (+ acc) to
в [v] (+ prep) in
для [dlya] (+ gen) for
до [do] (+ gen) before; until
за [za] (+ acc) behind; beyond; after; over
за [za] (+ instr) behind; beyond; at
между [myeJdoo] (+ instr) between; among
на [na] (+ acc) to

на [na] (+ prep) on
над [nat] (+ instr) above
напротив [naproteef] (+ gen) opposite
о [o] (+ prep) about
около [okala] (+ gen) about; near
от [ot] (+ gen) from
перед [pyeryed] (+ instr) in front of; before
по [po] (+ dat) on; along
под [pot] (+ instr) under
после [poslyeh] (+ gen) after
при [pree] (+ prep) by; at
с [s] (+ instr) with
через [chyeryes] (+ acc) through, via

ADJECTIVES

Adjectives agree in case, gender and number with the nouns to which they refer.

Most Russian adjectives end in -ый and change as follows:

	masculine	singular feminine	neuter	plural
красивый [kraseevi] beautiful				
nom	красивый	красивая	красивое	красивые
	kraseevi	kraseeva-ya	kraseeva-yeh	kraseevi-yeh
acc	красивый	красивую	красивое	красивые
	kraseevi	kraseevoo-yoo	kraseeva-yeh	kraseevi-yeh
gen	красивого	красивой	красивого	красивых
	kraseevava	kraseevi	kraseevava	kraseeviH
dat	красивому	красивой	красивому	красивым
	kraseevamoo	kraseevi	kraseevamoo	kraseevim
instr	красивым	красивой	красивым	красивыми
	kraseevim	kraseevi	kraseevim	kraseevimee
prep	красивом	красивой	красивом	красивых
	kraseevam	kraseevi	kraseevam	kraseeviH

Some adjectives ending in -ий (often preceded by г, ж, к, х, ч, ш, щ) change as follows:

		singular		plural
	masculine	feminine	neuter	
зимний [z**ee**mnee] winter, winter's				
nom	**зимний**	**зимняя**	**зимнее**	**зимние**
	z**ee**mnee	z**ee**mnya-ya	z**ee**mnyeh-yeh	z**ee**mnee-yeh
acc	**зимний**	**зимнюю**	**зимнее**	**зимние**
	z**ee**mnee	z**ee**mnyoo-yoo	z**ee**mnyeh-yeh	z**ee**mnee-yeh
gen	**зимнего**	**зимней**	**зимнего**	**зимних**
	z**ee**mnyeva	z**ee**mnyay	z**ee**mnyeva	z**ee**mneeн
dat	**зимнему**	**зимней**	**зимнему**	**зимним**
	z**ee**mnyemoo	z**ee**mnyay	z**ee**mnyemoo	z**ee**mneem
instr	**зимним**	**зимней**	**зимним**	**зимними**
	z**ee**mneem	z**ee**mnyay	z**ee**mneem	z**ee**mneemee
prep	**зимнем**	**зимней**	**зимнем**	**зимних**
	z**ee**mnyem	z**ee**mnyay	z**ee**mnyem	z**ee**mneeн

		singular		plural
	masculine	feminine	neuter	
хороший Har**o**shi good				
nom	**хороший**	**хорошая**	**хорошее**	**хорошие**
	Har**o**shi	Har**o**sha-ya	Har**o**sheh-yeh	Har**o**shi-yeh
acc	**хороший**	**хорошую**	**хорошее**	**хорошие**
	Har**o**shi	Har**o**shoo-yoo	Har**o**sheh-yeh	Har**o**shi-yeh
gen	**хорошего**	**хорошей**	**хорошего**	**хороших**
	Har**o**sheva	Har**o**shay	Har**o**sheva	Har**o**shiн
dat	**хорошему**	**хорошей**	**хорошему**	**хорошим**
	Har**o**shemoo	Har**o**shay	Har**o**shemoo	Har**o**shim
instr	**хорошим**	**хорошей**	**хорошим**	**хорошими**
	Har**o**shim	Har**o**shay	Har**o**shim	Har**o**shimee
prep	**хорошем**	**хорошей**	**хорошем**	**хороших**
	Har**o**shem	Har**o**shay	Har**o**shem	Har**o**shiн

Some adjectives ending in -ой (when the stress is on the ending) change as follows:

	masculine	singular feminine	neuter	plural
большой [balsh**oy**] big				
nom	**большой** balsh**oy**	**большая** balsha-ya	**большое** balsho-yeh	**большие** balsh**iy**-yeh
acc	**большой** balsh**oy**	**большую** balsh**oo**-yoo	**большое** balsho-yeh	**большие** balsh**iy**-yeh
gen	**большого** balsh**o**va	**большой** balsh**oy**	**большого** balshova	**больших** balsh**iy**н
dat	**большому** balsh**o**moo	**большой** balsh**oy**	**большому** balsho-moo	**большим** balsh**iy**m
instr	**большим** balsh**iy**m	**большой** balsh**oy**	**большим** balsh**iy**m	**большими** balsh**iy**mee
prep	**большом** balsh**o**m	**большой** balsh**oy**	**большом** balshom	**больших** balsh**iy**н

красивая картина
kras**ee**va-ya kart**ee**na
a beautiful picture

мне нравится русское пиво
mnyeh nr**a**veetsa r**oo**ska-yeh
p**ee**va
I like Russian beer

это хорошая гостиница
eta нar**o**sha-ya gast**ee**neetsa
it's a good hotel

Comparatives

The comparative of adjectives is generally formed by adding the words 'more' or 'less' in front of the adjective and noun:

более [b**o**lyeh-yeh] more
менее [m**ye**nyeh-yeh] less

более интересный
b**o**lyeh-yeh eentyer**ye**sni
more interesting

менее дорогой
m**ye**nyeh-yeh darag**oy**
less expensive

Some common adjectives have irregular comparatives:

большой [balsh**oy**] big
больше [b**o**lsheh] bigger
маленький [m**a**lyenkee]
  small
меньше [m**ye**nsheh] smaller
старый [st**a**ri] old
старше [st**a**rsheh] older
дорогой [darag**oy**] dear
дороже [dar**o**Jeh] dearer
дешёвый [dy**e**shovi] cheap
дешевле [dyesh**e**vlyeh]
  cheaper

'Than' is **чем** [chyem]:

это дешевле, чем я думал
eta dyesh**e**vlyeh, chyem ya d**oo**mal
it's cheaper than I thought

Superlatives

To form the superlative, add the adverb **наиболее** [na-eebolyeh-yeh] or the particle **самый** [sami] in front of the adjective and noun:

> **наиболее удобный**
> na-eebolyeh-yeh oodobni
> the most convenient

> **самый популярный**
> sami papoolyarni
> the most popular

ADVERBS

To form the adverb, remove the final -ый or -ий from the adjective and add -о:

хороший	хорошо
Haroshi	Harasho
good	well

медленный	медленно
myedlyen-ni	myedlyen-na
slow	slowly

DEMONSTRATIVES

The demonstratives are:

этот	эти
this (one)	these

тот	те
that (one)	those

In Russian, the demonstrative agrees with the gender and case of the noun to which it refers. этот and эти change as follows:

	masculine	feminine	neuter	plural
nom	этот	эта	это	эти
	etat	eta	eta	etee
acc	этот	эту	это	эти
	etat	etoo	eta	etee
gen	этого	этой	этого	этих
	etava	etI	etava	eteeH
dat	этому	этой	этому	этим
	etamoo	etI	etamoo	eteem
instr	этим	этой	этим	этими
	eteem	etI	eteem	eteemee
prep	этом	этой	этом	этих
	etam	etI	etam	eteeH

я этого не заказывал
ya etava nyeh zakazival
I didn't order this

эти открытки, пожалуйста
etee atkriytkee, paJalsta
these cards please

тот and **те** change as follows:

	masculine	feminine	neuter	plural
nom	**тот**	**та**	**то**	**те**
	tot	ta	to	tyeh
acc	**тот**	**ту**	**то**	**те**
	tot	too	to	tyeh
gen	**того**	**той**	**того**	**тех**
	tavo	toy	tavo	tyeh
dat	**тому**	**той**	**тому**	**тем**
	tamoo	toy	tamoo	tyem
instr	**тем**	**той**	**тем**	**теми**
	tyem	toy	tyem	t**ye**mee
prep	**том**	**той**	**том**	**тех**
	tom	toy	tom	tyeh

я зайду в тот магазин
ya zīd**oo** ftot magaz**ee**n
I'll pop into that shop

можна взглянуть на ту книгу?
mo**J**na vzglyan**oo**t na too kn**ee**goo?
can I see that book?

POSSESSIVES

Possessive adjectives and pronouns are as follows:

мой	[moy]	my; mine	**наш**	[nash]	our; ours
твой	[tvoy]	your (fam); yours	**ваш**	[vash]	your (sing pol or
его	[yevo]	his/its			pl); yours
её	[yeh-yo]	her; hers	**их**	[eeн]	their; theirs

See page 22 for more on the use of **твой** and **ваш**.

	masculine	feminine	neuter	plural
nom	**мой**	**моя**	**моё**	**мои**
	moy	ma-y**a**	ma-y**o**	ma-**ee**
acc	**мой**	**мою**	**моё**	**мои**
	moy	ma-y**oo**	ma-y**o**	ma-**ee**
gen	**моего**	**моей**	**моего**	**моих**
	ma-yev**o**	ma-**yay**	ma-yev**o**	ma-**ee**н

	masculine	feminine	neuter	plural
dat	моему	моей	моему	моим
	ma-yemoo	ma-yay	ma-yemoo	ma-eem
instr	моим	моей	моим	моими
	ma-eem	ma-yay	ma-eem	ma-eemee
prep	моём	моей	моём	моих
	ma-yom	ma-yay	ma-yom	ma-eeн

твой [tvoy] (your, yours) declines in the same way as мой (my, mine).

	masculine	feminine	neuter	plural
nom	наш	наша	наше	наши
	nash	nasha	nasheh	nashi
acc	наш	нашу	наше	наши
	nash	nashoo	nasheh	nashi
gen	нашего	нашей	нашего	наших
	nasheva	nashay	nasheva	nashiн
dat	нашему	нашей	нашему	нашим
	nashemoo	nashay	nashemoo	nashim
instr	нашим	нашей	нашим	нашими
	nashim	nashay	nashim	nashimee
prep	нашем	нашей	нашем	наших
	nashem	nashay	nashem	nashiн

ваш [vash] (your, yours) declines in the same way as наш (our, ours).

отнесите это в мой номер
atnyeseetyeh eta vmoy nomyer
take this to my room

вы не видели нашего гида?
viy nyeh veedyelee nasheva geeda?
have you seen our guide?

возвращаю вашу ручку
vazvrash-cha-yoo vashoo roochkoo
I'm returning your pen

The following possessives are invariable:

его [yevo]	his/its
её [yeh-yo]	her; hers
их [eeн]	their; theirs

это её сумка
eta yeh-yo soomka
it's her bag

я его друг
ya yevo drook
I'm his friend

это их автобус
eta eeн aftoboos
it's their bus

The possessive adjective **свой** [svoy] is used when the object possessed relates directly to the subject of the sentence. It declines like **мой**.

The possessives can be omitted when the object possessed relates directly to the subject of the sentence:

> я скучаю по родителям
> ya skooch**a**-yoo pa rad**ee**tyelyam
> I miss my parents

> я потерял свой ключ
> ya patyer**ya**l svoy klyooch
> I've lost my key

> мы живём в своём
>   собственном доме
> miy Jiv**yo**m fsva-**yo**m s**o**pstvyen-
>   nam **do**myeh
> we live in our own house

PRONOUNS

Personal Pronouns

я	[ya]	I		мы	[miy]	we
ты	[tiy]	you (fam)		вы	[viy]	you (sing pol or pl)
он	[on]	he				
она	[an**a**]	she		они	[an**ee**]	they
оно	[an**o**]	it				

Personal pronouns change according to case as follows:

nom	**я**	**ты**	**он/оно**	**она**
	ya	tiy	on/an**o**	an**a**
acc	**меня**	**тебя**	**его**	**её**
	myen**ya**	tyeb**ya**	yev**o**	yeh-**yo**
gen	**меня**	**тебя**	**его**	**её**
	myen**ya**	tyeb**ya**	yev**o**	yeh-**yo**
dat	**мне**	**тебе**	**ему**	**ей**
	mn**yeh**	tyeb**yeh**	yem**oo**	yay
instr	**мной**	**тобой**	**им**	**ей**
	mn**oy**	tab**oy**	eem	yay
prep	**мне**	**тебе**	**нём**	**ней**
	mn**yeh**	tyeb**yeh**	ny**om**	ny**ay**

GRAMMAR

nom	**мы**	**вы**	**они**
	miy	viy	an**ee**
acc	**нас**	**вас**	**их**
	nas	vas	eeH
gen	**нас**	**вас**	**их**
	nas	vas	eeH
dat	**нам**	**вам**	**им**
	nam	vam	eem
instr	**нами**	**вами**	**ими**
	n**a**mee	v**a**mee	**ee**mee
prep	**нас**	**вас**	**них**
	nas	vas	neeH

The third person singular and plural pronouns take the prefix **н** after prepositions i.e.:

для них
dlya neeH
for them

'You'

There are two words for 'you' in Russian: the polite/plural form **вы** [viy] and the familiar/singular form **ты** [tiy]. **Вы** is used when you are addressing someone you do not know at all, do not know well enough to consider a friend, as a sign of respect to an elder, or if you are addressing more than one person. **Ты** is used when addressing a child or a friend. The corresponding possessives are: **ваш** for the singular polite or plural and **твой** for the familiar form (see page 19–20.)

Reflexive Pronouns

The reflexive pronoun **себя** can mean myself, yourself, himself, herself, itself, ourselves, yourselves or themselves, depending on the context in which it is used. It changes according to case as follows:

acc	**себя**
	syeb**ya**
gen	**себя**
	syeb**ya**
dat	**себе**
	syeb**yeh**
instr	**собой**
	sab**oy**
prep	**себе**
	syeb**yeh**

Interrogative Pronouns

кто (who) and что (what)
decline as follows:

nom	**кто** kto
acc	**кого** kav**o**
gen	**кого** kav**o**
dat	**кому** kam**oo**
instr	**кем** kyem
prep	**ком** kom
nom	**что** shto
acc	**что** shto
gen	**чего** chyev**o**
dat	**чему** chyem**oo**
instr	**чем** chyem
prep	**чём** chom

VERBS

Verb Aspects

The basic form of the verb
given in the dictionaries in this
book is the infinitive (e.g. to
do, to go, to read etc). Most
Russian verbs have two forms
known as the imperfective and

perfective aspects. In the
English-Russian and Russian-
English sections of this book,
where useful, the two aspects
of common verbs are given in
this order: imperfective/
perfective. For example the
verb 'to do' is:

делать [d**ye**lat]/сделать
[zd**ye**lat]

The imperfective aspect is
generally used to form what in
English would be the present
and imperfect (continuous)
tenses and the future (with the
future tense of быть (to be)).
The perfective aspect is
generally used to form what in
English would be expressed
by the perfect tense.

Russian regular verbs usually
have one of two endings and
are known as first conjugation
and second conjugation verbs:

first conjugation
-ать   делать to do

second conjugation
-ить   говорить to speak, to
say

To form the various tenses,
the ending of the verb is
removed and appropriate
endings are added to the basic
stem.

Present Tense

The present tense corresponds to 'I leave' and 'I am leaving' in English. Using the imperfective aspect of the verb, the conjugation patterns for the present tense are as follows:

first conjugation	second conjugation
делать	**говорить**
dyelat	gavareet
to do	to speak, to say
я читаю	**я говорю**
ya dyela-yoo	ya gavaryoo
ты делаешь	**ты говоришь**
tiy dyela-yesh	tiy gavareesh
он/она делает	**он/она говорит**
on/ana dyela-yet	on/ana gavareet
мы делаем	**мы говорим**
miy dyela-yem	miy gavareem
вы делаете	**вы говорите**
viy dyela-yetyeh	viy gavareetyeh
они делают	**они говорят**
anee dyela-yoot	anee gavaryat

Most verbs ending in -ать or -ять conjugate in the same way as делать. The following are some common exceptions:

слышать	**спать**
sliyshat	spat
to hear	to sleep
я слышу	**я сплю**
ya sliyshoo	ya splyoo
ты слышишь	**ты спишь**
tiy sliyshish	tiy speesh
он/она слышит	**он/она спит**
on/ana sliyshit	on/ana speet
мы слышим	**мы спим**
miy sliyshim	miy speem
вы слышите	**вы спите**
viy sliyshityeh	viy speetyeh
они слышат	**они спят**
anee sliyshat	anee spyat

ждать	брать
Jdat	brat
to wait	to take

я жду	я беру
ya Jdoo	ya byer**oo**
ты ждёшь	ты берёшь
tiy Jdyosh	tiy byer**yo**sh
он/она ждёт	он/она берёт
on/on**a** Jdyot	on/on**a** byer**yo**t
мы ждём	мы берём
miy Jdyom	miy byer**yo**m
вы ждёте	вы берёте
viy Jd**yo**tyeh	viy byer**yo**tyeh
они ждут	берут
anee Jdoot	anee byer**oo**t

Most verbs ending in -ить and -еть are conjugated in a similar
way to говорить. However, the first person singular may change
slightly in that there may also be consonant changes or the
addition of an л between the verb stem and ending:

видеть	любить
vee**d**yet	lyoob**eet**
to see	to like

я вижу	я люблю
ya vee**J**oo	ya lyoobl**yoo**
ты видишь	ты любишь
tiy vee**d**eesh	tiy l**yoo**beesh
он/она видит	он/она любит
on/on**a** vee**d**eet	on/on**a** l**yoo**beet
мы видим	мы любим
miy vee**d**eem	miy l**yoo**beem
вы видите	вы любите
viy vee**d**eetyeh	viy l**yoo**beetyeh
они видят	они любят
anee vee**d**yat	anee l**yoo**byat

платить	просить
plat**eet**	pras**eet**
to pay for	to ask

я плачу	я прошу
ya plach**oo**	prash**oo**
ты платишь	ты просишь
tiy plat**eesh**	tiy pr**o**seesh
он/она платит	он/она просит
on/an**a** plat**eet**	on/an**a** pr**o**seet
мы платим	мы просим
miy plat**eem**	miy pr**o**seem
вы платите	вы просите
viy plat**eetyeh**	viy pr**o**seetyeh
они платят	они просят
anee pl**a**tyat	anee pr**o**syat

сидеть [seed**yet**] (to sit) and all forms of the verb ходить [Had**eet**] (to walk) are conjugated like видеть.

The following verbs are irregular in the present tense:

есть	хотеть	пить	жить
yest	Hat**yet**	peet	Jiyt
to eat	to want	to drink	to live, to stay

я ем	я хочу	я пью	я живу
ya yem	ya Hach**oo**	ya pyoo	ya Jiv**oo**
ты ешь	ты хочешь	ты пьёшь	ты живёшь
tiy yesh	tiy H**o**chyesh	tiy pyosh	tiy Jiv**yo**sh
он/она ест	он/она хочет	он/она пьёт	он/она живёт
on/an**a** yest	on/an**a** H**o**chyet	on/an**a** pyot	on/an**a** Jiv**yo**t
мы едим	мы хотим	мы пьём	мы живём
miy yed**eem**	miy Hat**eem**	miy pyom	miy Jiv**yo**m
вы едите	вы хотите	вы пьёте	вы живёте
viy yed**ee**tyeh	viy Hat**ee**tyeh	viy p**yo**tyeh	viy Jiv**yo**tyeh
они едят	они хотят	они пьют	они живут
anee yed**ya**t	anee Hat**ya**t	anee pyoot	anee Jiv**oo**t

The Past Tense: Imperfective and Perfective Forms

There are two types of past tense formed by the imperfective and the perfective of the verb.

The imperfective form describes an action which is seen as continuing:

> они покупали сувениры
> an**ee** pakoopalee soovyen**ee**ri
> they were buying souvenirs

The perfective form describes an action which is seen as completed:

> они купили сувениры
> an**ee** koop**ee**lee soovyen**ee**ri
> they bought souvenirs

Some perfective verbs can be formed by adding various prefixes to the imperfective form:

imperfective	perfective
делать	сделать to do
d**ye**lat	zd**ye**lat
платить	заплатить to pay for
plat**ee**t	zaplat**ee**t

Other perfective forms may be a different verb altogether:

imperfective	perfective
брать	взять to take
brat	vzyat
говорить	сказать to speak, to say
gavar**ee**t	skaz**a**t

Perfective verbs can sometimes be identified because they look like a simpler form of the imperfective, for example:

imperfective	perfective
открывать	открыть to open
atkriv**a**t	atkr**iy**t
давать	дать to give
dav**a**t	dat

To form the past tense of both the imperfective and perfective forms, remove the ending from the infinitive and add the appropriate ending for masculine, feminine, neuter or plural subjects:

masculine	feminine	neuter	plural
-л	-ла	-ло	-ли
-l	-la	-lo	-lee

> вчера шёл дождь
> fchyer**a** shol dosht
> it was raining yesterday

> я только что поела (said by woman)
> ya t**o**lka shto pa-**yeh**la
> I've only just eaten

время пролетело очень
быстро
v**rye**mya pralyet**ye**la **o**chyen
b**iy**stra
time flew by

мы побывали в Кремле
miy pabival**ee** fkryeml**yeh**
we visited the Kremlin

masculine	feminine	neuter	plural

идти [eet-t**ee**] to go

шёл	шла	шло	шли
shol	shla	shlo	shlee

нести [nyest**ee**] to carry

нёс	несла	несло	несли
nyos	nyesl**a**	nyesl**o**	nyesl**ee**

вести [vyest**ee**] to lead

вёл	вела	вело	вели
vyol	vyel**a**	vyel**o**	vyel**ee**

Future Tense

There are two ways of forming
the future tense in Russian.
The imperfective future is
formed with the infinitive of
the main verb (imperfective
aspect) and the future tense of
the verb 'to be' быть (see next
column.)

он будет встречать нас в
аэропорту
on b**oo**dyet fstryech**a**t nas va-
erapart**oo**
he'll be meeting us at the
airport

The future can also be
expressed using the 'present'
tense of perfective verbs. The
conjugation patterns are the
same as those for the Present
Tense on page 24.

завтра мы поедем в Суздаль
z**a**ftra miy pa-**ye**dyem fs**oo**zdal
tomorrow we'll go to Suzdal

'To Be'

In Russian, there is no
equivalent of the verb 'to be'
in the present tense; it is not
translated:

я уверен/уверена
ya oov**ye**ryen/oov**ye**ryena
I'm sure (said by man/woman)

он здесь?
on zdyes?
is he here?

The past tense of the verb 'to
be' is as follows:

masculine	feminine	neuter	plural
был	была	было	были
biyl	bil**a**	b**iy**la	b**iy**lee

The future tense of the verb
'to be' is as follows:

я буду	мы будем
ya b**oo**doo	miy b**oo**dyem
ты будешь	вы будете
tiy b**oo**dyesh	viy b**oo**dyetyeh
он/она будет	они будут
on/an**a** b**oo**dyet	an**ee** b**oo**doot

'To Have'

'To have' is translated in Russian using the preposition y followed by the genitive of the noun or pronoun; the object possessed is in the nominative:

у меня была простуда
oo myen**ya** bil**a** prast**oo**da
I had a cold

у вас есть другие?
oo vas yest droog**ee**-yeh?
do you have any others?

у нас будет достаточно
времени для покупок
oo nas b**oo**dyet dast**a**chna
vr**ye**myenee dlya pak**oo**pak
we'll have enough time for
shopping

Negatives

To form a negative sentence, insert не (not, no) in front of the verb:

In phrases, using 'have not', 'had not' or 'will not', нет, не было and не будет are used respectively as follows:

у меня нет талонов
oo men**ya** nyet tal**o**naf
I don't have any bus tickets

у меня не хватило денег на
подарки
oo myen**ya** nyeh нvat**ee**la
d**ye**nyek na pad**a**rkee
I hadn't enough money to
buy presents

у меня не будет времени на
это
oo myen**ya** nyeh b**oo**dyet
vr**ye**myenee na **e**ta
I won't have time for that

Double negatives are common:

ничего
neechyev**o**
nothing

я ничего не хочу
ya neechyev**o** nyeh нach**oo**
I don't want anything

никогда
neekagd**a**
never

я никогда там не был/была
ya neekagd**a** tam nyeh biyl/bil**a**
I've never been there (said by man/woman)

Imperative

The imperative form of the verb is used to express a command such as 'come here!', 'sit down' etc. The imperative is formed by taking the second person (ты form) of the verb (either the imperfective or perfective depending on the context), removing the last three letters and adding the endings as follows:

	stem ending in consonant	stem ending in vowel
fam	-и, or -ь	-й
pol/pl	-ите, or ьте	-йте

иди сюда!
eedee syooda!
come here!

идите сюда!
eedeetyeh syooda!
come here!

открой дверь
atkroy dvyer
open the door

откройте дверь
atkroytyeh dvyer
open the door

перестань кричать
pyeryestan kreechat
stop shouting

перестаньте кричать
pyeryestantyeh kreechat
stop shouting

Reflexive Verbs

Reflexive verbs such as 'to wash oneself', 'to get dressed' etc are formed by adding -ся to verbs ending in a consonant or -сь to verbs ending in a vowel:

одевать
adyevat
to dress

одеваться
adyevatsa
to get dressed

The same endings are used for myself, yourself, himself, themselves etc.

Some verbs only exist in the reflexive form:

бояться [ba-**ya**tsa] to be afraid of
надеяться [nad**yeh**-yatsa] to hope
нравиться [n**ra**veetsa] to like
смеяться [smyeh-**ya**tsa] to laugh

QUESTIONS

A statement can be turned into a question by using a questioning intonation:

мы возвращаемся в гостиницу
miy vazvrash-cha-yemsya vgasteeneetsoo
we are returning to the hotel

мы возвращаемся в гостиницу?
miy vazvrash-cha-yemsya vgasteeneetsoo?
are we returning to the hotel?

DATES

Use the neuter form of the ordinal numbers on pages 33–34 to express the date. These decline like adjectives see pages 15–17.

> второе ноября
> ftaro-yeh na-yabrya
> the second of November

> тридцать первое января
> treetsat pyerva-yeh yanvarya
> the thirty-first of January

DAYS

Sunday воскресенье
  [vaskryesyenyeh]
Monday понедельник
  [panyedyelneek]
Tuesday вторник [ftorneek]
Wednesday среда [sryeda]
Thursday четверг [chyetvyerk]
Friday пятница [pyatneetsa]
Saturday суббота [soobota]

MONTHS

January январь [yanvar]
February февраль [fyevral]
March март [mart]
April апрель [apryel]
May май [mı]
June июнь [ee-yoon]
July июль [ee-yool]
August август [avgoost]
September сентябрь [syentyabr]
October октябрь [aktyabr]
November ноябрь [na-yabr]
December декабрь [dyekabr]

TIME

what time is it? который час?
  [katori chas?]
(it's) one o'clock час [chas]
(it's) two o'clock два часа [dva
  chasa]
(it's) three o'clock три часа [tree
  chasa]
(it's) four o'clock четыре часа
  [chyetiyryeh chasa]
(it's) five o'clock* пять часов
  [pyat chasof]

* For numbers of five and above, use часов. See Numbers and Cases page 10.

five past one** пять минут
  второго [pyat meenoot ftarova]
ten past two** десять минут
  третьего [dyesyat meenoot
  tryetyeva]
quarter past one** четверть
  второго [chyetvyert ftarova]
quarter past two** четверть
  третьего [chyetvyert tryetyeva]
half past one** половина
  второго [palaveena ftarova]
half past two** половина
  третьего [palaveena tryetyeva]

** For time past the hour, refer to the next hour.
половина второго 'half past one' literally means 'half of the second'.

twenty to ten без двадцати
десять [byez dvatsat**ee** d**ye**sat]
quarter to two без четверти два
[byez ch**ye**tvyertee dva]
quarter to ten без четверти
десять [byez ch**ye**tvyertee
d**ye**sat]
at one o'clock в час [fchas]
at two/three/four o'clock в два/
три/четыре часа [v dva/tree/
chyet**iy**ryeh chas**a**]
at five o'clock в пять часов [fpyat
chas**of**]
at half past four в половине
пятого [fpalave**e**nyeh p**ya**tava]
14.00 hours четырнадцать
ноль-ноль [chyet**iy**rnatsat nol-
nol]
17.30 семнадцать тридцать
[syemn**a**tsat tr**ee**tsat]
noon полдень [p**o**ldyen]
midnight полночь [p**o**lnach]
am утра [ootra]
pm (in the afternoon) дня [dnya]
(in the evening) вечера
[v**ye**chyera]
hour час [chas]
minute минута [meen**oo**ta]
second секунда [syek**oo**nda]
quarter of an hour четверть часа
[ch**ye**tvyert chas**a**]
half an hour полчаса [polchas**a**]
three quarters of an hour сорок
пять минут [s**o**rak pyat
meen**oo**t]

NUMBERS

See Numbers and Cases page
10.

0	ноль [nol]
1	один m, одна f, одно n [ad**ee**n, adna, adn**o**]
2	два m/n, две f [dva, dvyeh]
3	три [tree]
4	четыре [chyet**iy**ryeh]
5	пять [pyat]
6	шесть [shest]
7	семь [syem]
8	восемь [v**o**syem]
9	девять [d**ye**vyat]
10	десять [d**ye**syat]
11	одиннадцать [ad**ee**natsat]
12	двенадцать [dvyen**a**tsat]
13	тринадцать [treen**a**tsat]
14	четырнадцать [chyet**iy**rnatsat]
15	пятнадцать [pyatn**a**tsat]
16	шестнадцать [shesn**a**tsat]
17	семнадцать [syemn**a**tsat]
18	восемнадцать [vasyemn**a**tsat]
19	девятнадцать [dyevyatn**a**tsat]
20	двадцать [dv**a**tsat]
21	двадцать один/одна/одно [dv**a**tsat ad**ee**n/adna/ adn**o**]
22	двадцать два/две [dv**a**tsat dva/dvyeh]
30	тридцать [tr**ee**tsat]
40	сорок [s**o**rak]
50	пятьдесят [pyadyes**ya**t]
60	шестьдесят [shesdyes**ya**t]
70	семьдесят [s**ye**mdyesyat]

80	восемьдесят [**vo**syemdyesyat]
90	девяносто [dyevyan**o**sta]
100	сто [sto]
101	сто один/одна/одно [sto ad**ee**n/adn**a**/adn**o**]
102	сто два/две [sto dva/dvyeh]
200	двести [dv**ye**stee]
300	триста [**tree**sta]
400	четыреста [chyet**iy**ryesta]
500	пятьсот [pyats**o**t]
600	шестьсот [shes-s**o**t]
700	семьсот [syems**o**t]
800	восемьсот [vasyems**o**t]
900	девятьсот [dyevyats**o**t]
1,000	тысяча [t**iy**syacha]
2,000	две тысячи [dvyeh t**iy**syachi]
3,000	три тысячи [tree t**iy**syachi]
4,000	четыре тысячи [chyet**iy**ryeh t**iy**syachi]
5,000	пять тысяч [pyat t**iy**syach]
10,000	десять тысяч [d**ye**syat t**iy**syach]
20,000	двадцать тысяч [dv**a**tsat t**iy**syach]
100,000	сто тысяч [sto t**iy**syach]
1,000,000	миллион [meelee-**o**n]

Ordinals

1st	первый [p**ye**rvi]
2nd	второй [ftar**oy**]
3rd	третий [tr**ye**tee]
4th	четвёртый [chyetv**yo**rti]
5th	пятый [p**ya**ti]
6th	шестой [shest**oy**]
7th	седьмой [syedm**oy**]
8th	восьмой [vasm**oy**]
9th	девятый [dyev**ya**ti]
10th	десятый [dyes**ya**ti]
11th	одиннадцатый [ad**ee**natsati]
12th	двенадцатый [dvyen**a**tsati]
13th	тринадцатый [treen**a**tsati]
14th	четырнадцатый [chyet**iy**rnatsati]
15th	пятнадцатый [pyatn**a**tsati]
16th	шестнадцатый [shesn**a**tsati]
17th	семнадцатый [syemn**a**tsati]
18th	восемнадцатый [vasyemn**a**tsati]
19th	девятнадцатый [dyevyatn**a**tsati]
20th	двадцатый [dvats**a**ti]
21st	двадцать первый [dv**a**tsat p**ye**rvi]
22nd	двадцать второй [dv**a**tsat ftar**oy**]
23rd	двадцать третий [dv**a**tsat tr**ye**tee]
24th	двадцать четвёртый [dv**a**tsat chyetv**yo**rti]
25th	двадцать пятый [dv**a**tsat p**ya**ti]

		BASIC PHRASES

26th двадцать шестой [dv**a**tsat shest**oy**]

27th двадцать седьмой [dv**a**tsat syedm**oy**]

28th двадцать восьмой [dv**a**tsat vasm**oy**]

29th двадцать девятый [dv**a**tsat dyev**ya**ti]

30th тридцатый [tr**ee**ts**a**ti]

31st тридцать первый [tr**ee**tsat p**ye**rvi]

yes
да
da

no
нет
nyet

OK
хорошо
Harash**o**

hello
здравствуйте
zdr**a**svooytyeh

good morning
доброе утро
d**o**bra-yeh **oo**tra

good evening
добрый вечер
d**o**bri v**ye**chyer

good night (when leaving)
до свидания
da sveed**a**nya
(when going to bed)
спокойной ночи
spak**oy**ni n**o**chee

goodbye
до свидания
da sveed**a**nya

hi! (hello)
привет!
preev**ye**t!

cheerio!
пока!
pa**ka**!

see you!
пока!
pa**ka**!

please
пожалуйста
pa**ja**lsta

yes please
да, спасибо
da, spas**ee**ba

thank you, thanks
спасибо
spas**ee**ba

no, thank you
нет, спасибо
nyet, spas**ee**ba

thank you very much
большое спасибо
balsh**o**-yeh spas**ee**ba

don't mention it
не за что
n**yeh**-za-shta

how do you do?
здравствуйте
zdr**a**svooytyeh

how are you?
как дела?
kak dy**e**la?

fine, thanks
хорошо, спасибо
Harash**o**, spas**ee**ba

nice to meet you
приятно познакомиться
pree-**ya**tna paznak**o**meetsa

excuse me (to get past, to say
sorry)
извините
eezveen**ee**tyeh
(to get attention)
простите!
prast**ee**tyeh!
(addressing someone with
question)
извините, пожалуйста ...
eezveen**ee**tyeh, pa**ja**lsta ...

(I'm) sorry
прошу прощения
prash**oo** prash-ch**ye**nee-ya

sorry?/pardon me? (didn't
understand)
простите?
prast**ee**tyeh?

what?
что?
shto?

what did you say?
что вы сказали?
shto viy skaz**a**lee?

I see (I understand)
понятно
pan**ya**tna

I don't understand
я не понимаю
ya nyeh paneema-yoo

do you speak English?
вы говорите по-английски?
viy gava**ree**tyeh pa-ang**lee**skee?

I don't speak Russian
я не говорю по-русски
ya nyeh gavar**yoo** pa-**roo**skee

could you speak more slowly?
вы не могли бы говорить
помедленнее?
viy nyeh mag**lee**bi gava**reet**
pam**ye**dlyenyeh-yeh?

could you repeat that?
повторите, пожалуйста
paftar**ee**tyeh, pa**ʌ**lsta

could you write it down?
запишите, пожалуйста
zapeesh**iy**tyeh, pa**ʌ**lsta

I'd like ... (said by man/woman)
я бы хотел/хотела ...
 ya biy Hat**yel**/Hat**ye**la ...

can I have ...?
можно, пожалуйста ...?
mo**ʌ**na, pa**ʌ**lsta ...?

do you have ...?
у вас есть ...?
oo vas yest ...?

how much is it?
сколько это стоит?
skolka **e**ta s**to**-eet?

cheers! (toast)
ваше здоровье!
vasheh zdar**o**vyeh!

it is ...
это ...
eta ...

where is the ...?
где ...?
gdyeh ...?

is it far from here?
это далеко отсюда?
eta dalyek**o** ats**yoo**da?

what's the time?
который час?
ka**to**ri chas?

CONVERSION TABLES

| 1 centimetre = 0.39 inches | 1 inch = 2.54 cm |

1 metre = 39.37 inches =
  1.09 yards

1 foot = 30.48 cm

1 yard = 0.91 m

1 kilometre = 0.62 miles =
  5/8 mile

1 mile = 1.61 km

km	1	2	3	4	5	10	20	30	40	50	100
miles	0.6	1.2	1.9	2.5	3.1	6.2	12.4	18.6	24.8	31.0	62.1

miles	1	2	3	4	5	10	20	30	40	50	100
km	1.6	3.2	4.8	6.4	8.0	16.1	32.2	48.3	64.4	80.5	161

1 gram = 0.035 ounces

g	100	250	500
oz	3.5	8.75	17.5

1 kilo = 1000 g = 2.2 pounds

1 oz = 28.35 g

1 lb = 0.45 kg

kg	0.5	1	2	3	4	5	6	7	8	9	10
lb	1.1	2.2	4.4	6.6	8.8	11.0	13.2	15.4	17.6	19.8	22.0

kg	20	30	40	50	60	70	80	90	100
lb	44	66	88	110	132	154	176	198	220

lb	0.5	1	2	3	4	5	6	7	8	9	10	20
kg	0.2	0.5	0.9	1.4	1.8	2.3	2.7	3.2	3.6	4.1	4.5	9.0

1 litre = 1.75 UK pints / 2.13 US pints

| 1 UK pint = 0.57 l | 1 UK gallon = 4.55 l |
| 1 US pint = 0.47 l | 1 US gallon = 3.79 l |

centigrade / Celsius

$C = (F - 32) \times 5/9$

C	-5	0	5	10	15	18	20	25	30	36.8	38
F	23	32	41	50	59	65	68	77	86	98.4	100.4

Fahrenheit

$F = (C \times 9/5) + 32$

F	23	32	40	50	60	65	70	80	85	98.4	101
C	-5	0	4	10	16	18	21	27	29	36.8	38.3

English-Russian

A

a, an*

about: about 20 около
двадцати [**o**kala dvatsat**ee**]
it's about 5 o'clock около
пяти часов [**o**kala pyat**ee**
chas**o**f]
a film about Russia фильм о
России [f**ee**lm a rass**ee**-ee]

above над [nad]

abroad за границей [za
gran**ee**tsay]

absolutely! конечно!
[kan**ye**shna!]

absorbent cotton вата [**v**ata]

accelerator акселератор
[aksyelyer**a**tar]

accept принимать/принять
[preeneem**a**t/preen**ya**t]

accident несчастный случай
[nyesh-ch**a**sni sl**oo**chee]
there's been an accident
произошёл несчастный
случай [pra-eezash**o**l nyesh-
ch**a**sni sl**oo**chee]

accommodation жильё [Jil**yo**]

Private accommodation for
tourists is best arranged in advance from abroad, as doing it
through local bureaux may be a
bit hit and miss. Most agencies
offer bed and breakfast in a Russian home. Your hosts may vol-
unteer to act as guides or driv-
ers, and are often keen to offer
insights into Russian life. Most
→

people in the habit of renting
rooms to foreigners speak some
English or another foreign language.
The cost varies depending on
factors such as location and
whether you opt for bed and
breakfast or full board, so it definitely pays to shop around. If
possible, you should try to get
the address of the flat and check
how far it is from the centre and
the nearest metro station.
see **room** and **hotel**

ache боль f [bol]
my back aches у меня болит
спина [oo men**ya** bal**ee**t
speen**a**]

across: across the road через
дорогу [ch**ye**ryes dar**o**goo]

adaptor адаптер [ad**a**pter]

address адрес [**a**drys]
what's your address? какой
ваш адрес? [kak**oy** vash
adrys?]

When addressing letters, Russians start with the country, followed by the town/city along
with a six-digit postal code on
the next line, then the street,
block and apartment number,
and finally the addressee's
name; the sender's details are
usually written at the bottom of
the envelope. The number of
the house, block or complex may
→

be preceded by дом (dom), abbreviated as д. (d). Two numbers separated by an oblique dash (for example, 16/21) usually indicates a corner, the second number being the address on the smaller side street. Buildings encompassing more than one number are also written like this (for example, 4/6). Floors are numbered in the American fashion; the ground floor is known as the first floor (etash1).

One final oddity is that some names are preceded by an ordinal number, for example: 2-ой Кадашевский пер. 1-ая or 1-ый (pronounced 'pyerva-ya' or 'pyervi') means '1st'; 2-ая or 2-ой ('ftara-ya' or 'ftaroy') '2nd', and so on. This usually applies to a series of parallel lanes or side streets.

Here is an address, as a Russian would write it:

**Россия
173060 г. Новгород
ул. Менделеева, д. 12,
 корп. 2, кв. 126
Сидоров Б. А.**

Russia
173060 Novgorod
12 Mendelayev Street, Block 2, Flat 126
B. A. Sidorov

address book алфавитная записная книжка [alfaveetna-ya zapeesna-ya kneeshka]

admission charge: how much is the admission charge? сколько стоит билет? [skolka sto-eet beelyet?]

adult взрослый человек [vzrosli chyelavyek]

advance: in advance заранее [zaranyeh-yeh]

aeroplane самолёт [samalyot]

after после [poslyeh]
 after you после вас [poslyeh vas]
 after lunch после обеда [poslyeh abyeda]

afternoon: in the afternoon днём [dnyom]
 this afternoon сегодня днём [syevodnya dnyom]

aftershave лосьон после бритья [lasyon poslyeh breetya]

aftersun cream крем после загара [kryem poslyeh zagara]

afterwards потом [patom]

again снова [snova]

against против [proteef]

age возраст [vozrast]

ago: a week ago неделю назад [nyedyelyoo nazat]
 an hour ago час назад [chas nazat]

agree: I agree (said by man/woman) я согласен/согласна [ya saglasyen/saglasna]

Aids СПИД [speed]

air воздух [**vo**zd**oo**h]
by air самолётом
[samal**yo**tam]
air-conditioning: with
air-conditioning
с кондиционером
[skandeetsi-an**ye**ram]
airline авиалиния [**a**vee-a-
leenee-ya]
airmail: by airmail авиапочтой
[**a**vee-a-**po**chtI]
airmail envelope
международный конверт
[mye**J**doona**ro**dni kan**vye**rt]
airport аэропорт [a-era**po**rt]
to the airport, please в
аэропорт, пожалуйста [va-
era**po**rt, pa**J**alsta]
airport bus автобус-экспресс в
аэропорт [af**to**boos-eks**pre**s va-
era**po**rt]
aisle seat место у прохода
[m**ye**sto oo pra**ho**da]
alcohol спиртное
[speert**no**-yeh]
alcoholic: is it alcoholic? это
спиртное? [eta speert**no**-yeh?]
all* (things) всё [fsyo]
(people) все [fsyeh]
all the children все дети [fsyeh
d**ye**tee]
all of it всё [fsyo]
all of them все [fsyeh]
all day весь день [vyes dyen]
that's all, thanks это всё,
спасибо [eta fsyo, spas**ee**ba]
allergic: I'm allergic to ... у меня
аллергия на ... [oo men**ya**
alyer**gee**-ya na ...]

allowed: is smoking allowed
here? можно ли здесь
курить? [m**o**Jnalee zdyes
koor**ee**t?]
all right хорошо [Harash**o**]
I'm all right со мной всё в
порядке [samn**oy** fsyo
fpar**ya**tkyeh]
are you all right? с вами всё в
порядке? [s**va**mee fsyo
fpar**ya**tkyeh?]
almond миндаль m [meend**al**]
almost почти [pach**tee**]
alone (man/woman) один/одна
[ad**ee**n/adn**a**]
alphabet алфавит [alfav**ee**t]

а ah	к ka	ц tseh
б beh	л el	ч chyeh
в veh	м em	ш sha
г geh	н en	щ sh-chya
д deh	о o	ъ tv**yo**rdi
е yeh	п peh	znak
ё yo	р er	ы iy
ж Jeh	с es	ь m**ya**Hkee
з zeh	т teh	znak
и ee	у oo	э e
й ee k**ra**tka-	ф ef	ю yoo
yeh	х Ha	я ya

already уже [oo**Je**h]
also тоже [t**o**Jeh]
although хотя [Hat**ya**]
altogether всего [fsyev**o**]
always всегда [fsyegd**a**]
a.m.: at seven a.m. в семь часов
утра [fsyem chas**of** oo**tra**]
amazing (surprising)
удивительный
[oodeev**ee**tyelni]

(very good) потрясающий
[patryas**a**-yoosh-chee]
ambulance скорая помощь
[sk**o**ra-ya p**o**mash-ch]
call an ambulance! вызовите
скорую помощь!
[v**iy**zaveetyeh sk**o**r**oo**-yoo
p**o**mash-ch!]

Public ambulances (dial 03)
leave a lot to be desired, but in
many places there is still no al-
ternative. If you are staying in
Moscow or St Petersburg, however, there are now a number of
private healthcare companies
which can provide reliable fee-
paying ambulance and emergency services.

America Америка [am**y**ereeka]
American (adj) американский
[amyereek**a**nskee]
I'm American (man/woman) я
американец/американка [ya
amyereek**a**nyets/amyereek**a**nka]
among среди [sryed**ee**]
amount количество
[kal**ee**chyestva]
(money) сумма [s**oo**m-ma]
amp: 13-amp fuse
предохранитель на
тринадцать ампер
[predaнran**ee**tyel na treen**a**tsat
amp**y**er]
and и [ee]
angry сердитый [syerd**ee**ti]
animal животное
[Jiv**o**tna-yeh]

ankle лодыжка [lad**iy**shka]
anniversary (wedding) юбилей
[yoobeel**yay**]
annoy: this man's annoying me
этот человек мне досаждает
[**e**tat chyelav**y**ek mn**yeh**
dasaJd**a**-yet]
annoying: it's annoying это
раздражает [**e**ta razdraJ**a**-yet]
another другой [droog**oy**]
can we have another room?
можно другой номер? [m**o**Jna
droog**oy** n**o**myer?]
another beer, please ещё одно
пиво, пожалуйста [yesh-ch**o**
adn**o** p**ee**va, paJ**a**lsta]
antibiotics антибиотики
[anteebee-**o**teekee]
antifreeze антифриз
[anteefr**ee**s]
antihistamine антигистамин
[anteegeestam**ee**n]
antique антиквариат
[anteekvaree-**a**t]
antique shop антикварный
магазин [anteekv**a**rni
magaz**ee**n]
antiseptic антисептическое
средство [anteesept**ee**chyeska-
yeh sr**y**etstva]
**any: have you got any bread/
tomatoes?** у вас есть хлеб/
помидоры? [oo vas yest Hlyep/
pameed**o**ri?]
do you have any ...? у вас
есть ...? [oo vas yest ...?]
sorry, I don't have any
извините, у меня нет
[eezveen**ee**tyeh, oo men**ya** nyet]

anybody кто-нибудь [kto-neeboot]

does anybody speak English? кто-нибудь говорит по-английски? [kto-neeboot gavareet pa-angleeskee?]

there wasn't anybody there там никого не было [tam neekavo nyebila]

anything что-нибудь [shto-neeboot]

•••••• DIALOGUES ••••••

anything else? что-нибудь ещё? [shto-neeboot yesh-cho?]

nothing else, thanks больше ничего, спасибо [bolsheh neechyevo, spaseeba]

would you like anything to drink? вы хотите что-нибудь выпить? [viy Hateetyeh shto-neeboot viypeet?]

I don't want anything, thanks спасибо, я ничего не хочу [spaseeba, ya neechyevo nyeh Hachoo]

apart from кроме [kromyeh]
apartment квартира [kvarteera]
apartment block многоквартирный дом [mnogakvarteerni dom]
aperitif аперитив [apyereeteef]
apology извинение [eezveenyenee-yeh]
appendicitis аппендицит [apyendeetsiyt]
appetizer закуска [zakooska]
apple яблоко [yablaka]

appointment приём [preeyom]

•••••• DIALOGUE ••••••

good morning, how can I help you? доброе утро, чем я могу вам помочь? [dobra-yeh ootra, chyem ya magoo vam pamoch?]

I'd like to make an appointment (said by man/woman) я бы хотел/хотела записаться на приём [yabi Hatyel/Hatyela zapeesatsa na preeyom]

what time would you like? какое время для вас удобно? [kako-yeh vryemya dlya vas oodobna?]

three o'clock в три часа [ftree chasa]

I'm afraid that's not possible, is four o'clock all right? боюсь, что в три часа не получится, в четыре вас устроит? [bayoos, shto ftree chasa nyeh paloocheetsa, fchyetiyryeh vas oostro-eet?]

yes, that will be fine да, это меня устроит [da, eta myenya oostro-eet]

the name was ...? ваше имя ...? [vasheh eemya ...?]

apricot абрикос [abreekos]
April апрель m [apryel]
area район [rI-on]
area code междугородный код [myeJdoogarodni kod]
arm рука [rooka]
arrange: will you arrange it for us? вы организуете это для нас? [viy arganeezoo-yetyeh eta dlya nas?]
arrival прибытие [preebyitee-yeh]

arrive приезжать/приехать
[pree-yeJJ**a**t/pree-**ye**Hat]
  when do we arrive? когда мы
  приезжаем? [kagd**a** miy pree-
  yeJ-J**a**-yem?]
  has my fax arrived yet? ещё не
  пришёл факс для меня?
  [yesh-ch**o** nyeh preesh**o**l faks
  dlya men**ya**?]
  we arrived today мы
  приехали сегодня [miy
  pree-**ye**Halee syev**o**dnya]
art искусство [eesk**oo**stva]
art gallery картинная галерея
  [kart**ee**n-na-ya galyer**yeh**-ya]
artist художник [Hood**o**Jneek]
as: **as big as** такой же большой
  как ... [tak**oy**Jeh balsh**oy** kak ...]
  as soon as possible как
  можно быстрее [kak m**o**Jna
  bistr**yeh**-yeh]
ashtray пепельница
  [p**ye**pyelneetsa]
ask спрашивать/спросить
  [spr**a**shivat/spras**ee**t]
  I didn't ask for this (said by man/
  woman) это не то, что я
  заказал/заказала [eta nyeh to,
  shto ya zakaz**a**l/zakaz**a**la]
  could you ask him to ...?
  попросите его,
  пожалуйста ... [papras**ee**tyeh
  yev**o**, paJ**a**lsta ...]
asleep: **she's asleep** она спит
  [an**a** speet]
aspirin аспирин [aspeer**ee**n]
asthma астма [**a**stma]
astonishing поразительный
  [paraz**ee**tyelni]

at: **at the hotel** в гостинице
  [vgast**ee**neetseh]
  at the station на станции [na
  st**a**ntsi-ee]
  at six o'clock в шесть часов
  [fshest chas**o**f]
  at Sasha's у Саши [oo s**a**shi]
athletics атлетика [atl**ye**teeka]
ATM банкомат [bankam**a**t]
attractive привлекательный
  [preevlyek**a**tyelni]
aubergine баклажан [baklaJ**a**n]
August август [**a**vgoost]
aunt тётя [t**yo**tya]
Australia Австралия
  [afstr**a**lee-ya]
Australian (adj) австралийский
  [afstral**ee**skee]
  I'm Australian (man/woman) я
  австралиец/австралийка [ya
  afstral**ee**-yets/afstral**ee**ka]
Austria Австрия [**a**fstree-ya]
automatic (adj) автоматический
  [aftamat**ee**chyeskee]
  (noun: car) с автоматической
  коробкой передач
  [saftamat**ee**chyeski kar**o**pkı
  pyeryed**a**ch]
autumn осень f [**o**syen]
  in the autumn осенью
  [**o**senyoo]
avenue аллея [al**yeh**-ya]
average (not good)
  посредственный
  [pasr**ye**tstvyen-ni]
  on average в среднем
  [fsr**ye**dnyem]
awake: **is he awake?** он
  проснулся? [on prasn**oo**lsya?]

away: go away! уходите!
[ooHad**ee**tyeh!]
is it far away? это далеко? [eta
dalyek**o**?]
awful ужасный [oo**J**asni]

B

baby-sitter няня [n**ya**nya]
baby ребёнок [ryeb**yo**nak]
baby food детское питание
[d**ye**tska-yeh peet**a**nee-yeh]
baby's bottle бутылочка для
кормления ребёнка
[boot**iy**lachka dlya karml**ye**nee-
ya ryeb**yo**nka]
back (of body) спина [sp**ee**na]
(back part) задняя часть
[z**a**dnya-ya ch**a**st]
at the back сзади [z-z**a**dee]
I'd like my money back (said by
man/woman) я хотел/хотела бы
получить обратно деньги [ya
Hat**ye**l/Hat**ye**la biy palooch**ee**t
abr**a**tna d**ye**ngee]
to come back возвращаться/
вернуться [vazvrash-ch**a**tsa/
vyern**oo**tsa]
to go back (by transport)
уезжать/уехать [oo-yeJ-J**a**t/oo-
yeHat]
(on foot) возвращаться/
вернуться [vazvrash-ch**a**tsa/
vyern**oo**tsa]
backache боль в спине [bol
fspeen**ye**h]
bacon бекон [b**ye**kon]
bad плохой [plan**oy**]
not bad неплохо [nyepl**o**Ha]

a bad headache сильная
головная боль [s**ee**lna-ya
galavn**a**-ya bol]
badly плохо [pl**o**Ha]
bag сумка [s**oo**mka]
(handbag) дамская сумка
[d**a**mska-ya s**oo**mka]
(suitcase) чемодан [chyemad**a**n]
baggage багаж [bag**a**sh]
baggage check room
камера хранения
[k**a**myera Hran**ye**nee-ya]
baggage claim выдача багажа
[v**iy**dacha bag**a**Ja]
bakery булочная [b**oo**lachna-ya]
balcony балкон [balk**o**n]
a room with a balcony номер с
балконом [n**o**myer zbalk**o**nam]
bald лысый [l**iy**si]
ball мяч [myach]
ballet балет [bal**ye**t]
ballpoint pen шариковая ручка
[sh**a**reekava-ya r**oo**chka]
banana банан [ban**a**n]
band (orchestra) оркестр
[ark**ye**str]
bandage бинт [beent]
Bandaid® пластырь m [pl**a**stir]
bank (money) банк [bank]

As the exchange rate (koors) is
now set by market forces and
the black market offers nothing
but risks, there's no reason to
change money anywhere other
than in an official bank or currency exchange booth: обмен
валюты (abm**ye**n val**yoo**ti).
These are to be found all over
→

town and inside hotel foyers, shops and restaurants (they usually keep the same hours as the shop or restaurant). Exchange rates vary slightly from place to place and most banks charge a maximum of a few hundred roubles commission, if anything at all. You should make sure you have your passport with you if you intend to change money.

bank account банковский счёт [b**a**nkofskee sh-chot]
banknote банкнота [bankn**o**ta]
bar бар [bar]

Although there are now a good many bars and particularly English/Irish-style pubs in Moscow and St Petersburg, watering holes in the regional centres are still relatively few and far between, and on the whole tend to be frequented by the local Mafia. Due to prohibitive prices in Western-style bars, Russians often buy from a kiosk/shop and drink at home.

There are still the old Soviet-style beer halls (peevn**oy** b**à**r, otherwise known as peevn**oo**shka), which are fairly grim. Although you can find bottled or canned imported beer in cafés now, to drink a decent pint in pleasant surroundings you really →

need to go to a Western-run bar. Nowadays you can buy alcohol almost anywhere: in cafés, restaurants, theatres, and street kiosks. The kiosks sell vodka, spirits, trashy brands of imported spirits, and Moldovan, Crimean or Bulgarian wines. More basically, you'll just find someone dispensing beer bottles from a pile of crates: it costs a little more to take the stuff away (s sab**oy**) than to drink it on the spot (na m**ye**styeh). Many kiosks are open 24 hours.

a bar of chocolate плитка шоколада [pl**ee**tka shakal**a**da]
barber's парикмахерская [pareeHm**a**Hyerska-ya]
bargaining

•••••• DIALOGUE ••••••
how much is this? сколько это стоит? [sk**o**lka **e**ta st**o**-eet?]
100,000 roubles сто тысяч рублей [sto t**i**ysyach roobl**yay**]
that's too expensive это слишком дорого [**e**ta sl**ee**shkam d**o**raga]
how about 70,000? как насчёт семидесяти тысяч? [kak nash-ch**o**t syem**ee**dyestee t**i**ysyach?]
I'll let you have it for 90,000 отдам за девяносто тысяч [ad-d**a**m za dyevyan**o**sta t**i**ysyach]
can you reduce it a bit more?/OK, it's a deal сбросьте ещё немного/ладно, идёт [sbr**o**styeh yesh-ch**o** nyemn**o**ga/l**a**dna, eed**yo**t]

basket корзина [karz**ee**na]
bath ванна [v**an**-na]
  can I have a bath? можно ли
  принять ванну? [m**o**Jnalee
  preen**ya**t v**an**-noo?]
bathhouse баня [b**a**nya]

The Russian bathhouse is as
much a national institution as
the sauna is in Scandinavia.
Some bathhouses have separate
floors for men and women, while
others operate on different days
for each sex but, whatever the
set-up, there's no mixed bathing except in special deluxe
saunas (available for private
rental). Towels are provided;
other things such as shampoo
should be brought with you. At
the entrance you can buy a
'**vye**neek' – a leafy bunch of
birch twigs – with which bath-
ers flail themselves (and each
other) in the steam room, to
open up the pores and improve
the circulation.
Hand your coat and valuables to
the cloakroom attendant before
going into the changing rooms.
Beyond these lies a washroom
with a cold plunge pool or bath;
the metal basins are for soaking your '**vye**neek' to make it
supple. Finally you enter the hot
room (par**ee**lka), with its tiers
of benches – it gets hotter
the higher you go. Novices
→

---

shouldn't try to stick it out for
more than five to seven minutes.
After a dunk in the cold bath and
a rest, you repeat the process all
over again.

---

bathroom ванная [v**an**-na-ya]
  with a private bathroom с
  ванной [sv**an**-nı]
bath towel банное полотенце
  [b**an**-na-yeh palat**ye**ntseh]
bathtub ванна [v**an**-na]
battery (for radio) батарейка
  [batar**yay**ka]
  (for car) аккумулятор
  [akoomool**ya**tar]
bay бухта [b**oo**Hta]
be* быть [biyt]
beach пляж [plyash]
  on the beach на пляже [na
  pl**ya**Jeh]
beach mat пляжная подстилка
  [pl**ya**Jna-ya patst**ee**lka]
beach umbrella пляжный зонт
  [pl**ya**Jni zont]
beans фасоль (f, sing) [fas**ol**]
  French beans фасоль [fas**ol**]
  broad beans бобы [bab**iy**]
beard борода [barad**a**]
beautiful красивый [kras**ee**vi]
because потому что
  [patam**oo**shta]
  because of из-за [**ee**z-za]
bed кровать f [krav**at**]
  I'm going to bed now я
  ложусь спать [ya laJ**oo**s
  spat]
bed and breakfast проживание

и завтрак [praJivanee-yeh ee zaftrak]
see **accommodation** and **hotel**

bedroom спальня [spalnya]
beef говядина [gavyadeena]
beer пиво [peeva]
  two beers, please два пива, пожалуйста [dva peeva, paJalsta]

Beer can be good if it's fresh, but few cafés sell it and it's sold and drunk mostly at street kiosks. The most common brands are **Очаковское** (achakafska-yeh), **Жигулёвское** (Jigool-yofska-yeh) and **Московское** (maskofska-yeh), which is best described as light ale; the various **Балтика** (balteeka) beers come in dark, pale and now even alcohol-free varieties and are increasingly popular. The best readily available dark beer is **Тверское** (tversko-yeh).
see **bar**

---

before перед [pyeryet]
begin начинаться/начаться [nacheenatsa/nachatsa]
  when does it begin? когда начало? [kagda nachala?]
beginner (man/woman) начинающий/начинающая [nacheena-yoosh-chee/nacheena-yoosh-cha-ya]
beginning: at the beginning в начале [vnachalyeh]

behind за [za]
  behind me за мной [za mnoy]
Belgium Бельгия [byelgee-ya]
believe верить/поверить [vyereet/pavyereet]
below под [pod]
belt ремень [ryemyen]
bend (in road) поворот [pavarot]
berth (on ship) койка [koyka]
beside: beside the ... рядом с ... [ryadam s ...]
best лучший [loochshi]
better лучше [loochsheh]
  are you feeling better? вам лучше? [vam loochsheh?]
between между [myeJdoo]
beyond за [za]
bicycle велосипед [vyelaseepyet]
big большой [balshoy]
  too big слишком большой [sleeshkam balshoy]
  it's not big enough недостаточно большой [nyedastatachna balshoy]
bike велосипед [vyelaseepyet]
  (motorbike) мотоцикл [matatsiykl]
bill счёт [sh-chot]
  (US: banknote) банкнота [banknota]
  could I have the bill, please? счёт, пожалуйста [sh-chot, paJalsta]
bin мусорное ведро [moosarna-yeh vyedro]
bird птица [pteetsa]
birthday день рождения [dyen raJdyenee-ya]
  happy birthday! с днём

рождения! [sdnyom raJdyenee-ya!]

biscuit печенье [pyechyenyeh]

bit: a little bit немножко [nyehmnoshka]

a big bit большой кусок [balshoy koosok]

a bit of ... кусочек ... [koosochyek ...]

a bit expensive дороговато [daragavata]

bite (by insect) укус (насекомого) [ookoos (nasyekomava)]

(by dog) укус (собаки) [ookoos (sabakee)]

bitter (taste) горький [gorkee]

black чёрный [chorni]

black market чёрный рынок [chorni riynak]

Black Sea Чёрное море [chorna-yeh moryeh]

blanket одеяло [adyeh-yala]

bleach (for toilet) хлорка [Hlorka]

bless you! будьте здоровы! [boot-tyeh zdarovi!]

blind слепой [slyepoy]

blinds шторы [shtori]

blocked (road) перегороженный [pyeryegaroJen-ni]

(sink) засоренный [zasoryen-ni]

blond (adj) белокурый [byelakoori]

blood кровь f [krof]

high blood pressure высокое давление [visoka-yeh davlyenee-yeh]

blouse блузка [blooska]

blow-dry укладка феном [ooklatka fyenam]

I'd like a cut and blow-dry пожалуйста, постригите и сделайте укладку феном [paJalsta, pastreegeetyeh ee sdyelItyeh ooklatkoo fyenam]

blue синий [seenee]

blue eyes голубые глаза [galoobiy-yeh glaza]

blusher румяна pl [roomyana]

boarding pass посадочный талон [pasadachni talon]

boat лодка [lotka]

(for passengers) корабль m [karabl]

when is the next boat to ...? когда следующий рейс в ...? [kagda slyedoo-sh-chee ryays v ...?]

body тело [tyela]

boil: do we have to boil the water? нужно ли кипятить воду? [nooJnalee keepyateet vodoo?]

boiled egg варёное яйцо [varyona-yeh yItso]

boiled water кипячёная вода [keepyachona-ya vada]

boiler кипятильник [keepyateelneek]

bone кость [kost]

bonnet (of car) капот [kapot]

book (noun) книга [kneega]

(verb) заказывать/заказать [zakazivat/zakazat]

can I book a seat? могу ли я заказать билет [magoolee ya zakazat beelyet?]

•••••• DIALOGUE ••••••

I'd like to book a table for two (said by man/woman) я хотел/хотела бы заказать столик на двоих [ya Hatyel/Hatyela biy zakazat stoleek na dva-eeн]

what time would you like it booked for? на какое время? [na kako-yeh vryemya?]

half past seven на половину восьмого [na palaveenoo vasmova]

that's fine хорошо [Harasho]

and your name? ваше имя? [vasheh eemya?]

bookshop, bookstore книжный магазин [kneeжni magazeen]

boot (footwear) ботинок [bateenak]

(of car) багажник [bagaжneek]

border (of country) граница [graneetsa]

bored: I'm bored мне скучно [mnyeh skooshna]

boring скучный [skooshni]

born: I was born in Manchester (said by man/woman) я родился/родилась в Манчестере [ya radeelsa/radeelas vmanchyesteryeh]

I was born in 1960 (said by man/woman) я родился/родилась в тысяча девятьсот шестидесятом году [ya radeelsa/radeelas ftiysyacha dyevyatsot shesteedyesyatam gadoo]

borrow занимать/занять [zaneemat/zanyat]

may I borrow ...? вы не одолжите ...? [viy nyeh adalжiyteh ...?]

both оба [oba]

bother: sorry to bother you извините за беспокойство [eezveeneetyeh za byespakoystva]

bottle бутылка [bootiylka]

a bottle of vodka бутылка водки [bootiylka votkee]

bottle-opener открывалка [atkrivalka]

bottom (of person) зад [zat]

at the bottom of ... (street etc) в конце ... (улицы) [fkantseh (ooleetsi)]

(hill) у подножия ... [oo padnoжi-ya ...]

bouncer вышибала [vishibala]

bowl тарелка [taryelka]

box коробка [karopka]

box office театральная касса [tyeh-atralna-ya kas-sa]

boy мальчик [malcheek]

boyfriend друг [drook]

bra бюстгальтер [byoostgalter]

bracelet браслет [braslyet]

brake тормоз [tormas]

brandy коньяк [kanyak]

bread хлеб [нlyep]

white bread белый хлеб [byeli нlyep]

brown bread чёрный хлеб [chorni нlyep]

rye bread ржаной хлеб [rжanoy нlyep]

wholemeal bread хлеб из непросеянной муки [нlyep

eez nyepras**yeh**-yanı mook**ee**]

Bread (Hlyep) is available from bakeries **булочная** (b**oo**la-chna-ya), and is one of Russia's culinary strong points. 'Black' bread (known as 'ch**o**rni' or 'rJan**oy**') is the traditional rye bread. French-style baguettes **батон** (bat**o**n) are also popular. On the whole, you still have to queue at the 'k**a**s-sa' to pay and then queue again for the bread.

break (verb) ломать/сломать [lam**a**t/slam**a**t]
   I've broken the ... (said by man/woman) я сломал/сломала ... [ya slam**a**l/slam**a**la]
   I think I've broken my wrist (said by man/woman) кажется, я сломал/сломала запястье [ka**J**etsa, ya slam**a**l/slam**a**la zap**ya**styeh]
break down ломаться/сломаться [lam**a**tsa/slam**a**tsa]
   I've broken down у меня сломалась машина [oo men**ya** slam**a**las mash**i**yna]
breakdown поломка [pal**o**mka]
breakdown service экстренная техпомощь [**e**kstryen-na-ya tye**н**p**o**mosh-ch]
breakfast завтрак [z**a**ftrak]
break-in: I've had a break-in мою комнату обокрали [ma-**yoo** k**o**mntoo abak**ra**lee]
breast грудь f [gr**oo**d]

breathe дышать [dish**a**t]
breeze ветерок [vyetyer**o**k]
bribe взятка [vz**ya**tka]
bridge (over river) мост [mosst]
brief краткий [kr**a**tkee]
briefcase портфель m [partf**ye**l]
bright (light etc) яркий [**ya**rkee]
   bright red ярко-красный [**ya**rka-kr**a**sni]
brilliant (idea, person) блестящий [blyest**ya**sh-chee]
bring приносить/принести [preenas**ee**t/preenyest**ee**]
   I'll bring it back later я верну это позже [ya vyern**oo** **e**ta po**J**-Jeh]
Britain Великобритания [vyeleeka-breet**a**nee-ya]
British британский [breet**a**nskee]
brochure брошюра [brash**oo**ra]
broken сломанный [sl**o**man-ni]
bronchitis бронхит [bran**H**eet]
brooch брошь f [brosh]
broom метла [myetl**a**]
brother брат [brat]
brother-in-law (husband's brother) деверь [d**ye**vyer]
   (wife's brother) шурин [sh**oo**reen]
brown коричневый [kar**ee**chnyevi]
   brown hair каштановые волосы [kasht**a**navi-yeh v**o**lasi]
   brown eyes карие глаза [k**a**ree-yeh glaz**a**]
bruise синяк [seen**ya**k]
brush щётка [sh-ch**o**tka]
   (artist's) кисть f [keest]
bucket ведро [vyedr**o**]

buffet (on train etc) буфет
[boof**yet**]
(in restaurant) шведский стол
[shv**e**tskee stol]
buggy (for child) детская коляска
[d**ye**tska-ya kal**ya**ska]
building здание [zd**a**nee-yeh]
bulb (light bulb) лампочка
[l**a**mpachka]
Bulgaria Болгария [balg**a**ree-ya]
bumper бампер [b**a**mpyer]
bunk койка [k**oy**ka]
bureau de change обмен
валюты [abm**ye**n val**yoo**ti]
see **bank**
burglary ограбление
[agrabl**ye**nee-yeh]
burn (noun) ожог [a**J**ok]
(verb) гореть/сгореть [gar**yet**/
sgar**yet**]
this is burnt это горелое [**e**ta
gar**ye**la-yeh]
burst: a burst pipe
лопнувшая труба [l**o**pnoofsha-
ya tr**oo**ba]
bus автобус [aft**o**boos]
what number bus is it to ...?
какой автобус идёт до ...?
[kak**oy** aft**o**boos eed**yo**t
da ...?]
when is the next bus to ...?
когда следующий автобус
до ...? [kagd**a** sl**ye**doosh-chee
aft**o**boos da ...?]
what time is the last bus?
когда приходит последний
автобус? [kagd**a** pree**H**odeet
pasl**ye**dnee aft**o**boos?]

Tickets (tal**o**ni) for buses,
trams and trolley buses are
available from some street kiosks and vendors, or from the
driver of the vehicle, who sells
them in batches of ten. You
must use a separate 'tal**on**' each
time you board, punching it on
one of the archaic gadgets
mounted inside the vehicle.
Roaming plain-clothes inspec-
tors will issue on-the-spot fines
to anyone caught without a
ticket.

To save money, most Russians
buy a monthly travel pass
(yed**ee**ni beel**ye**t), which goes
on sale in metro stations and kiosks towards the end of the calendar month (in Moscow, from
the 20th). This covers all forms
of transport, although it is possible to buy a pass just for the
metro or for surface transport.
On buses, trams and trolley
buses, you only need to produce
the pass at the request of an inspector.

Stops tend to be few and far between, so getting off at the
wrong one can mean a lengthy
walk. Bus stops are marked with
an 'A' (for aft**o**boos) and trolley bus stops with a 'T' (for
tral**yay**boos). The signs for
tram stops (bearing a 'T' for
tramv**I**) are suspended from the
overhead cables.

→

In addition to the services outlined above, there are special express buses (eks**pre**s) on certain routes. These are not to be confused with minibuses, which Russians call 'marsh**roo**tna-yeh tak**see**'. The latter tend to leave from metro or mainline stations and serve outlying destinations, like the airports, with limited stops. On both, you pay the driver instead of using a 'tal**on**', and the fares are a lot higher than on regular buses.

• • • • • DIALOGUE • • • • • •

does this bus go to ...? идёт ли этот автобус до ...? [eed**yo**tlee **e**tat aft**o**boos da ...?]

no, you need a number ... нет, вам нужен номер ... [nyet, vam n**oo**Jen n**o**myer ...]

business бизнес [b**ee**znes]
bus station автобусная станция [aft**o**boosna-ya st**a**ntsi-ya]
bus stop остановка автобуса [astan**o**fka aft**o**boosa]
bust бюст [byoost]
busy (restaurant etc) оживлённый [aJivl**yon**-ni]
I'm busy tomorrow (said by man/woman) я буду занят/занята завтра [ya bood**oo** zanyat/z**a**nyata z**a**ftra]
but но [no]
butcher's мясной магазин [myasn**oy** magaz**een**]

butter масло [m**a**sla]
button пуговица [p**oo**gaveetsa]
buy покупать/купить [pakoop**a**t/koop**ee**t]
where can I buy ...? где можно купить ...? [gdyeh m**o**Jna koop**ee**t ...?]
by: by train/by car/by plane на поезде/на машине/на самолёте [na p**o**-yezdyeh/na mash**iy**nyeh/na samal**yo**tyeh]
the book is written by ... книга написана ... [kn**ee**ga nap**ee**sana ...]
by the window около окна [**o**kala akn**a**]
by the sea у моря [oo m**o**rya]
by Thursday к четвергу [kchyetvyerg**oo**]
bye! пока! [pak**a**]

C

cabaret кабаре [kabar**eh**]
cabbage капуста [kap**oo**sta]
cabin (on ship) каюта [ka-y**oo**ta]
cable car фуникулёр [fooneekool**yor**]
café кафе [kaf**eh**]

Cafés always serve some sort of food, at much lower prices than full-blown restaurants, and seldom require bookings. Most cafés, like restaurants, sell vodka and cognac, which usually come in large measures of

→

100 grams (sto gram), as well as beer.
see **bar**

cagoule куртка от дождя [k**oo**rtka ad-daJd**ya**]
cake торт [tort]
  a piece of cake кусок торта [koos**o**k t**o**rta]
cake shop кондитерская [kand**ee**tyerska-ya]
call (verb) звать/позвать [zvat/ pazv**a**t]
  (verb: to phone) звонить/ позвонить [zvan**ee**t/ pazvan**ee**t]
  what's it called? как это называется? [kak **e**ta naz**ee**va-yetsa?]
  he/she is called ... его/её зовут ... [yev**o**/ye-**yo** zav**oo**t ...]
  please call the doctor вызовите, пожалуйста, врача [v**i**yzaveetyeh, paJ**a**lsta, vrach**a**]
  please give me a call at 7.30 a.m. tomorrow позвоните мне, пожалуйста, завтра в семь тридцать утра [pazvan**ee**tyeh mnyeh, paJ**a**lsta, z**a**ftra fsy**e**m tr**ee**tsat ootr**a**]
  please ask him to call me пожалуйста, попросите его мне позвонить [paJ**a**lsta, papras**ee**tyeh yev**o** mnyeh pazvan**ee**t]
call back: I'll call back later я вернусь позже [ya vyern**oo**s poJ-Jeh]

(phone back) я перезвоню попозже [ya pyeryezvan**yoo** pap**o**J-Jeh]
call round: I'll call round tomorrow я зайду завтра [ya zId**oo** z**a**ftra]
camcorder видеокамера [veedyeh-ok**a**myera]
camera фотоаппарат [f**o**ta-apar**a**t]
camera shop магазин кино- и фотоаппаратуры [magaz**ee**n keena-ee-f**o**ta-aparat**oo**ri]
camp (verb) жить в палатках [Jiyt fpal**a**tkaH]
  can we camp here? можно ли здесь разбить лагерь? [m**o**Jnalee zdyes razb**ee**t l**a**gyer?]
  see **hotel**
camping gas газовый баллончик [g**a**zavi bal**o**ncheek]
campsite кемпинг [ky**e**mpeeng]
can банка [b**a**nka]
  a can of beer банка пива [b**a**nka p**ee**va]
can*: can you ...? вы можете ...? [viy m**o**Jetyeh ...?]
  can you show me ...? вы можете показать мне ...? [viy m**o**Jetyeh pakaz**a**t mnyeh ...?]
  can I have ...? можно мне, пожалуйста ... [m**o**Jna mnyeh, paJ**a**lsta ...]
  I can't ... я не могу ... [ya nyeh mag**oo** ...]
Canada Канада [kan**a**da]
Canadian канадский [kan**a**tskee]
  I'm Canadian (man/woman) я

канадец/канадка [ya
kanadyets/kanatka]

canal канал [kanal]

cancel отменять/отменить
[atmyenyat/atmyeneet]

candies конфеты [kanfyeti]

candle свеча [svyecha]

can-opener открывалка
[atkrivalka]

cap (hat) шапка [shapka]
    (of bottle) крышка [kriyshka]

car машина [mashiyna]
    by car на машине [na
    mashiynyeh]

carafe графин [grafeen]
    a carafe of white wine, please
    графин белого вина,
    пожалуйста [grafeen byelava
    veena, paJalsta]

card (birthday etc) открытка
[atkriytka]
    here's my (business) card моя
    карточка, пожалуйста [ma-ya
    kartachka, paJalsta]
    cards карты [karti]

cardigan кофта [kofta]

cardphone телефон,
принимающий карточки
[tyelyefon, preeneema-yoosh-
chee kartachkee]

careful осторожный [astaroJni]
    be careful! осторожно!
    [astaroJna!]

caretaker (man/woman) сторож
[storash]

car ferry автопаром [aftaparom]

car park стоянка [sta-yanka]

carpet ковёр [kavyor]

car rental прокат автомобилей

[prakat aftamabeeleeyay]

A growing number of car rental
agencies offer Western models,
with or without a driver. You
should seriously consider hiring
a driver: it could spare you a lot
of anxiety, and may not cost a lot
more than straightforward car
rental. Most rental agencies prefer payment by credit card and
require the full range of docu-
mentation for self-drive rental.
Most places tend to charge about
the same after you take all the
hidden charges into account, so
you might as well go for a well-
known firm rather than an ob-
scure one, where possible.

---

carriage (of train) вагон [vagon]

carrier bag сумка [soomka]

carrot морковь f [markof]

carry нести [nyestee]

carry-cot переносная кроватка
[pyeryenasna-ya kravatka]

carton пакет [pakyet]

case (suitcase) чемодан
[chyemadan]

cash наличные деньги
[naleechni-yeh dyengee]
    will you cash this for me?
    (travellers' cheque) обменяйте,
    пожалуйста, на наличные
    [abmyenyaytyeh, paJalsta, na
    naleechni-yeh]

cash desk касса [kas-sa]

cash dispenser банкомат
[bankamat]

cassette кассета [kas-syeta]

cassette recorder кассетный магнитофон [kas-syetni magneetafon]

castle замок [zamak]

casualty department палата скорой помощи [palata skori pomash-chee]

cat кошка [koshka]

catch (verb: ball) ловить/ поймать [laveet/pimat]
   where do we catch the bus to ...? откуда идёт автобус до ...? [atkooda eedyot aftoboos da ...?]

cathedral собор [sabor]

Catholic (adj) католический [kataleechyeskee]

cauliflower цветная капуста [tsvyetna-ya kapoosta]

cave пещера [pyesh-chyera]

caviar икра [eekra]
   red caviar красная икра [krasna-ya eekra]
   black caviar чёрная икра [chorna-ya eekra]

ceiling потолок [patalok]

celery сельдерей [syeldyeryay]

cemetery кладбище [kladbeesh-chyeh]

centigrade по Цельсию [pa tselsee-yoo]

centimetre сантиметр [santeemyetr]

central центральный [tsentralni]

central heating центральное отопление [tsentralna-yeh ataplyenee-yeh]

centre центр [tsentr]
   how do we get to the city centre? как попасть в центр города? [kak papast ftsentr gorada?]

cereal сухой завтрак [sooHoy zaftrak]

certainly да, конечно [da, kanyeshna]
   certainly not ни в коем случае [nee fko-yem sloocha-yeh]

chair стул [stool]

champagne шампанское [shampanska-yeh]

> Russian champagne, some of which is good if served chilled, is extremely cheap compared with the French variety. The two types to go for are 'sooHo-yeh' and 'bryoot', which are both reasonably dry; 'poloosooHo-yeh' or 'medium dry' is actually very sweet, and 'slatka-yeh' extremely sweet.

change (noun: money) мелочь [myelach]
(verb: money) обменивать/ обменять [abmyeneevat/ abmyenyat]
   can I change this for ...? можно обменять это на ...? [moJna abmyenyat eta na ...?]
   I don't have any change у меня нет мелочи [oo menya nyet myelachee]
   can you give me change for a 10,000 rouble note? вы не

могли бы разменять десять тысяч? [viy nyeh mag**lee**bi razmyen**yat** d**ye**syat t**iy**sych?]

•••••• DIALOGUE ••••••

do we have to change (trains)? нужно ли нам сделать пересадку? [**noo**Jnalee nam zd**ye**lat pyeryes**at**koo?]

yes, change at St Petersburg/no, it's a direct train да, сделайте пересадку в Санкт-Петербурге/ нет, это прямой поезд [da, zd**ye**lityeh pyeryes**at**koo fsankt-peetyerb**oo**rgyeh/nyet, eta pryam**oy** po-yest]

changed: to get changed переодеваться/переодеться [pyeryeh-adyev**at**sa/pyeryeh-ad**ye**tsa]

charge (noun) цена [ts**en**a] (verb) назначать/назначить цену [naznach**at**/nazn**a**cheet ts**en**oo]

cheap дешёвый [d**ye**shovi]

do you have anything cheaper? у вас нет ничего подешевле? [oo vas nyet neech**ye**vo padyesh**ev**lyeh?]

check (US: bill) счёт [sh-chyot] (US: cheque) чек [chyek]

check (verb) проверять/ проверить [pravver**yat**/ pr**av**yereet]

could you check the ..., please? проверьте ..., пожалуйста [prav**yer**tyeh ..., pa**Jal**sta]

check in регистрироваться/

зарегистрироваться [ryegeestr**ee**ravatsa/ zaryegeestr**ee**ravatsa]

where do we have to check in? где проходит регистрация? [gdyeh pra**Ho**deet ryegeestr**at**si-ya?]

check-in регистрация [ryegeestr**at**si-ya]

cheek щека [sh-chy**ek**a]

cheerio! пока! [pak**a**!]

cheers! (toast) ваше здоровье! [**va**sheh zdar**ov**yeh!]

cheese сыр [siyr]

chemist's аптека [apt**ye**ka] see pharmacy

cheque чек [chyek]

do you take cheques? вы принимаете чеки? [viy preen**ee**ma-yetyeh chy**ek**ee?]

cheque book чековая книжка [chy**ek**ava-ya kn**ee**shka]

cheque card чековая карточка [chy**ek**ava-ya k**ar**tachka]

cherry вишня [v**ee**shnya]

chess шахматы [sh**a**Hmati]

chest грудь f [grood]

chewing gum жвачка [Jv**ach**ka]

chicken цыплёнок [tsipl**yo**nak]

chickenpox ветрянка [vyetr**ya**nka]

child ребёнок [ryeb**yo**nak] children дети [d**ye**tee]

Disposable nappies are now available in many supermarkets, which usually also stock baby food, but it's best to bring a →

small supply to tide you over,
particularly if you're travelling
outside the big cities. Note
that breast-feeding in public is
totally unacceptable. Children
up to the age of seven ride free
on all forms of transport.

child minder няня [**nya**nya]
children's pool бассейн для
детей [bas**ay**n dlya dyet**yay**]
children's portion детская
порция [d**ye**tska-ya p**o**rtsi-ya]
chin подбородок [padbar**o**dak]
China Китай [Keet**ı**]
Chinese (adj) китайский
[keet**ı**skee]
chips картофель фри [kart**o**fyel
free]
(US: crisps) чипсы [**chee**psi]
chocolate шоколад [shakal**a**t]
milk chocolate молочный
шоколад [mal**o**chni shakal**a**t]
plain chocolate шоколад
[shakal**a**t]
hot chocolate горячий
шоколад [gar**ya**chee shakal**a**t]
choose выбирать/выбрать
[vibeer**a**t/v**iy**brat]
Christian name имя [**ee**mya]
Christmas Рождество
[raЈdyestv**o**]
Christmas Eve канун
рождества [kan**oo**n
raЈdyestv**a**]
merry Christmas! счастливого
Рождества! [sh-chasl**ee**vava
raЈdyestv**a**!]

church церковь f [ts**e**rkaf]

During Soviet times, many
places of worship were con-
verted into museums or work-
shops or simply left to fall into
ruin. Though the majority have
now reverted to their original
function, many are only open for
services.
Visitors are expected to dress
modestly; women should wear
headscarves and men remove
their hats in church.

cider сидр [**see**dr]
cigar сигара [seeg**a**ra]
cigarette сигарета [seegar**ye**ta]
(Russian non-filter) папироса
[papeer**o**sa]

Nearly all Western cigarette
brands are available, though
many of the packets sold from
kiosks are made under licence
(or counterfeited) in Russia or
Turkey; Marlboro kiosks and
hotel shops are likely to stock
the genuine article. Traditional
Soviet brands like Беломор
(byelam**o**r) are what are called
'papeer**o**si', with an inch of tobacco at the end of a long cardboard tube that is twisted to
make a crude filter. It is not
unusual to be approached by
strangers asking for a light
(sp**ee**chka nyeh n**ı**d**yo**tsa?) or
→

a cigarette (oo vas nyeh nidyotsa zakooreet?). While museums and public transport are no-smoking zones, Russians smoke everywhere else.

cigarette lighter зажигалка [zaЛigalka]

cinema кино [keeno]

circle круг [krook]
   (in theatre) ярус [yaroos]

CIS СНГ [es-en-geh]

city город [gorat]

city centre центр города [tsentr gorada]

clean (adj) чистый [cheesti]
   can you clean these for me? вы можете почистить это [viy moЛetyeh pacheesteet eta?]

cleaning solution (for contact lenses) раствор для линз [rastvor dlya leenz]

cleansing lotion очищающий лосьон [acheesh-cha-yoosh-chee lasyon]

clear (obvious) ясный [yasni]

clever умный [oomni]

cliff скала [skala]

climbing альпинизм [alpeeneezm]

clinic клиника [kleeneeka]

cloakroom (for coats) гардероб [gardyerop]

clock часы [chasiy]

close (verb) закрывать/закрыть [zakrivat/zakriyt]

• • • • • • DIALOGUE • • • • • •

what time do you close? когда вы закрываетесь? [kagda viy zakriva-yetyes?]

we close at 8pm on weekdays and 6pm on Saturdays мы закрываемся в восемь в будние дни и в шесть по субботам [miy zakriva-yemsya vvosyem vboodnee-yeh dnee ee fshest pa soobotam]

do you close for lunch? у вас есть обеденный перерыв? [oo vas yest abyedyen-ni pyereriyf?]

yes, between 1 and 2pm да, с часу до двух [da, schasoo da dvooн]

closed закрыто [zakriyta]

cloth (fabric) ткань f [tkan]
   (for cleaning etc) тряпка [tryapka]

clothes одежда [adyeJda]

cloud облако [oblaka]

cloudy облачный [oblachni]

clutch сцепление [stseplyenee-yeh]

coach междугородный автобус [myeJdoo-garodni aftoboos]
   (on train) вагон [vagon]

coach trip автобусная экскурсия [aftoboosna-ya ekskoorsee-ya]

coast берег [byeryek]
   on the coast на побережье [na pabyeryeJeh]

coat пальто [palto]
   (jacket) куртка [koortka]

coathanger вешалка [vyeshalka]

cockroach таракан [tarakan]

cocoa какао [kaka-o]

code (for phoning) код [kod]
**what's the (dialling) code for
Moscow?** какой код для
Москвы? [kak**oy** kod dlya
maskv**iy**?]
coffee кофе m [k**o**fyeh]
two coffees, please две чашки
кофе, пожалуйста [dvyeh
ch**a**shkee k**o**fyeh, pa**J**alsta]

Coffee is readily available and
often of reasonable quality.
Many places offer imported
espresso brands like Lavazza
and occasionally you will be
served an approximation of
an espresso or, better still, a
Turkish coffee – both served
strong and black. Note that coffee is usually served with sugar
already added, so you should
make it clear when you order if
you don't want sugar (byes
s**a**Hara, pa**J**alsta).

---

coin монета [man**ye**ta]
Coke® Кока-кола [k**o**ka-k**o**la]
cold холодный [н**a**l**o**dni]
(noun) простуда [prast**oo**da]
I'm cold мне холодно [mnyeh
н**o**ladna]
I have a cold у меня простуда
[oo men**ya** prast**oo**da]
collapse: **he's collapsed** он
потерял сознание [on
patyer**ya**l saznanee-yeh]
collar воротник [varatn**ee**k]
collect: **I've come to collect ...**
(said by man/woman) я пришёл/

пришла за ... [ya preesh**o**l/
preeshl**a** za ...]
collect call звонок с оплатой
вызываемым абонентом
[zvan**o**k sapl**a**tı visiva-yemim
aban**ye**ntam]
college колледж [kal**e**dj]
colour цвет [tsvyet]
**do you have this in other
colours?** у вас есть это
другого цвета? [oo vas yest **e**ta
droog**o**va tsvy**e**ta?]
colour film цветная плёнка
[tsvyetn**a**-ya pl**yo**nka]
comb расчёска [rash-ch**o**ska]
come приходить/прийти
[preeHad**ee**t/pree**t**ee]

•••••• DIALOGUE ••••••

where do you come from? вы
откуда? [viy atk**oo**da?]
I come from Edinburgh я из
Эдинбурга [ya eez edeenb**oo**rga]

come back возвращаться/
вернуться [vazvrash-ch**a**tsa/
vyern**oo**tsa]
I'll come back tomorrow я
вернусь завтра [ya vyern**oo**s
z**a**ftra]
come in входить/войти
[fHad**ee**t/v**ı**t**ee**]
comfortable удобный [ood**o**bni]
communism коммунизм
[kamoon**ee**zm]
communist (adj)
коммунистический
[kamooneest**ee**chyeskee]
Communist party
коммунистическая партия

[kamooneesteechyeska-ya
partee-ya]

compact disc компакт-диск
[kampakt-deesk]

company (business) компания
[kampanee-ya]

compartment (on train) купе
[koopeh]

complain жаловаться/
пожаловаться [Jalavatsa/
paJalavatsa]

complaint жалоба [Jalaba]
I have a complaint у меня есть
жалоба [oo myenya yest
Jalaba]

completely совершенно
[savyershen-na]

computer компьютер
[kampyooter]

concert концерт [kantsert]

concierge (in hotel) дежурная
[dyeJoorna-ya]
see hotel

conditioner (for hair)
опаласкиватель m
[apalaskeevatyel]

condom презерватив
[pryezyervateef]

conference конференция
[kanfyeryentsi-ya]

confirm подтверждать/
подтвердить [patvyerJdat/
patverdeet]

congratulations! поздравляю!
[pazdravlya-yoo!]

connecting flight стыковочный
рейс [stikovachni ryays]

connection (transport) пересадка
[pyeryesatka]

conscious в сознании
[fsaznanee-ee]

constipation запор [zapor]

consulate консульство
[konsoolstva]

contact (verb) связаться с
[svyazatsa s]

contact lenses контактные
линзы [kantaktni-yeh leenzi]

contraceptive
противозачаточное средство
[proteevazachatachna-yeh
sryetstva]

convenient удобный [oodobni]
that's not convenient это не
удобно [eta nyeh oodobna]

cook (verb) готовить/
приготовить [gatoveet/
preegatoveet]
the meat is not cooked мясо
не прожарено [myasa nyeh
praJaryena]

cooker плита [pleeta]

cookie печенье [pyechyenyeh]

cooking utensils кухонная
посуда [kooHan-na-ya
pasooda]

cool прохладный [praHladni]

cork пробка [propka]

corkscrew штопор [shtopar]

corner: on the corner на углу [na
oogloo]
in the corner в углу [voogloo]

cornflakes кукурузные
хлопья [kookooroozni-yeh
Hlopya]

correct (right) правильный
[praveelni]

corridor коридор [kareedor]

cosmetics косметика
[kasmyeteeka]

cost (noun) стоимость f
[sto-eemast]

 how much does it cost?
сколько это стоит? [skolka
eta sto-eet?]

cot детская кроватка
[dyetska-ya kravatka]

cottage (in the country) дача
[dacha]

cotton хлопок [Hlopak]

cotton wool вата [vata]

couch (sofa) диван [deevan]

couchette спальное место
[spalna-yeh myesta]

cough (noun) кашель m
[kashel]

cough medicine средство от
кашля [sryedstva at kashlya]

could: could you ...? вы не
могли бы ..? [viy nyeh
magleebi ...?]

 could I have ...? можно
мне ...? [moɹna mnyeh ...?]

country страна [strana]
 (countryside) деревня
[dyeryevnya]

 in the country за городом
[zagaradam]

countryside деревня
[dyeryevnya]

couple (two people) пара [para]
 a couple of hours пару часов
[paroo chasof]

courgette кабачок [kabachok]

courier курьер [kooryer]

course (main course etc) блюдо
[blyooda]

of course конечно [kanyeshna]

of course not конечно, нет
[kanyeshna, nyet]

cousin (male/female) кузен/
кузина [koozen/koozeena]

cow корова [karova]

cracker крекер [krekyer]

craft shop художественный
салон [HoodoJestvyen-ni salon]

crash (noun) авария [avaree-ya]

 I've had a crash (said by man/
woman) я попал/попала в
аварию [ya papal/papala
vavaree-yoo]

crazy сумасшедший
[soomashetshi]

cream (in coffee etc) сливки pl
[sleefkee]

 (in cake, lotion) крем [kryem]

 (colour) кремовый [kryemavi]

soured cream сметана
[smyetana]

creche ясли pl [yaslee]

credit card кредитная карточка
[kryedeetna-ya kartachka]

 do you take credit cards? вы
принимаете кредитные
карточки? [viy preeneema-
yetyeh kryedeetni-yeh
kartachkee?]

Credit cards are becoming more
widely accepted in restaurants
and shops in Moscow and St
Petersburg, but are still not accepted in the majority of outlets
in regional towns and cities.
Many places only take one or

→

two types of card – mostly Visa, Mastercard or Amex (in that order). You will usually need to show your passport or some other form of identification. Always make sure that the transaction is properly recorded, keep the receipt and check that the carbons are destroyed.

Holders of Visa or Amex cards can obtain cash advances in Moscow and St Petersburg (in dollars or roubles) at several venues, notably Dialogbank and Credobank. Alternatively, in these cities, you can use cash dispensers/ATMs which accept Eurocard, Mastercard and bankcards on the Cirrus network, and pay out in dollars or roubles.

•••••• DIALOGUE ••••••

can I pay by credit card? могу ли я заплатить кредитной карточкой? [mag**oo**lee ya zaplat**eet** kryed**eet**nı k**a**rtachkı?]

which card do you want to use? какой карточкой вы хотите заплатить? [kak**oy** k**a**rtachkı viy Hat**ee**tyeh zaplat**eet**?]

Mastercard/Visa

yes, sir да, пожалуйста [da, pa**J**alsta]

what's the number? какой номер? [kak**oy** n**o**myer?]

and the expiry date? когда истекает срок действия? [kagd**a** eestyek**a**-yet srok d**yey**stvee-ya?]

crime
Moscow, in particular, is often viewed as a city overrun by gangsters, with shootings on every corner. Although such dangers are exaggerated by the Western media, visitors should certainly observe obvious precautions like not flashing money or cameras around, or going off with strangers. At night, stick to the well-lit and busier parts of town. Try to blend in whenever possible: the less you look like a tourist, the smaller the risk of trouble. The main targets of crime are rich Russian businessmen, compared with whom foreign tourists are considered small fry. The Mafia is less of a hazard than petty crime (mostly thefts from cars and hotel rooms).

If you are unlucky enough to have something stolen, you will need to go to the police to report it. It's unlikely that there'll be anyone who speaks English, and even less likely that your belongings will be retrieved, but at the very least you should get a statement detailing what you've lost for your insurance claim.

Crimea Крым [kriym]
crisps хрустящий картофель [Hroost**ya**sh-chee kart**o**fyel]
crockery посуда [pas**oo**da]

crossing (by sea, across river) переправа [pyeryeprava]

crossroads перекрёсток [pyeryekryostak]

crowd толпа [talpa]

crowded переполненный [pyeryepolnyen-ni]

crown (on tooth) коронка [karonka]

cruise круиз [kroo-ees]

crutches костыли [kastilee]

cry (verb) плакать/заплакать [plakat/zaplakat]

cucumber огурец [agooryets]

  pickled cucumber солёный огурец [salyoni agooryets]

cup чашка [chashka]

  a cup of tea, please чашку чая, пожалуйста [chashkoo cha-ya, paJalsta]

cupboard шкаф [shkaf]

cure (verb) лечить/вылечить [lyecheet/viylyecheet]

curly кудрявый [koodryavi]

current (electrical) ток [tok]

curtains занавески [zanavyeskee]

cushion подушка [padooshka]

custom обычай [abiychee]

Customs таможня [tamoJnya]

Over the last couple of years, border controls have relaxed considerably. However, all foreigners entering Russia still have to fill in a currency declaration form stating exactly how much money they are bringing into the country. The form will →

be stamped at Customs. When leaving the country, you must fill in a duplicate form stating how much currency you are taking out of Russia and submit it to the Customs officer along with the form you filled out on entry, the aim being to prevent you taking out more than you took in. The entry form is probably as important as your passport, since without it you will have serious problems getting through Customs, so it should be kept in a safe place at all times. As a tourist, you can take out, tax-free, goods worth up to fifty times the minimum wage; on anything over this amount, you'll have to pay sixty per cent tax on the difference. You can expect to encounter serious problems if you try to export any artwork, military souvenirs, electrical goods or antique samovars.

Customs form таможенная декларация [tamoJen-na-ya dyeklaratsi-ya]

cut (noun) порез [paryes] (verb) резать/разрезать [ryezat/razryezat]

  I've cut myself (said by man/woman) я порезался/порезалась [ya paryezalsa/paryezalas]

cutlery столовые приборы

[stalovi-yeh preebori]
cycling велоспорт [vyelasport]
cyclist (man/woman)
велосипедист/
велосипедистка
[vyelaseepyedeest/
vyelaseepyedeestka]
Czech Republic Чешская
республика [chyeshska-ya
ryespoobleeka]

D

dad папа [papa]
daily ежедневно [yeJednyevna]
(adj) ежедневный
[yeJednyevni]
damage (verb) повреждать/
повредить [pavryeJdat/
pavryedeet]
it's damaged это повреждено
[eta pavryeJdyeno]
I'm sorry, I've damaged this
(said by man/woman) извините, я
повредил/повредила это
[eezveeneetyeh, ya pavryedeel/
pavryedeela eta]
damn! чёрт! [chort!]
damp сырой [siroy]
dance (noun) танец [tanyets]
(verb) танцевать [tantsevat]
would you like to dance?
можно пригласить вас на
танец? [moJna preeglaseet vas
na tanyets?]
dangerous опасный [apasni]
Danish (adj) датский [datskee]
dark (adj: colour) тёмный
[tyomni]

dark green тёмно-зелёный
[tyomna-zyelyoni]
it's getting dark темнеет
[tyemnyeh-yet]
date*: what's the date today?
какое сегодня число?
[kako-yeh syevodnya cheeslo?]
let's make a date for next
Monday договоримся на
следующий понедельник
[dagavareemsya na slyedoosh-
chee panyedyelneek]

You may wonder why the Great
October Revolution always used
to be celebrated in November.
The reason is that at the time
of the Revolution the Russians
were still using the Julian calendar, which lagged behind the
Gregorian calendar (used by the
rest of Europe) by a good two
weeks. The Bolsheviks switched
to the Gregorian calendar in
February 1918, leaping straight
forward from January 31 to
February 14.

dates (fruit) финики [feeneekee]
daughter дочь [doch]
daughter-in-law невестка
[nyevyestka]
dawn рассвет [ras-svyet]
at dawn на рассвете [na ras-
svyetyeh]
day день m [dyen]
the day before накануне
[nakanoonyeh]
the day after tomorrow

послезавтра [**po**slyeh-z**a**ftra]
the day before yesterday
позавчера [pazafch**ye**ra]
next day на следующий день
[na sl**ye**doosh-chee dyen]
every day каждый день [k**a**jdi
dyen]
all day весь день [vyes dyen]
in two days' time через два
дня [ch**ye**ryes dva dnya]
have a nice day всего
хорошего! [fsyevo H**a**rosheva!]
day trip однодневная
экскурсия [adnadn**ye**vna-ya
eksk**oo**rsee-ya]
dead мёртвый [m**yo**rtvi]
deaf глухой [glooH**oy**]
deal (business) сделка [zd**ye**lka]
it's a deal (said by man/woman)
согласен/согласна [sagl**a**syen/
sagl**a**sna]
death смерть f [smyert]
decaffeinated coffee кофе без
кофеина [k**o**fyeh byes kafyeh-
eena]
December декабрь m [dyek**a**br]
decide решать/решить [ryesh**a**t/
ryesh**iy**t]
we haven't decided yet мы
ещё не решили [miy yesh-ch**o**
nyeh ryesh**iy**lee]
decision решение [ryeshen**ee**-
yeh]
deck (on ship) палуба [p**a**looba]
deckchair шезлонг [shezl**o**ng]
deep глубокий [gloob**o**kee]
definitely: we'll definitely come
мы обязательно придём [miy
abyaz**a**tyelna preed**yo**m]

it's definitely not possible это
совершенно невозможно
[**e**ta savyershen-na
nyevazm**o**Jna]
degree (qualification) диплом
[deepl**o**m]
delay (noun) задержка
[zad**ye**rshka]
delay: the flight was delayed
рейс задержался [ryays
zadyerJ**a**lsa]
deliberately умышленно
[oom**iy**shlen-na]
delicatessen кулинария
[kooleenar**ee**-ya]
delicious вкусный [fk**oo**sni]
deliver доставлять/доставить
[dastavl**ya**t/dast**a**veet]
delivery (of mail) доставка
[dast**a**fka]
democratic демократический
[dyemakrat**ee**chyeskee]
Denmark Дания [d**a**nee-ya]
dental floss нитка для чистки
зубов [n**ee**tka dlya ch**ee**stkee
zoob**o**f]
dentist зубной врач [zoobn**oy**
vrach]

· · · · · · DIALOGUE · · · · · ·
it's this one here вот этот [vot **e**tat]
this one? этот? [**e**tat?]
no that one нет, вот этот [nyet, vot
etat]
here здесь [zdyes]
yes да [da]

dentures зубной протез
[zoobn**oy** prat**e**s]
deodorant дезодорант

[dyezadarant]

department отдел [ad-dyel]

department store универмаг
[ooneevyermak]

departure (train) отправление
[atpravlyenee-yeh]
(plane) вылет [viylyet]

departure lounge зал ожидания
[zal ajidanee-ya]

depend: it depends как сказать
[kak skazat]
it depends on ... это зависит
от ... [eta zaveeseet at ...]

deposit (as security) задаток
[zadatak]
(as part payment) взнос [vznos]

dessert десерт [dyesyert]

**destination: what's your
destination?** куда вы едете?
[kooda viy yedeetyeh?]

develop проявлять/проявить
[pra-yavlyat/pra-yaveet]

•••••• DIALOGUE ••••••

could you develop these films? вы
можете проявить эти плёнки? [viy
moJetyeh pra-yaveet etee
plyonkee?]

yes, certainly да, конечно [da,
kanyeshna]

when will they be ready? когда
они будут готовы? [kagda anee
boodoot gatovi?]

tomorrow afternoon завтра днём
[zaftra dnyom]

how much is the four-hour service?
сколько стоит проявить за
четыре часа? [skolka sto-eet pra-
yaveet za chyetiyryeh chasa?]

diabetic (noun) диабетик
[dee-abyeteek]

dial (verb) набирать/набрать
номер [nabeerat/nabrat
nomyer]

dialling code код [kod]

To ring abroad from Russia, dial
8, wait for the tone, then dial 10
plus the following country codes:

Australia	61
Ireland	353
New Zealand	64
UK	44
US & Canada	1

---

diamond бриллиант
[breelee-ant]

diaper пелёнка [pyelyonka]

diarrhoea понос [panos]
**do you have something for
diarrhoea?** у вас есть
что-нибудь от поноса? [oo
vas yest shto-neeboot at
panosa?]

diary (for personal experiences)
дневник [dnyevneek]
(business) записная книжка
[zapeesna-ya kneeshka]

dictionary словарь m [slavar]

didn't*
see **not**

die умирать/умереть
[oomeerat/oomyeryet]

diesel дизельное топливо
[deezyelna-yeh topleeva]

diet диета [dee-yeta]
I'm on a diet я на диете [ya na

dee-**ye**tyeh]
I have to follow a special diet
(said by man/woman) я должен/
должна соблюдать особую
диету [ya do**l**Jen/dal**J**na
sablyoo**d**at aso**b**oo-yoo dee-
yetoo]
difference разница [**ra**zneetsa]
what's the difference? в чём
разница? [fchom **ra**zneetsa?]
different разный [**ra**zni]
they are different они разные
[a**n**ee **ra**zni-yeh]
a different table другой
столик [droo**goy st**oleek]
difficult трудный [**tr**oodni]
difficulty трудность f [**tr**oodnast]
dining room столовая
[sta**lo**va-ya]
dinner (evening meal) ужин
[**oo**Jin]
to have dinner ужинать/
поужинать [**oo**Jinat/
pa**oo**Jinat]
direct (adj) прямой [prya**moy**]
is there a direct train? есть ли
прямой поезд? [**ye**stlee
prya**moy** po-yest?]
direction направление
[napravl**ye**nee-yeh]
which direction is it? в каком
это направлении? [fka**ko**m eta
napravl**ye**nee-ee?]
is it in this direction? это в
этом направлении? [eta
v**e**tam napravl**ye**nee-ee?]
directory enquiries справочная
[**s**pravachna-ya]
dirt грязь f [gryas]

dirty грязный [**gr**yazni]
disabled инвалид [eenval**ee**t]
**is there access for the
disabled?** есть ли доступ для
инвалидов? [**ye**stlee d**o**stoop
dlya eenval**ee**daf?]
disappear исчезать/исчезнуть
[eeschyez**at**/eesch**ye**znoot]
my watch has disappeared
мои часы пропали [ma-ee
cha-s**iy** pra**p**alee]
disappointed: I am disappointed
(said by man/woman) я
разочарован/разочарована
[ya razacha**ro**van/
razacha**ro**vana]
disappointing неважный
[nye**va**Jni]
disaster катастрофа [kata**st**rofa]
disco дискотека [deeskat**ye**ka]
discount скидка [**s**keetka]
is there a discount? нет ли
скидки? [n**ye**tlee **s**keetkee?]
disease болезнь [bal**ye**zn]
disgusting отвратительный
[atvrat**ee**tyelni]
dish блюдо [bl**yoo**da]
dishcloth кухонное полотенце
[**koo**Han-na-yeh palat**ye**ntseh]
disinfectant дезинфицирующее
средство
[dyezeen-feets**iy**roo-yoosh-
chyeh-yeh s**rye**tstva]
disk (for computer) диск [deesk]
disposable diapers/nappies
одноразовые пелёнки
[adna**ra**zavi-yeh pyel**yo**nkee]
distance расстояние
[rasta-**ya**nee-yeh]

in the distance на расстоянии
[na rasta-**ya**nee-ee]
district район [rɪ-**o**n]
disturb беспокоить [byespako-
eet]
diversion (detour) объезд
[ab**ye**st]
divorced: I'm divorced (said by
man/woman) я разведён/
разведена [ya razvyed**yo**n/
razvyedyen**a**]
dizzy: I feel dizzy у меня
кружится голова [oo myen**ya**
kroo**J**itsa galav**a**]
do делать/сделать [d**ye**lat/
sd**ye**lat]
  what shall we do? что нам
  делать? [shto nam d**ye**lat?]
  how do you do it? как это
  делается? [kak **e**ta
  d**ye**la-yetsa?]
  will you do it for me?
  пожалуйста, сделайте это
  для меня [pa**J**alsta, zd**ye**lɪtyeh
  eta dlya men**ya**]

•••••• DIALOGUES ••••••
how do you do? здравствуйте!
[zdr**a**stvooytyeh!]
nice to meet you приятно
познакомиться [pree-**ya**tna
paznak**o**meetsa]
what do you do? (work) кем вы
работаете? [kyem viy rab**o**ta-yetyeh?]
I'm a teacher, and you? (said by
man/woman) я учитель/
учительница, а вы? [ya ooch**ee**tyel/
ooch**ee**tyelneetsa, a**viy**?]
I'm a student (said by man/woman) я

студент/студентка [ya stood**ye**nt/
stood**ye**ntka]
what are you doing this evening?
что вы делаете сегодня вечером?
[shto viy d**ye**la-yetyeh syev**o**dnya
v**ye**chyeram?]
we're going out for a drink, do you
want to join us? мы идём куда-
нибудь выпить, не хотите пойти
с нами? [miy eed**yo**m kood**a**-neeboot
v**iy**peet, nyeh Hat**ee**tyeh pɪt**ee**
sn**a**mee?]

do you want cream? вы хотите
сливки? [viy Hat**ee**tyeh sl**ee**fkee?]
I do, but she doesn't я да, а она
нет [ya da, a an**a** nyet]

doctor врач [vrach]
  (title) доктор [d**o**ktar]
  we need a doctor нам нужен
  врач [nam n**oo**Jen vrach]
  please call a doctor вызовите,
  пожалуйста, врача
  [v**iy**zaveetee, pa**J**alsta, vrach**a**]

The standard of doctors varies
enormously so seek recommen-
dations before consulting one. If
your condition is serious, public hospitals will provide free
emergency treatment to foreigners on production of a passport
(but may charge for medica-
tion). Standards of hygiene and
expertise can be low by Western
standards.
If you don't want to go to a
Russian hospital, then the only
→

option is a private clinic charging US rates, which means that it's vital to take out travel insurance before you leave home. Ideally this should also cover you for medical evacuation if you require it.

•••••• DIALOGUE ••••••

where does it hurt? где у вас болит? [gdyeh oo vas baleet?]

right here здесь [zdyes]

does that hurt now? а теперь больно? [atyepyer bolna?]

yes да [da]

take this to the chemist получите это в аптеке [paloocheetyeh eta vaptyekyeh]

document документ [dakoomyent]

dog собака [sabaka]

doll кукла [kookla]

domestic flight внутренний рейс [vnootryen-nee ryays]

don't!* (to adult/child) перестаньте/перестань! [pyeryestantyeh/pyeryestan!]

don't do that! (to adult/child) не делайте/делай этого! [nyeh dyeltyeh/dyeli etava!]

door дверь f [dvyer]

doorman швейцар [shvyaytsar]

double двойной [dvinoy]

double bed двуспальная кровать [dvoospalna-ya kravat]

double room двухместный номер [dvooHmyesni nomyer]

doughnut пончик [poncheek]

down вниз [vnees]

put it down over there положите там [palajiytyeh tam]

it's down there on the right это там, справа [eta tam, sprava]

it's further down the road это дальше по дороге [eta dalsheh pa darogyeh]

downmarket (restaurant etc) дешёвый [dyeshovi]

downstairs внизу [vneezoo]

dozen дюжина [dyooJina]

half a dozen полдюжины [poldyooJini]

draught beer бочковое пиво [bachkova-yeh peeva]

draughty: it's draughty дует [doo-yet]

drawer ящик [yash-cheek]

drawing рисунок [reesoonak]

dreadful ужасный [ooJasni]

dream сон [son]
(aspiration) мечта [myechta]

dress (noun) платье [platyeh]

dressed: to get dressed одеваться/одеться [adyevatsa/adyetsa]

dressing (for cut) перевязка [pyeryevyaska]
(for salad) приправа [preeprava]

dressing gown халат [Halat]

drink (noun) напиток [napeetak]
(verb) пить/выпить [peet/viypeet]

a cold drink прохладительный напиток [praHladeetyelni napeetak]

can I get you a drink? не хотите ли что-нибудь

выпить? [nyeh Hat**ee**tyehlee sht**o**-neeboot v**iy**peet?]
what would you like (to drink)?
что бы вы хотели (выпить)? [shtobi viy Hat**ye**lee (v**iy**peet)?]
no thanks, I don't drink
спасибо, я не пью [spas**ee**ba, ya nyeh pyoo]
I'll just have a drink of water
стакан воды, пожалуйста [stak**a**n vad**iy**, paJ**a**lsta]
see **bar**

drinking water питьевая вода [peetyev**a**-ya vad**a**]
is this drinking water? это питьевая вода? [**e**ta peetyev**a**-ya vad**a**?]

drive водить машину [vad**ee**t mash**iy**noo]
we drove here мы приехали сюда на машине [miy pree-**ye**Halee syood**a** na mash**iy**nyeh]
I'll drive you home я отвезу вас домой [ya atvez**oo** vas dam**oy**]

driver водитель m [vad**ee**tyel]
driving licence водительские права [vad**ee**tyelskee-yeh prav**a**]

drop: just a drop, please (of drink) чуть-чуть, пожалуйста [choot-ch**oo**t, paJ**a**lsta]
drug (medical) лекарство [lyek**a**rstva]
drugs (narcotics) наркотики [nark**o**teekee]
drunk (adj) пьяный [p**ya**ni]
dry (adj) сухой [sooH**oy**]
dry-cleaner's химчистка [Heemch**ee**stka]

duck утка [**oo**tka]
due: he was due to arrive yesterday он должен был приехать вчера [on dolJen biyl pree-**ye**Hat fchyer**a**]
when is the train due? когда приходит поезд? [kagd**a** preeH**o**deet p**o**-yest?]
dull (pain) тупой [toop**oy**]
(weather) пасмурный [p**a**smoorni]
dummy (baby's) пустышка [poost**iy**shka]
during в течение [ftyech**ye**nee-yeh]
dust пыль [piyl]
dustbin мусорный ящик [m**oo**sarni **ya**sh-cheek]
dusty пыльный [p**iy**lni]
duty-free беспошлинный [byesp**o**shleen-ni]
duty-free shop магазин беспошлинной торговли [magaz**ee**n byesp**o**shleen-ni targ**o**vlee]

Duty-free allowances from Russia into EU countries are currently 250 cigarettes, two litres of wine or champagne, and one litre of spirits; into the US and Australia, allowances are 200 cigarettes, one litre of wine or spirits, and goods up to the value of $400. These allowances may change in the future, so check with Customs before you leave the country.

duvet одеяло [adye-**ya**la]

E

each (every) каждый [**ka**Jdi]
how much are they each?
сколько стоит каждый?
[sk**o**lka st**o**-eet k**a**Jdi?]
ear ухо [**oo**Ha]
earache: I have earache у меня
болит ухо [oo men**ya** bal**ee**t
ooHa]
early рано [**ra**na]
early in the morning рано
утром [**ra**na **oo**tram]
I called by earlier (said by man/
woman) я заходил/заходила
раньше [ya zaHad**ee**l/
zaHad**ee**la **ra**nsheh]
earrings серьги [s**ye**rgee]
east восток [vast**ok**]
in the east на востоке [na
vast**o**kyeh]
Easter Пасха [**pa**sHa]
eastern восточный
[vast**o**chni]
Eastern Europe Восточная
Европа [vast**o**chna-ya
yevr**o**pa]
easy лёгкий [l**yo**Hkee]
eat есть/поесть [yest/pa-**ye**st]
we've already eaten, thanks
мы уже поели, спасибо [miy
ooJ**eh** pa-**ye**lee, spas**ee**ba]

---

eating habits
At home, most Russians take
breakfast (z**a**ftrak) seriously,
tucking into buckwheat pancakes (bleen**iy**) or porridge

→

(k**a**sha), with curd cheese
(tv**o**rok) and sour cream
(smet**a**na) – though some simply settle for a cup of tea and a
slice of bread. Hotels usually
serve an approximation of the
Continental breakfast, probably
just fried egg, bread, butter and
jam; however, ritzier hotels in
the big cities may provide a buffet and offer a Western-style
brunch on Sundays.

Savoury pies (peerashk**ee**) are
often sold on the streets from
late morning – the best are filled
with cabbage, curd cheese or
rice; steer clear of the meat
ones.

Russians are very fond of cakes
(tort). There are over sixty varieties, but the main ingredients
are fairly standard: a sponge
dough, a good deal of honey and
a distinctive spice like cinnamon or ginger or lots of buttery
cream and jam. Russians eat ice
cream (maroJena-yeh) whatever the season; it's sold from
kiosks in most towns.

Despite the increasing popular-
ity of fast food and foreign cuisine, most Russians remain
loyal to their culinary heritage
– above all, to 'zak**oo**skee'.
These small dishes are con-
sumed before a big meal, as an
accompaniment to vodka, or on
their own as a light snack at any

→

time of day. Salted fish, like sprats or herring, are a firm favourite, as are gherkins, assorted cold meats and salads. Hard-boiled eggs or 'bleen**iy**', both served with caviar (eekr**a**), are also available.

At the weekends and when on holiday, many Russians eat their main meal of the day at lunchtime (ab**y**et), between 1 and 4 p.m., and have only 'zak**oo**skee' and tea for supper (**oo**Jin), although restaurants concentrate on evening meals and may close for part of the afternoon.

Most menus start with a choice of soup or 'zak**oo**skee'. Soup has played an important role in Russian cuisine. Cabbage soup (sh-chee), served with sour cream, and beetroot soup (borsh-ch) are common.

Main courses are overwhelmingly based on meat (m**ya**sa), usually beef, mutton or pork, sometimes accompanied by a simple sauce (mushroom, sour cream or cheese). Meat may also make its way into 'pyelm**y**eni', which are dumplings similar in form to ravioli, and often served in a broth.

eau de toilette туалетная вода [too-al**y**etna-ya vad**a**]
economy class экономический класс [ekanam**ee**chyeskee klass]

Edinburgh Эдинбург [edeenb**oo**rk]
egg яйцо [yltts**o**]
eggplant баклажан [bakla**J**an]
either: either ... or ... или ... или ... [**ee**lee ... **ee**lee ...]
   either of them любой из них [lyoob**oy** eez neen]
elastic (noun) резинка [ryez**ee**nka]
elastic band резинка [ryez**ee**nka]
elbow локоть m [l**o**kat]
electric электрический [elyektr**ee**chyeskee]
electrical appliances электрические приборы [elyektr**ee**chyeskee-yeh preeb**o**ri]
electric fire электрокамин [elyektrakam**ee**n]
electrician электрик [el**y**ektreek]
electricity электричество [elyektr**ee**chyestva]
   see **voltage**
elevator лифт [leeft]
else: something else что-то другое [sht**o**-ta droog**o**-yeh]
   somewhere else где-нибудь в другом месте [gd**yeh**-neeboot vdroog**om** m**y**estyeh]

•••••• DIALOGUE ••••••
would you like anything else? вы хотите ещё что-нибудь? [viy нат**ee**tyeh yesh-ch**o** sht**o**-neeboot?]
no, nothing else, thanks нет, спасибо, больше ничего [nyet, spas**ee**ba, b**o**lsheh neechyev**o**]

embassy посольство [pasolstva]

emergency критическая ситуация [kreeteechyeska-ya seetoo-atsi-ya]

this is an emergency! требуется неотложная помощь! [tryeboo-yetsa nyeh-atloJna-ya pomash-ch!]

emergency exit запасной выход [zapasnoy viyHat]

empty пустой [poostoy]

end (noun) конец [kanyets]

at the end of the street в конце улицы [fkantseh ooleetsi]

when does it end? когда это заканчивается? [kagda eta zakancheeva-yetsa?]

engaged (toilet/telephone) занято [zanyata]

(to be married: man/woman) помолвлен/помолвлена [pamolvlyen/pamolvlyena]

engine (car) двигатель m [dveegatyel]

England Англия [anglee-ya]

English (adj) английский [angleeskee]

(language) английский язык [angleeskee yaziyk]

I'm English (man/woman) я англичанин/англичанка [ya angleechaneen/angleechanka]

do you speak English? вы говорите по-английски? [vi gavareet-yeh pa-angleeskee?]

enjoy: to enjoy oneself хорошо проводить/провести время [Harasho pravadeet/pravyestee vryemya]

• • • • • DIALOGUE • • • • •

how did you like the film? вам понравился фильм? [vam panraveelsya feelm?]

I enjoyed it very much, did you enjoy it? мне очень понравился, а вам? [mnyeh ochyen panraveelsa, a vam?]

enjoyable приятный [pree-yatni]

enlargement (of photo) увеличение [oovyeleechyenee-yeh]

enormous огромный [agromni]

enough достаточно [dastatachna]

that's enough достаточно [dastatachna]

that's not enough этого недостаточно [etava nyedastatachna]

it's not big enough это не достаточно большое [eta nyeh dastatachna balsho-yeh]

entrance вход [fHot]

(to house) подъезд [padyest]

envelope конверт [kanvyert]

epileptic эпилептик [epeelyepteek]

equipment оборудование [abaroodavanee-yeh]

(for climbing etc) снаряжение [snaryaJenee-yeh]

(for photography) фотоаппаратура [fota-ap-paratoora]

error ошибка [ashiypka]

escalator эскалатор [eskalatar]

especially особенно [asobyen-na]

essential основной [asnavnoy]
it is essential that ...
необходимо, чтобы ...
[nyeh-apHadeema, shtobi ...]

ethnic (restaurant, dress etc)
национальный [natsi-analni]

EU Европейский Союз
[yevrapyayskee sa-yoos]

Europe Европа [yevropa]

European (adj) европейский
[yevrapyayskee]

even даже [daJeh]
even if ... даже если [daJeh
yeslee]

evening вечер [vyechyer]
this evening сегодня
вечером [syevodnya
vyechyeram]
in the evening вечером
[vyechyeram]

evening meal ужин [ooJin]

eventually в конце концов
[fkantseh kantsof]

ever когда-нибудь
[kagda-neeboot]

• • • • • DIALOGUE • • • • • •

have you ever been to Novgorod?
вы когда-нибудь были в
Новгороде? [viy kagda-neeboot
biylee vnovgaradyeh?]

yes, I was there two years ago
(said by man/woman) да, я там был/
была два года назад [da, ya tam
biyl/bila dva goda nazat]

every каждый [kaJdi]
every-day каждый день [kaJdi
dyen]

everyone все [fsyeh]

everything всё [fsyo]

everywhere везде [vyezdyeh]

exactly! совершенно верно
[savyershen-na vyerna]

exam экзамен [ekzamyen]

example пример [preemyer]
for example например
[napreemyer]

excellent отличный
[atleechni]
excellent! отлично!
[atleechna!]

except кроме [kromyeh]

excess baggage излишек
багажа [eezleeshek bagaJa]

exchange rate обменный курс
[abmyen-ni koors]

exciting увлекательный
[oovlyekatyelni]

excuse me (to get past, to say
sorry) извините!
[eezveeneetyeh!]
(to get attention) простите!
[prasteetyeh!]
(addressing someone with
question) извините,
пожалуйста ... [eezveeneetyeh,
paJalsta ...]

exhausted: I'm exhausted (said by
man/woman) я очень устал/
устала [ya ochyen oostal/
oostala]

exhaust pipe выхлопная труба
[viHlapna-ya trooba]

exhibition выставка [viystafka]

exit выход [**viy**Hat]
  where's the nearest exit? где
  ближайший выход? [gdyeh
  bleeJIshi **viy**Hat?]
expect ожидать [aJid**at**]
expensive дорогой [darag**oy**]
experienced опытный [**o**pitni]
explain объяснять/объяснить
  [abyasny**at**/abyasn**ee**t]
  can you explain that? вы
  можете это объяснить? [viy
  mo**J**etyeh **e**ta abyasn**ee**t?]
express (mail) срочное письмо
  [s**ro**chna-yeh peesm**o**]
  (train, bus) экспресс [ekspr**es**]
extension (telephone)
  добавочный (номер)
  [dab**a**vachni (**no**myer)]
  extension 221, please
  добавочный двести двадцать
  один, пожалуйста
  [dab**a**vachni dv**ye**stee dv**a**tsat
  ad**ee**n, paJ**a**lsta]
extension lead удлинитель
  [oodleen**ee**tyel]
extra: can we have an extra
  one? можно ещё один?
  [m**o**Jna yesh-cho ad**ee**n?]
  do you charge extra for that?
  вы берёте дополнительную
  плату за это? [viy byery**o**tyeh
  dapaln**ee**tyelnoo-yoo pl**a**too za
  eta?]
extraordinary удивительный
  [oodeev**ee**tyelni]
extremely крайне [kr**I**nyeh]
eye глаз [glas]
  will you keep an eye on my
  suitcase for me?

присмотрите, пожалуйста,
за моим чемоданом
[preesmatr**ee**tyeh, paJ**a**lsta, za
ma-**ee**m chyemad**a**nam]
eyebrow pencil карандаш для
бровей [karand**a**sh dlya
brav**yay**]
eye drops глазные капли
[glazn**iy**-yeh k**a**plee]
eyeglasses очки [ach**kee**]
eyeliner карандаш для глаз
[karand**a**sh dlya glas]
eye shadow тени для век pl
[t**ye**nee dlya vyek]

F

face лицо [leets**o**]
factory фабрика [**fa**breeka]
faint (verb) падать/упасть в
  обморок [**pa**dat/oop**a**st
  v**o**bmarak]
  she's fainted она упала в
  обморок [an**a** oop**a**la
  v**o**bmarak]
  I feel faint мне дурно [mnyeh
  d**oo**rna]
fair (funfair) парк аттракционов
  [park at-traktsi-**o**naf]
  (trade) выставка [**viy**stafka]
  (adj: just) справедливый
  [sprav**ye**dl**ee**vi]
fairly довольно [d**a**volna]
fake подделка [pad-d**ye**lka]
fall (verb) падать/упасть [**pa**dat/
  oop**a**st]
  she's had a fall она упала
  [an**a** oop**a**la]
fall (US: autumn) осень f [**o**syen]

in the fall осенью [**o**syenyoo]
false ложный [**lo**Jni]
family семья [syem**ya**]
famous знаменитый [znamyen**ee**ti]
fan (electrical) вентилятор [vyenteel**ya**tar]
(sport: man/woman) любитель/ любительница [lyoob**ee**tyel/ lyoob**ee**tyelneetsa]
fantastic замечательный [zamyech**a**tyelni]
far далеко [dalyek**o**]

• • • • • • DIALOGUE • • • • • •

is it far from here? это далеко отсюда? [eta dalyek**o** ats**yoo**da?]
no, not very far нет, не очень далеко [nyet, nyeh **o**chyen dalyek**o**]
well how far? как далеко? [kak dalyek**o**?]
it's about 20 kilometres примерно двадцать километров [preemy**e**rna dv**a**tsat keelamy**e**traf]

fare стоимость f проезда [st**o**-eemast pra-**ye**zda]
farm ферма [f**ye**rma]
fashionable модный [**mo**dni]
fast быстрый [**bi**ystri]
fat (person) толстый [**to**lsti]
(on meat) жир [Jir]
father отец [at**ye**ts]
father-in-law (wife's father) тесть [tyest]
(husband's father) свёкор [sv**yo**kar]
faucet кран [kran]
fault (mechanical) неисправность f

[nyeh-eespr**a**vnast]
sorry, it was my fault извините, это моя вина [eezveen**ee**tyeh, eta ma-**ya** veen**a**]
it's not my fault это не моя вина [eta nyeh ma-**ya** veen**a**]
faulty: this is faulty это не работает [eta nyeh rab**o**ta-yet]
favourite любимый [lyoob**ee**mi]
fax (noun) факс [faks]
(verb) посылать/послать по факсу [pasil**a**t/pasl**a**t pa f**a**ksoo]

Given the inadequacy of the postal system, it's better to use fax, telex, telegram or electronic mail.
Most large hotels, even those in the regional towns and cities, now have a business centre offering an immediate fax-sending service, via satellite link. Otherwise, it is usually possible to send a fax from the main post office. For a fee you can also arrange to receive faxes; if you leave your number, the post office should notify you when a fax arrives.

fax machine факс [faks]
February февраль m [fyevr**a**l]
feel чувствовать/ почувствовать [ch**oo**stvavat/ pach**oo**stvavat]
I feel hot мне жарко [mnyeh J**a**rka]

I feel unwell мне нехорошо [mnyeh nyeh-Harasho]

I feel like going for a walk мне хочется прогуляться [mnyeh Hochyetsa pragoolyatsa]

how are you feeling? как вы себя чувствуете? [kak viy syebya choostvoo-yetyeh?]

I'm feeling better мне лучше [mnyeh loochsheh]

felt-tip (pen) фломастер [flamastyer]

fence забор [zabor]

fender (of car) бампер [bampyer]

ferry паром [parom]

festival фестиваль m [fyesteeval]

fetch: I'll fetch him я схожу за ним [ya shaJoo za neem]

will you come and fetch me later? вы зайдёте за мной попозже? [viy zIdyotyeh za mnoy papoJ-Jeh?]

feverish: I'm feverish меня лихорадит [myenya leeHaradeet]

few: a few несколько [nyeskalka]

a few days несколько дней [nyeskalka dnyay]

fiancé жених [JeneeH]

fiancée невеста [nyevyesta]

field поле [polyeh]

fight (noun) драка [draka]

figs инжир [eenJiyr]

fill in заполнять/заполнить [zapalnyat/zapolneet]

do I have to fill this in? мне нужно это заполнить? [mnyeh nooJna eta zapolneet?]

fill up наполнять/наполнить [napalnyat/napolneet]

fill it up, please полный бак, пожалуйста [polni bak, paJalsta]

filling (in cake, sandwich) начинка [nacheenka]

(in tooth) пломба [plomba]

film (movie) фильм [feelm]

(for camera) плёнка [plyonka]

•••••• DIALOGUE ••••••

do you have this kind of film? у вас есть такая плёнка? [oo vas yest taka-ya plyonka?]

yes, how many exposures? да, на сколько кадров? [da, na skolka kadraf?]

36 тридцать шесть [treetsat shest]

film processing проявление плёнки [pra-yavlyenee-yeh plyonkee]

filthy грязный [gryazni]

find (verb) находить/найти [naHadeet/nItee]

I can't find it я не могу это найти [ya nyeh magoo eta nItee]

I've found it (said by man/woman) я нашёл/нашла это [ya nashol/nashla eta]

find out узнавать/узнать [ooznavat/ooznat]

could you find out for me? вы не могли бы узнать для меня [viy nyeh magleebi ooznat dlya myenya?]

fine (weather) хороший [Haroshi]

(punishment) штраф [shtraf]

•••••• D I A L O G U E S ••••••

how are you? как у вас дела? [kak oo vas dyel**a**?]

I'm fine thanks хорошо, спасибо [нarash**o**, spas**ee**ba]

is that OK? так хорошо? [tak нarash**o**?]

that's fine thanks хорошо, спасибо [нarash**o**, spas**ee**ba]

---

finger палец [p**a**lyets]

finish (verb) заканчивать/закончить [zak**a**ncheevat/zak**o**ncheet]

I haven't finished yet (said by man/woman) я ещё не закончил/закончила [ya yesh-ch**o** nyeh zak**o**ncheel/zak**o**ncheela]

when does it finish? когда это заканчивается? [kagd**a** eta zak**a**ncheeva-yetsa?]

Finland Финляндия [feenly**a**ndee-ya]

fire (in hearth) огонь m [ag**o**n]
(campfire) костёр [kast**yor**]
(blaze) пожар [paз**a**r]

fire! пожар! [paз**a**r!]

can we light a fire here? здесь можно разложить костёр? [zdyes m**o**зna razlaз**i**yt kast**yor**?]

my room is on fire! в моём номере пожар! [vma-**yom** n**o**myeryeh paз**a**r!]

fire alarm пожарная тревога [paз**a**rna-ya tryev**o**ga]

fire brigade пожарная команда [paз**a**rna-ya kam**a**nda]

To call out the fire brigade dial 01.

---

fire escape пожарная лестница [paз**a**rna-ya l**ye**sneetsa]

fire extinguisher огнетушитель m [agnyetoosh**iy**tyel]

first первый [p**ye**rvi]

I was first (said by man) я был первым [ya biyl p**ye**rvim]
(said by woman) я была первой [ya biyl**a** p**ye**rvi]

at first сначала [snach**a**la]

the first time первый раз [p**ye**rvi ras]

first turn on the left первый поворот налево [p**ye**rvi pavar**o**t nal**ye**va]

first aid первая помощь f [p**ye**rva-ya p**o**mash-ch]

first-aid kit походная аптечка [paн**o**dna-ya apt**ye**chka]

first class (travel etc) первым классом [p**ye**rvim kl**a**sam]

first floor второй этаж [ftar**oy** et**a**sh]
(US) первый этаж [p**ye**rvi et**a**sh]

first name имя [**ee**mya]

fish (noun) рыба [r**i**yba]

fit (attack) приступ [pr**ee**stoop]

fit: it doesn't fit me это мне не по размеру [eta mnyeh nyeh pa razm**ye**roo]

fitting room примерочная [pryem**ye**rachna-ya]

fix (verb: arrange) чинить/починить [cheen**ee**t/

pacheen**ee**t]

can you fix this? (repair) вы можете это починить? [viy moJetyeh eta pacheen**ee**t?]

fizzy газированный [gazeer**o**van-ni]

flag флаг [flag]

flash (for camera) вспышка [fsp**iy**shka]

flat (noun: apartment) квартира [kvart**ee**ra]

(adj) плоский [pl**o**skee]

I've got a flat tyre у меня спустила шина [oo men**ya** spoost**ee**la sh**iy**na]

flavour вкус [fk**oo**s]

flea блоха [blah**a**]

flight рейс [ryays]

flight number номер рейса [n**o**myer r**yay**sa]

flood наводнение [navadn**ye**nee-yeh]

floor (of room) пол [pol]

(storey) этаж [et**a**sh]

on the floor на полу [na pal**oo**]

florist цветочный магазин [tsvyet**o**chni magaz**ee**n]

flour мука [m**oo**ka]

flower цветок [tsvyet**o**k]

flu грипп [greep]

fluent: he speaks fluent Russian он бегло говорит по-русски [on b**ye**gla gavar**ee**t pa-r**oo**skee]

fly (noun) муха [m**oo**Ha]

(verb) лететь/полететь [lyet**ye**t/palyet**ye**t]

can we fly there? туда можно полететь? [tood**a** m**o**Jna palyet**ye**t?]

fog туман [toom**a**n]

foggy туманный [toom**a**n-ni]

folk dancing народные танцы pl [nar**o**dni-yeh t**a**ntsi]

folk music народная музыка [nar**o**dna-ya m**oo**zika]

follow следовать/последовать [sl**ye**davat/pasl**ye**davat]

follow me следуйте за мной [sl**ye**dooytyeh za mnoy]

food еда [yed**a**]

food poisoning пищевое отравление [peesh-chyev**o**-yeh atravl**ye**nee-yeh]

food shop/store гастроном [gastran**o**m]

foot (of person) ступня [stoopn**ya**]

on foot пешком [pyeshk**o**m]

football (game) футбол [footb**o**l]

(ball) футбольный мяч [footb**o**lni myach]

football match футбольный матч [footb**o**lni match]

for: do you have something for a headache/diarrhoea? у вас есть что-то от головной боли/поноса? [oo vas yest sht**o**-ta at galavn**oy** b**o**lee/pan**o**sa?]

•••••• D I A L O G U E S ••••••

who's the chicken Kiev for? для кого котлеты по-Киевски [dlya kav**o** katl**ye**ti pa-kee-**ye**fskee?]

that's for me это для меня [eta dlya men**ya**]

and this one? а это? [a eta?]

that's for her это для неё [eta dlya nyeh-**yo**]

where do I get the bus for Belorussky station? откуда идёт автобус до Белорусского вокзала? [atk**oo**da eed**yo**t aft**o**boos da byelar**oo**skava vakz**a**la?]

the bus for the railway station leaves from Tverskaya street автобус до вокзала идёт с Тверской улицы [aft**o**boos da vakz**a**la eed**yo**t stvyersk**oy oo**leetsi]

how long have you been here? вы давно приехали? [viy davn**o** pree-**ye**Halee?]

I've been here for two days, how about you? я здесь уже два дня, а вы? [ya zdyes ooJ**eh** dva dnya, a viy?]

I've been here for a week я здесь уже неделю [ya zdyes ooJ**eh** nyed**ye**lyoo]

forehead лоб [lop]
foreign иностранный [eenastr**a**n-ni]
foreigner (man/woman) иностранец/иностранка [eenastr**a**nyets/eenastr**a**nka]
forest лес [lyes]
forget забывать/забыть [zabiv**a**t/zab**i**yt]
  I forget, I've forgotten (said by man/woman) я забыл/забыла [ya zab**i**yl/zab**i**yla]
fork (for eating) вилка [v**ee**lka]
form (document) бланк [blank]
formal (dress) вечерний [vyech**ye**rnee]
fortnight две недели [dvyeh nyed**ye**lee]

fortunately к счастью [ksh-ch**a**styoo]
forward: could you forward my mail? вы не могли бы переслать мне мою почту [viy nyeh magl**ee**bi pyeryesl**a**t mnyeh ma-**yoo** p**o**chtoo]
forwarding address адрес для пересылки [**a**dryes dlya pyeryes**i**ylkee]
foundation (make-up) тональный крем [tan**a**lni kryem]
fountain фонтан [fant**a**n]
foyer (hotel, theatre) фойе [fay-**yeh**]
fracture перелом [pyeryel**o**m]
France Франция [fr**a**ntsi-ya]
free (no charge) бесплатный [byespl**a**tni]
  is it free (of charge)? это бесплатно? [**e**ta byespl**a**tna?]
freeway автострада [aftastr**a**da]
freezer морозилка [maraz**ee**lka]
French (adj, language) французский [frants**oo**skee]
French fries картофель фри [kart**o**fyel free]
frequent частый [ch**a**sti]
  how frequent is the bus to Suzdal? как часто ходят автобусы в Суздаль? [kak ch**a**sta H**o**dyat aft**o**boosi fs**oo**zdal?]
fresh (weather, breeze) прохладный [praHl**a**dni]
  (fruit etc) свежий [sv**ye**Ji]
fresh orange juice свежий

апельсиновый сок [svyeJi
apyelseenavi sok]
Friday пятница [pyatneetsa]
fridge холодильник
[Haladeeelneek]
fried жареный [Jaryeni]
fried egg яичница
[ya-eeshneetsa]
friend (male/female) друг/подруга
[drook/padrooga]
friendly дружеский [drooJeskee]
**from: when does the next train
from Yaroslavl arrive?** когда
приходит следующий поезд
из Ярославля? [kagda
preeHodeet slyedoosh-chee
po-yest eez yaraslavlya?]
from Monday to Friday с
понедельника до пятницы
[spanyedyelneeka da
pyatneetsi]
from Moscow to Tver от
Москвы до Твери [at maskviy
da tvyeree]

• • • • • • DIALOGUE • • • • • •

where are you from? вы откуда?
[viy atkooda?]
I'm from England я из Англии [ya
eez anglee-ee]

front передняя часть
[pyeryednya-ya chast]
in front впереди [fpyeryedee]
in front of впереди [fpyeryedee]
in front of the hotel перед
гостиницей [pyeryed
gasteeneetsay]
at the front спереди
[spyeryedee]
frost мороз [maros]

frozen замёрзший [zamyorshi]
frozen food замороженные
продукты [zamaroJeni-yeh
pradookti]
fruit фрукты [frookti]
fruit juice фруктовый сок
[frooktovi sok]
frying pan сковородка
[skavarotka]
FSS ФСБ (Федеральная
Служба Безопасности)
[ef-es-beh (fyedyeralna-ya
slooJba byezapasnastee)]
full полный [polni]
this fish is full of bones в этой
рыбе одни кости [vetI riybyeh
adnee kostee]
I'm full (said by man/woman) я
наелся/наелась [ya na-yelsya/
na-yelas]
full board полный пансион
[polni pansee-on]
fun: it was fun было весело
[biyla vyesyela]
funeral похороны pl
[poHarani]
funny (strange) странный [stran-
ni]
(amusing) забавный [zabavni]
fur мех [myeH]
fur hat меховая шапка
[myeHava-ya shapka]
furniture мебель f [myebyel]
further дальше [dalsheh]
it's further down the road это
дальше по улице [eta dalsheh
pa ooleetseh]

how much further is it to Klin?
далеко ли ещё до Клина?
[dalyek**o**lee yesh-ch**o** da kl**ee**na?]

about 5 kilometres около пяти
километров [**o**kala pyat**ee**
keelam**ye**traf]

fuse предохранитель m
[pryeda**H**ran**ee**tyel]
the lights have fused свет
перегорел [svyet pyeryega**rye**l]
fuse wire проволока для
предохранителя [**pro**valaka
dlya pryeda**H**ran**ee**tyelya]
future будущее
[b**oo**doosh-chyeh-yeh]
in future в будущем
[vb**oo**doosh-chyem]

G

game (cards etc) игра [eegr**a**]
  (match) матч [match]
  (meat) дичь f [deech]
garage (for fuel) бензоколонка
  [byenzakal**o**nka]
  (for repairs) станция
  техобслуживания [st**a**ntsi-ya
  tyeHapsl**oo**Jivanee-ya]
  (for parking) гараж [gar**a**sh]
garden сад [sat]
garlic чеснок [chyesn**o**k]
gas газ [gas]
  (US: petrol) бензин [byenz**ee**n]
gas cylinder (camping gas)
  газовый баллон [g**a**zavi
  bal**o**n]
gas permeable lenses

газопроницаемые линзы
[gazapraneets**a**-yemi-yeh l**ee**nzi]
gas station бензоколонка
[byenzakal**o**nka]
gate ворота [var**o**ta]
  (at airport) выход [v**iy**Hat]
gay гомосексуалист
[gomaseksoo-al**ee**st]
gay bar бар для
  гомосексуалистов [bar dlya
  gomaseksoo-**a**leestaf]
gear передача [pyeryed**a**cha]
gearbox коробка передач
[kar**o**pka pyeryed**a**ch]
general (adj) общий [**o**psh-chee]
general delivery до
  востребования
  [da vastr**ye**bavanee-ya]
gents' toilet мужской туалет
[mooshsk**oy** too-al**ye**t]
genuine (antique etc) подлинный
[p**o**dleen-ni]
German (adj) немецкий
[nyem**ye**tskee]
Germany Германия
[gyerm**a**nee-ya]
get (fetch) приносить/принести
[preenas**ee**t/preenyest**ee**]
**could you get me another one,
please?** принесите,
  пожалуйста, ещё один
  [preenyes**ee**tyeh, pa**J**alsta,
  yesh-ch**o** ad**ee**n]
how do I get to ...? как
  попасть в ...? [kak pap**a**st
  v ...?]
**do you know where I can get
them?** вы не знаете, где я
  могу их достать [viy nyeh

zna-yetyeh, gdyeh ya mag**oo** eeH
dast**at**?]

•••••• **DIALOGUE** ••••••

can I get you a drink?? что вы
будете пить? [shto viy b**oo**dyetyeh
peet?]

no, I'll get this one, what would
you like? нет, позвольте мне, что
бы вы хотели? [nyet, pazv**o**ltyeh
mnyeh, shto biy viy H**a**t**ye**lee?]

a glass of red wine бокал
красного вина [bak**a**l kr**a**snava
veen**a**]

get back (return) возвращаться/
вернуться [vazvrash-ch**a**tsa/
vyern**oo**tsa]

get in (arrive) приезжать/
приехать [pree-yeJ-J**a**t/
pree-**ye**Hat]

get off выходить/выйти
[viHad**ee**t/**viy**tee]

where do I get off? где мне
выходить? [gdyeh mnyeh
viHad**ee**t?]

get on (to train etc) садиться/
сесть [sad**ee**tsa/syest]

get out (of car etc) выходить/
выйти [viHad**ee**t/**viy**tee]

get up (in the morning) вставать/
встать [fstav**a**t/fstat]

gift подарок [pad**a**rak]

gift shop магазин сувениров
[magaz**ee**n soovyen**ee**raf]

gin джин [djin]

a gin and tonic, please джин с
тоником, пожалуйста [djin
st**o**neekam, paJ**a**lsta]

girl (child) девочка [d**ye**vachka]

(young woman) девушка
[d**ye**vooshka]

girlfriend подруга [padr**oo**ga]

give давать/дать [dav**a**t/dat]

can you give me some
change? вы не разменяете?
[viy nyeh razmyen**ya**-yetyeh?]

I gave it to him (said by man/
woman) я отдал/отдала ему
это [ya ad-d**a**l/ad-dal**a** yem**oo**
eta]

will you give this to ...?
передайте это,
пожалуйста, ... [pyeryed**i**tyeh
eta, paJ**a**lsta, ...]

•••••• **DIALOGUE** ••••••

how much do you want for this?
сколько вы хотите за это? [sk**o**lka
viy H**a**t**ee**tyeh za **e**ta?]

40,000 roubles сорок тысяч
рублей [s**o**rak t**iy**syach roobly**ay**]

I'll give you 30,000 roubles я дам
вам тридцать тысяч [ya dam vam
tr**ee**tsat t**iy**syach]

give back возвращать/вернуть
[vazvrash-ch**a**t/vyern**oo**t]

glad: I'm glad (said by man/woman)
я рад/рада [ya rat/r**a**da]

glass (material) стекло [st**ye**klo]

(for drinking) стакан [stak**a**n]

a glass of wine бокал вина
[bak**a**l veen**a**]

glasses очки [achk**ee**]

gloves перчатки [pyerch**a**tkee]

glue (noun) клей [klyay]

go (on foot) идти/пойти [eet-
tee/p**i**tee]

(by transport) ехать/поехать

[**ye**Hat/pa-**ye**Hat]
we'd like to go to the Kremlin
мы хотели бы сходить в
Кремль [miy Hat**ye**leebi
sHad**ee**t fk**rye**ml]
where are you going? куда вы
идёте? [kood**a** viy eed**yo**tyeh?]
where does this bus go? куда
идёт этот автобус? [kood**a**
eed**yo**t etat aft**o**boos?]
let's go! пойдемте!
[pId**yo**mtyeh!]
she's gone (left) она ушла
[an**a** ooshl**a**]
where has he gone? куда он
ушёл? [kood**a** on oosh**o**l?]
I went there last week (said by
man/woman) я там был/была
на прошлой неделе [ya tam
biyl/bil**a** na pr**o**shlI nyed**ye**lyeh]
hamburger to go гамбургер на
вынос [g**a**mboorgyer na v**i**ynas]
go away уходить/уйти
[ooHad**ee**t/ooyt**ee**]
go away! уходите!
[ooHad**ee**tyeh!]
go back (return) возвращаться/
вернуться [vazvrash-ch**a**tsa/
vyern**oo**tsa]
go down (the stairs etc)
спускаться/спуститься
[spoosk**a**tsa/spoost**ee**tsa]
go in входить/войти [fHad**ee**t/
vIt**ee**]
**go out: do you want to go out
tonight?** вы не хотите куда-
нибудь пойти сегодня
вечером? [viy nyeh Hat**ee**tyeh
kood**a**-neebood pIt**ee** syev**o**dnya

vy**e**chyeram?]
go through проходить/пройти
[praHad**ee**t/prit**ee**]
go up (the stairs etc)
подниматься/подняться
[padneem**a**tsa/padn**ya**tsa]
goat коза [kaz**a**]
God бог [boH]
goggles защитные очки
[zash-ch**ee**tni-yeh achk**ee**]
gold золото [z**o**lata]
good хороший [Har**o**shi]
  good! хорошо! [Harash**o**!]
  it's no good это не годится
  [eta nyeh gad**ee**tsa]
goodbye до свидания [da
sveed**a**nya]
good evening добрый вечер
[d**o**bri v**ye**chyer]
Good Friday Страстная
Пятница [strasn**a**-ya
p**ya**tneetsa]
good morning доброе утро
[d**o**bra-yeh **oo**tra]
good night (leaving) до свидания
[da sveed**a**nya]
  (when going to bed) спокойной
  ночи [spak**o**ynI n**o**chee]
goose гусь m [goos]
got: we've got to leave нам
нужно идти [nam n**oo**Jna eet-
t**ee**]
  have you got any ...? у вас
  есть ... [oo vas yest ...]
government правительство
[prav**ee**tyelstva]
gradually постепенно
[pastyep**ye**n-na]
gram(me) грамм [gram]

grammar грамматика [gram-
meteeka]

granddaughter внучка
[vnoochka]

grandfather дедушка
[dyedooshka]

grandmother бабушка
[babooshka]

grandson внук [vnook]

grapefruit грейпфрут
[gryaypfroot]

grapefruit juice грейпфрутовый
сок [gryaypfrootavi sok]

grapes виноград [veenagrat]

grass трава [trava]

grateful благодарный
[blagadarni]

gravy соус [so-oos]

great (excellent) замечательный
[zamyechatyelni]

that's great! здорово!
[zdorava!]

a great success большой
успех [balshoy oospyeH]

Great Britain Великобритания
[vyeleekabreetanee-ya]

Greece Греция [gryetsi-ya]

greedy жадный [Jadni]

green зелёный [zyelyoni]

greengrocer's овощной
магазин [avash-chnoy
magazeen]

grey серый [syeri]

grilled жареный на рашпере
[Jaryeni na rashpyeryeh]

grocer's бакалейный магазин
[bakalyayni magazeen]

ground: on the ground на земле
[na zyemlyeh]

ground floor первый этаж
[pyervi etash]

group группа [groop-pa]

guarantee (noun) гарантия
[garantee-ya]

guest (man/woman) гость/гостья
[gost/gostya]

guesthouse дом для приезжих
[dom dlya pree-yeJ-JiH]
see hotel

guide (noun: man/woman) гид
[geet]

guidebook путеводитель m
[pooteevadeetyel]

guided tour экскурсия с гидом
[ekskoorsee-ya zgeedam]

guitar гитара [geetara]

gum (in mouth) десна [dyesna]

gun (pistol) пистолет
[peestalyet]

gym спортзал [sportzal]

gymnastics гимнастика
[geemnasteeka]

H

hair волосы pl [volasi]

hairbrush щётка для волос
[sh-chotka dlya valos]

haircut стрижка [streeshka]

hairdresser's парикмахерская
[pareeHmaHyerska-ya]

hairdryer фен [fyen]

hair gel гель для волос m [gyel
dlya valos]

hair grips шпильки [shpeelkee]

hairspray лак для волос [lak dlya
valos]

half* половина [palaveena]

half an hour полчаса
[pol-chas**a**]

half a litre пол-литра
[pol-l**ee**tra]

about half that примерно
половина от этого
[preem**ye**rna palav**ee**na at
et**a**va]

half board полупансион
[poloo-pansee-**on**]

half-bottle полбутылки
[polboot**iy**lkee]

half fare половинный тариф
[palav**ee**n-ni tar**ee**f]

half-price полцены [pol-tsen**iy**]

hamburger гамбургер
[g**a**mboorger]

ham ветчина [vyetcheen**a**]

hand рука [rook**a**]

handbag сумочка [s**oo**machka]

handbrake ручной тормоз
[roochn**oy** t**o**rmas]

handkerchief носовой платок
[nasav**oy** plat**ok**]

handle (on door, suitcase etc) ручка
[r**oo**chka]

hand luggage ручная кладь f
[roochn**a**-ya klat]

hangover похмелье
[paнm**ye**lyeh]

I've got a hangover я с
похмелья [ya spaнm**ye**lya]

happen случаться/случиться
[slooch**a**tsa/slooch**ee**tsa]

what's happening? что
нового? [shto n**o**vava?]

what has happened? что
случилось? [shto slooch**ee**las?]

happy счастливый

[sh-chastl**ee**vi]

I'm not happy about this мне
это не нравится [mnyeh **e**ta
nyeh nr**a**veetsa]

harbour порт [port]

hard твёрдый [tv**yo**rdi]
(difficult) трудный [tr**oo**dni]

hard-boiled egg яйцо вкрутую
[yıts**o** fkroot**oo**-yoo]

hard currency валюта [val**yoo**ta]

hard lenses жёсткие линзы
[J**o**skee-yeh l**ee**nsi]

hardly едва [yedv**a**]

hardly ever очень редко
[**o**chyen r**ye**tka]

hardware shop хозяйственный
магазин [нaz**iy**stvyen-ni
magaz**ee**n]

hat шляпа [shl**ya**pa]
(with flaps) шапка [sh**a**pka]

hate (verb) ненавидеть
[nyenav**ee**dyet]

have* иметь [eem**ye**t]

can I have ...? можно,
пожалуйста ...? [m**o**Jna,
paJ**a**lsta ...?]

do you have ...? у вас есть ...?
[oo vas yest ...?]

what'll you have? что бы вы
хотели? [shto biy viy нat**ye**lee?]

I have to leave now мне
нужно идти [mnyeh n**oo**Jna
eet-t**ee**]

do I have to ...? нужно ли
мне ...? [n**oo**Jnalee mnyeh ...?]

can we have some ...? можно,
пожалуйста ...? [m**o**Jna,
paJ**a**lsta ...?]

hayfever сенная лихорадка

[syen-n**a**ya leeH**a**r**a**tka]

hazelnuts фундук [foond**oo**k]

he* он [on]

head голова [gal**a**v**a**]

headache головная боль f
[galavn**a**-ya bol]

headlights фары [f**a**ri]

healthy здоровый [zdar**o**vi]

hear слышать/услышать
[sl**i**yshat/oosl**i**yshat]

•••••• **DIALOGUE** ••••••

can you hear me? вы меня
слышите? [viy myen**ya** sl**i**yshityeh?]

I can't hear you, could you repeat
that? я вас не слышу, повторите,
пожалуйста [ya vas nyeh sl**i**yshoo,
paftar**ee**tyeh, pa**J**alsta]

hearing aid слуховой аппарат
[slooHav**oy** aparat]

heart сердце [s**y**ertseh]

heart attack сердечный
приступ [syerd**y**echni
pr**ee**stoop]

heartburn изжога [eez**J**oga]

heat жара [**J**ara]

heater (in room, car)
обогреватель [abagryev**a**tyel]

heating отопление
[atapl**y**enee-yeh]

heavy тяжёлый [tye**J**oli]

heel (of foot) пятка [p**ya**tka]
(of shoe) каблук [kabl**oo**k]
please could you heel these?
вы можете поставьте сюда
набойки? [viy m**o**Jetyeh
past**a**veet syood**a** nab**oy**kee?]

heelbar мастерская по ремонту
обуви [mastyersk**a**-ya pa

ryem**o**ntoo **o**boovee]

height (of person) рост [rost]
(of mountain, building etc) высота
[visat**a**]

helicopter вертолёт [vyertaly**ot**]

hello здравствуйте
[zdr**a**stvooytyeh]
(answer on phone) алло [all**o**]

helmet (for motorcycle) шлем
[shlyem]

help (noun) помощь f
[p**o**mash-ch]
(verb) помогать/помочь
[pamag**a**t/pam**o**ch]
help! помогите!
[pamag**ee**tyeh]
can you help me? вы можете
мне помочь? [viy m**o**Jetyeh
mnyeh pam**o**ch?]
thank you very much for your
help большое спасибо за
помощь [balsh**o**-yeh spas**ee**ba
za p**o**mash-ch]

helpful полезный [pal**y**ezni]

hepatitis гепатит [gyepat**ee**t]

her*: I haven't seen her (said by
man/woman) я её не видел/
видела [ya yeh-**yo** nyeh
v**ee**dyel/v**ee**dyela]
to her ей [yay]
with her с ней [snyay]
for her для неё [dlya nyeh-**yo**]
that's her это она [eta ana]
that's her towel это её
полотенце [eta yeh-**yo**
palat**y**entseh]

herbal tea травяной чай
[travyan**oy** ch**i**]

herbs кухонные травы

[kooHan-ni-yeh travi]

here здесь [zdyes]

  here is/are ... вот ... [vot...]

  here you are вот, пожалуйста [vot, paJalsta]

hers* её [yeh-**yo**]

  that's hers это её [eta yeh-**yo**]

hey! эй! [ay!]

hi! (hello) привет! [preev**ye**t!]

hide (verb) прятаться/спрятаться [pr**ya**tatsa/spr**ya**tatsa]

high высокий [vis**o**kee]

highchair высокий детский стул [vis**o**kee d**ye**tskee stool]

highway (US) автострада [aftastr**a**da]

hill холм [Holm]

him*: I haven't seen him (said by man/woman) я его не видел/видела [ya yev**o** nyeh v**ee**dyel/v**ee**dela]

  to him ему [yem**oo**]

  with him с ним [sneem]

  for him для него [dlya nyev**o**]

  that's him это он [eta on]

hip бедро [byedr**o**]

hire брать/взять напрокат [brat/vzyat naprak**a**t]

  for hire напрокат [naprak**a**t]

  where can I hire a bike? где я могу взять напрокат велосипед? [gdyeh ya mag**oo** vzyat naprak**a**t vyelaseep**ye**t?]

  see rent

his*: it's his car это его машина [eta yev**o** mash**y**na]

  that's his это его [eta yev**o**]

hit (verb) ударять/ударить [oodar**ya**t/ood**a**reet]

hitch-hike путешествовать автостопом [pootyesh**e**stvavat aftast**o**pam]

hobby хобби n [н**o**b-bee]

hockey хоккей m [нak**ya**y]

hold (verb) держать/подержать [dyerJ**a**t/padyerJ**a**t]

hole дыра [dir**a**]

holiday праздник [pr**a**zneek]

  on holiday в отпуске [v**o**tpooskyeh]

Holland Голландия [gal**a**ndee-ya]

home дом [dom]

  at home (in my house etc) дома [d**o**ma]

  (in my country) на родине [na r**o**deenyeh]

  we go home tomorrow мы едем домой завтра [miy **ye**dyem dam**oy** z**a**ftra]

honest честный [ch**ye**sni]

honey мёд [myot]

honeymoon медовый месяц [myed**o**vi m**ye**syats]

hood (US: of car) капот [kap**o**t]

hope (verb) надеяться [nad**ye**-yatsa]

  I hope so надеюсь, что да [nad**yeh**-yoos, shto da]

  I hope not надеюсь, что нет [nad**yeh**-yoos, shto nyet]

hopefully надо надеяться [n**a**da nad**yeh**-yatsa]

horn (of car) гудок [good**o**k]

horrible ужасный [ooJ**a**sni]

horse лошадь f [l**o**shat]

horse riding верховая езда [vyerн**a**va-ya yezd**a**]

hospital больница [bal**nee**tsa]
hospitality гостеприимство
  [gastyepree-**ee**mstva]
  thank you for your hospitality
  спасибо за ваше
  гостеприимство
  [spas**ee**ba za v**a**sheh
  gastyepree-**ee**mstva]
hot (water, food) горячий
  [gar**ya**chee]
  (weather) жаркий [**J**a**rkee]
  (spicy) острый [**o**stri]
  I'm hot мне жарко [mnyeh
  Ja**rka]
  it's hot today сегодня жарко
  [syev**o**dnya **J**a**rka]
hotel гостиница [gast**ee**neetsa]

Most hotels are still unused to
coping with people just turning
up without booking. That's not
to say that they won't have a
room for you, but the price will
in all likelihood be far above the
rate charged to package tourists.
While joint-venture hotels are
comparable to their Western
four-and five-star counterparts,
wholly Russian places tend to
have lower standards than sug-
gested by the Intourist system of
two to four stars, which should
be taken with a pinch of salt.
Four-star hotels tend to date
from the 1980s and come clos-
est to matching the standards
(and prices) of their Western
counterparts. When checking in
→

you should receive a 'pro**poosk'**
or guest card that enables you
to get past the doorman and
claim your room key. Most hotels have a service bureau,
which can obtain theatre tickets,
arrange tours, rental cars and
the like. Each floor is monitored
by a 'dyeJ**oo**rna-ya' or concierge, who will keep your key
while you are away and can arrange to have your laundry done.
A small gift to her on arrival
should help resolve any ensuing
problems, but her presence is no
guarantee of security. Many hotels do not include breakfast in
the price, so it's always wise to
check beforehand. As hotels are
expensive, anyone on a tight
budget will be limited to the din-
giest, dodgiest ones, and will
almost certainly do better by
opting for a hostel or private
accommodation instead. Forget
about campsites, which are
miles outside the city, have poor
facilities and security, and only
function over the summer. In
summer, it's wise to reserve
hostel accommodation in advance.

hotel room номер [**no**myer]
hour час [chas]
house дом [dom]
hovercraft судно на воздушной
  подушке [**soo**dna na

vazd**oo**shnɪ pad**oo**shkyeh]
how как [kak]
  how many? сколько? [sk**o**lka?]
  how do you do? здравствуйте
  [zdr**a**stvooytyeh]

• • • • • • DIALOGUES • • • • • •

  how are you? как дела? [kak
  dy**e**la?]
  fine, thanks, and you? хорошо,
  спасибо, а у вас? [harash**o**,
  spas**ee**ba, a oo vas?]

  how much is it? сколько это
  стоит? [sk**o**lka eta st**o**-eet?]
  10,500 roubles десять тысяч
  пятьсот рублей [d**ye**syat t**iy**syach
  pyats**o**t roobl**yay**]
  I'll take it я возьму это [ya vazm**oo**
  eta]

humid влажный [vl**a**Jni]
Hungary Венгрия [v**y**engree-ya]
hungry голодный [gal**o**dni]
  are you hungry? вы голодны?
  [viy g**o**ladni?]
hurry (verb) спешить
  [spyesh**iy**t]
  I'm in a hurry я спешу [ya
  spyesh**oo**]
  there's no hurry это не к спеху
  [eta nyeh ksp**ye**Hoo]
  hurry up! быстрее!
  [bistr**yeh**-yeh]
hurt (verb) причинять/
  причинить боль
  [preecheen**ya**t/preecheen**ee**t
  bol]
  it hurts больно [b**o**lna]
  it really hurts очень больно

[**o**chyen b**o**lna]
husband муж [moosh]
hydrofoil судно на подводных
  крыльях [s**oo**dna na
  padv**o**dniH kr**iy**lyaH]

I

I я [ya]
ice лёд [lyot]
  with ice со льдом [sald**o**m]
  no ice, thanks безо льда,
  пожалуйста [byezald**a**,
  paJ**a**lsta]
ice cream мороженое
  [maroJena-yeh]
ice-cream cone рожок [raJ**o**k]
ice lolly эскимо [eskeem**o**]
ice rink каток [kat**o**k]
ice skates коньки [kank**ee**]
ice skating катание на
  коньках [kat**a**nee-yeh na
  kank**a**H]
icon икона [eek**o**na]
icy ледяной [lyedyan**oy**]
idea идея [eed**ye**h-ya]
idiot идиот [eedee-**o**t]
if если [**ye**slee]
ignition зажигание
  [zaJigan**ee**-yeh]
ill: he/she is ill он болен/она
  больна [on b**o**lyen/ona baln**a**]
  I feel ill мне плохо [mnyeh
  pl**o**Ha]
illness болезнь f [bal**ye**zn]
imitation (leather)
  искусственный
  [eesk**oo**stvyen-ni]
  (jewellery) подделка [pad-

dyelka]
immediately немедленно
[nyem**ye**dlyen-na]
important важный [va**J**ni]
it's very important это очень
важно [eta **o**chyen va**J**na]
it's not important это не
важно [eta nyeh va**J**na]
impossible: it's impossible это
невозможно [eta
nyevazm**o**Jna]
impressive впечатляющий
[fpyechatl**ya**-yoosh-chee]
improve улучшать/улучшить
[ooloochsh**a**t/ool**oo**chshit]
in: it's in the centre это в
центре [eta fts**e**ntryeh]
in my car в моей машине
[vma-**yay** mash**iy**nyeh]
in Moscow в Москве
[vmaskv**yeh**]
in two days from now через
два дня [ch**ye**ryez dva dnya]
in five minutes через пять
минут [ch**ye**ryes pyat
meen**oo**t]
in May в мае [vma-yeh]
in English по-английски
[pa-angl**ee**skee]
in Russian по-русски
[pa-r**oo**skee]
include включать/включить
[fklyoochat/fklyoocheet]
does that include meals? в это
входит стоимость питания?
[veta fH**o**deet st**o**-eemast
peet**a**nee-ya?]
is that included? это
включено в стоимость? [eta

fklyoochyen**o** fsto-eemast?]
inconvenient неудобный
[nyeh-ood**o**bni]
incredible поразительный
[paraz**ee**tyelni]
Indian (adj) индийский
[eend**ee**skee]
indicator указатель m
[ookaz**a**tyel]
indigestion несварение
[nyesvar**ye**nee-yeh]
indoor pool закрытый бассейн
[zakr**iy**ti bass**yay**n]
indoors в помещении
[fpamyesh-ch**ye**nee-ee]
inexpensive дешёвый [dyesh**o**vi]
infection инфекция
[eenf**ye**ktsi-ya]
infectious инфекционный
[eenfyektsi-**o**n-ni]
inflammation воспаление
[vaspal**ye**nee-yeh]
informal неофициальный
[nyeh-afeetsi-**a**lni]
information информация
[eenfarm**a**tsi-ya]
**do you have any information
about ...?** у вас есть какая-то
информация о ...? [oo vas yest
kaka-ya-ta eenfarm**a**tsi-ya a...?]
information desk справочный
стол [spr**a**vachni stol]
injection инъекция
[een**ye**ktsi-ya]
injured раненый [r**a**nyeni]
she's been injured она ранена
[ana r**a**nyena]
innocent: I'm innocent (said by
man/woman) я не виновен/

виновна [ya nyeh veenovyen/
veenovna]

insect насекомое
[nasyekoma-yeh]

insect bite укус насекомого
[ookoos nasyekomava]

**do you have anything for
insect bites?** у вас есть что-то
от укусов насекомых? [oo vas
yest shto-ta at ookoosaf
nasyekomiн?]

insect repellent средство от
насекомых [sryetstva at
nasyekomiн]

inside внутри [vnootree]

inside the hotel в гостинице
[vgasteeneetseh]

let's sit inside давайте сядем
внутри [davItyeh syadyem
vnootree]

insist настаивать [nasta-eevat]

I insist я настаиваю [ya
nasta-eeva-yoo]

instant coffee растворимый
кофе m [rastvareemi kofyeh]

instead вместо [vmyesta]

give me that one instead
дайте мне это взамен [dItyeh
mnyeh eta vzamyen]

instead of ... вместо ...
[vmyesta ...]

insurance страховка [straнofka]

intelligent умный [oomni]

interested: **I'm interested in ...**
меня интересует ... [myenya
eentyeryesoo-yet ...]

interesting интересный
[eentyeryesni]

that's very interesting это

очень интересно [eta ochyen
eentyeryesna]

international международный
[myeJdoonarodni]

interpreter (man/woman)
переводчик/переводчица
[pyeryevotcheek/
pyeryevotcheetsa]

intersection перекрёсток
[pyeryekryostak]

interval (at theatre) антракт
[antrakt]

into в [v]

I'm not into ... я не
увлекаюсь ... [ya nyeh
oovlyeka-yoos ...]

Intourist Интурист [eentooreest]

introduce знакомить/
познакомить [znakomeet/
paznakomeet]

may I introduce ...? разрешите
представить ... [razryeshiytyeh
pryetstaveet...]

invitation приглашение
[preeglashenee-yeh]

invite приглашать/пригласить
[preeglashat/preeglaseet]

Ireland Ирландия [eerlandee-ya]

Irish ирландский [eerlantskee]

I'm Irish (man/woman) я
ирландец/ирландка [ya
eerlandyets/eerlantka]

iron (for ironing) утюг [ootyook]

can you iron these for me? вы
не могли бы погладить это?
[viy nyeh magleebi pagladeet
eta?]

island остров [ostraf]

it это [eta]

it is ... это ... [eta ...]
is it ...? это ...? [eta ...?]
where is it? где это? [gdyeh
eta?]
it's him это он [eta on]
Italian (adj) итальянский
[eetalyanskee]
Italy Италия [eetalee-ya]
itch: it itches чешется
[chyeshetsa]

J

jack (for car) домкрат [damkrat]
jacket куртка [koortka]
 (tailored) пиджак [peedjak]
jam варенье [varyenyeh]
jammed: it's jammed заело
[za-yela]
January январь m [yanvar]
jar (noun) банка [banka]
jaw челюсть f [chyelyoost]
jazz джаз [djaz]
jealous ревнивый [ryevneevi]
jeans джинсы [djinsi]
jellyfish медуза [myedooza]
jersey джерси n [djersee]
jetty пристань f [preestan]
jeweller's ювелирный магазин
[yoovyeleerni magazeen]
jewellery ювелирные изделия
pl [yoovyeleerni-yeh
eezdyelee-ya]
Jewish еврейский [yevryayskee]
job работа [rabota]
jogging бег трусцой [byek
troostsoy]
 to go jogging бегать трусцой
[byegat troostsoy]

joke шутка [shootka]
journey путешествие
[pootyeshestvee-yeh]
 have a good journey!
счастливого пути!
[sh-chasleevava pootee!]
jug кувшин [koofshiyn]
 a jug of water кувшин воды
[koofshiyn vadiy]
juice сок [sok]
July июль m [ee-yool]
jump (verb) прыгать/прыгнуть
[priygat/priygnoot]
jumper джемпер [djempyer]
junction (of roads) перекрёсток
[pyeryekryostak]
 (on motorway) развилка
[razveelka]
June июнь m [ee-yoon]
just (only) только [tolka]
 just two только два [tolka dva]
 just for me только для меня
[tolka dlya myenya]
 just here именно здесь
[eemyen-na zdyes]
 not just now не сейчас [nyeh
syechas]
 we've just arrived мы только
что приехали [miy tolka shto
pree-yeHalee]

K

keep (verb) оставлять/оставить
[astavlyat/astaveet]
 keep the change сдачи не
надо [zdachee nyeh nada]
 can I keep it? я могу оставить
это себе? [ya magoo astaveet

eta seeb**yeh**?]
please keep it пожалуйста,
оставьте это себе [pa**ja**lsta,
as**taf**tyeh eta seeb**yeh**]
ketchup кетчуп [k**ye**tchoop]
kettle чайник [ch**i**neek]
key ключ [kl**yooch**]
　the key for room 201, please
　ключ от номера двести один,
　пожалуйста [kl**yooch** at
　n**o**myera dv**ye**stee ad**ee**n,
　pa**ja**lsta]
keyring кольцо для ключей
　[k**a**lts**o** dlya klyooch**yay**]
kidneys почки [**po**chkee]
kill (verb) убивать/убить
　[oobeev**a**t/oob**ee**t]
kilo килограмм [keelagr**a**m]
kilometre километр
　[keelam**ye**tr]
　how many kilometres is it to ...?
　сколько километров до ...
　[sk**o**lka keelam**ye**traf da ...]
kind (generous) добрый [d**o**bri]
　that's very kind вы очень
　любезны [viy **o**chyen
　lyoob**ye**zni]

• • • • • • DIALOGUE • • • • • •

which kind do you want? какой
　именно вы хотите? [kak**oy**
　ee**myen**-na viy Hat**ee**tyeh?]
I want this/that kind вот этот/тот,
　пожалуйста [vot **e**tat/tot,
　pa**ja**lsta]

kiosk киоск [kee-**o**sk]
kiss (noun) поцелуй m
　[patsel**ooy**]
　(verb) целовать/поцеловать

[tselav**a**t/patselav**a**t]
kitchen кухня [k**oo**Hnya]
Kleenex® бумажный носовой
　платок [boom**a**jni nasav**oy**
　plat**o**k]
knee колено [kal**ye**na]
knickers трусики [tr**oo**seekee]
knife нож [nosh]
knock (verb) стучать/постучать
　[stooch**a**t/pastooch**a**t]
knock down сбивать/сбить
　[zbeev**a**t/zbe**e**t]
　he's been knocked down by a
　car его сбила машина [yev**o**
　zbeela mash**i**yna]
knock over (object)
　опрокидывать/опрокинуть
　[aprak**ee**divat/aprak**ee**noot]
　(pedestrian) сбивать/сбить с
　ног [zbeev**a**t/zbeet snok]
know (somebody, something, a place)
　знать [znat]
　I don't know я не знаю [ya
　nyeh zna-yoo]
　I didn't know that (said by man/
　woman) я этого не знал/знала
　[ya **e**tava nyeh znal/zn**a**la]
　do you know where I can
　find ...? вы не знаете, где я
　могу найти ...? [viy nyeh
　zn**a**-yetyeh, gdyeh ya mag**oo**
　n**i**t**ee** ...?]
Kremlin Кремль m [kr**ye**ml]

L

label ярлык [yarl**i**yk]
ladies' room, ladies' toilets
　женский туалет [**j**enskee

too-al**ye**t]

ladies' wear женская одежда [**J**enska-ya ad**ye**Jda]

lady дама [**da**ma]

lager светлое пиво [s**vye**tla-yeh **pee**va]

see **beer**

lake озеро [**o**zyera]

lamb (meat) баранина [bar**a**neena]

lamp лампа [**la**mpa]

lane (narrow street) переулок [pyeryeh-**oo**lak]

(country road) дорожка [d**a**roshka]

(motorway) ряд [ryat]

language язык [yaz**iy**k]

language course курсы иностранного языка [**koo**rsi eenastr**a**n-nava yaz**i**ka]

large большой [balsh**oy**]

last последний [pasl**ye**dnee]

last week на прошлой неделе [na pr**o**shl**i** nyed**ye**lyeh]

last Friday в прошлую пятницу [fpr**o**shloo-yoo p**ya**tneetsoo]

last night (evening) вчера вечером [fch**ye**ra v**ye**chyeram]

what time is the last train to Omsk? когда отходит последний поезд в Омск? [kagd**a** at**н**odeet pasl**ye**dnee p**o**-yest vomsk?]

late: sorry I'm late извините за опоздание [eezveen**ee**tyeh za apazd**a**nee-yeh]

the train was late поезд опоздал [p**o**-yest apazd**a**l]

we must go, we'll be late нам нужно идти, а то опоздаем [nam n**oo**Jna eet-t**ee**, a to apazd**a**-yem]

it's getting late становится поздно [stan**o**veetsa p**o**zna]

later позже [p**o**J-Jeh]

I'll come back later я вернусь попозже [ya vyern**oo**s pap**o**J-Jeh]

see you later пока! [pak**a**!]

later on потом [pat**o**m]

latest последний [pasl**ye**dnee]

by Wednesday at the latest не позднее среды [nyeh pazn**ye**h-yeh sr**ye**diy]

laugh (verb) смеяться/ засмеяться [smyeh-**ya**tsa/ zasmyeh-**ya**tsa]

launderette, laundromat прачечная самообслуживания [pr**a**chyechna-ya sama-apsl**oo**Jivanee-ya]

laundry (clothes) бельё [byel**yo**]

(place) прачечная [pr**a**chyechna-ya]

Russians generally wash their clothes at home in the bathtub, and few would risk their garments at municipal laundries, which take a week (or longer) to return clothing.

If you're staying in a hotel where there aren't any formal laundry services available it's usually possible, for a small fee, to do →

a deal with your concierge (dye**joo**rna-ya) or cleaner. If you're staying in Moscow or St Petersburg you can get your washing done at the growing number of private laundries – the various free English-language newspapers provide information on these.

lavatory туалет [too-al**yet**]
law закон [zak**on**]
lawn газон [gaz**on**]
lawyer (man/woman) юрист [yoor**ee**st]
laxative слабительное [slab**ee**tyelna-yeh]
lazy ленивый [lyen**ee**vi]
lead (electrical) провод [pr**o**vat] (verb) вести/привести [vyest**ee**/preeveest**ee**]
  where does this lead to? куда это ведёт? [kood**a** eta vyedy**ot**?]
leaf лист [leest]
leaflet брошюрка [brash**oo**rka]
leak течь f [tyech]
  the roof leaks крыша течёт [kr**i**ysha tyech**ot**]
learn учиться [ooch**ee**tsa]
least: not in the least нисколько [neesk**o**lka]
  at least по крайней мере [pa kr**i**nyay m**ye**ryeh]
leather кожа [k**o**ja]
leave (verb: by transport) уезжать/уехать [oo-yeJ-J**at**/oo-**ye**Hat]

(on foot) уходить/уйти [ooHad**ee**t/ooyt**ee**]
I am leaving tomorrow я уезжаю завтра [ya oo-yeJJ**a**-yoo z**a**ftra]
he left yesterday он уехал вчера [on oo-**ye**Hal fchyer**a**]
may I leave this here? можно это здесь оставить? [m**o**Jna eta zdyes ast**a**veet?]
I left my coat in the bar (said by man/woman) я оставил/оставила пальто в баре [ya ast**a**veel/ast**a**veela palt**o** vb**a**ryeh]
when does the bus for Vladimir leave? когда отходит автобус во Владимир? [kagd**a** atH**o**deet aft**o**boos va vlad**ee**meer?]
leek лук-порей m [look-par**yay**]
left-handed левша [lyefsh**a**]
left левый [l**ye**vi]
  on the left слева [sl**ye**va]
  to the left налево [nal**ye**va]
  turn left поверните налево [pavyern**ee**tyeh nal**ye**va]
  there's none left ничего не осталось [neechyev**o** nyeh ast**a**las]
left luggage (office) камера хранения [k**a**myera Hran**ye**nee-ya]

Most train stations have lockers and/or a 24-hour left luggage office, but you would be tempting fate to use them.

leg нога [nag**a**]

lemon лимон [lee**mon**]
lemonade лимонад [leeman**at**]
lemon tea чай с лимоном m
[chI slee**mon**am]
lend одолжить [adalJ**iyt**]
will you lend me your pen ?
одолжите, пожалуйста, вашу
ручку [adalJ**iy**tyeh, pa**J**alsta,
va**sh**oo **roo**chkoo]
lens (of camera) объектив
[abyekt**eef**]
lesbian лесбиянка
[lyezbee-**ya**nka]
less меньше [m**ye**nsheh]
less than меньше, чем
[m**ye**nsheh, chyem]
less expensive менее дорогой
[m**ye**nyeh-yeh darag**oy**]
lesson урок [oo**rok**]
let (allow) позволять/
позволить [pazval**yat**/
pazv**o**leet]
will you let me know? вы мне
дадите знать? [viy mnyeh
dad**ee**tyeh znat?]
I'll let you know я дам вам
знать [ya dam vam znat]
let's go for something to eat
пойдёмте поедим
[pId**yom**tyeh pa-yed**ee**m]
to let сдаётся [sda-**yot**sa]
let off высаживать/высадить
[visa**J**ivat/**viy**sadeet]
let me off at the corner я
выйду на углу [ya **viy**doo na
oogl**oo**]
letter письмо [peesm**o**]
do you have any letters for
me? есть ли для меня

письма? [**ye**stlee dlya myen**ya**
p**ee**sma?]
letterbox почтовый ящик
[pacht**ov**i **ya**sh-cheek]

Letterboxes come in the form of
small blue-painted metal boxes,
usually fixed to walls and em-
bossed with the word **почта**
(mail).

lettuce салат [sal**at**]
lever (noun) рычаг [rich**ak**]
library библиотека
[beeblee-at**ye**ka]
licence (driver's) водительские
права pl [vad**ee**tyelskee-yeh
pr**av**a]
(permit) лицензия
[leets**en**zee-ya]
lid крышка [kr**iy**shka]
lie (verb: tell untruth) лгать/
солгать [lgat/salg**at**]
lie down лежать/лечь [lye**J**at/
lyech]
life жизнь f [Jizn]
lifebelt спасательный пояс
[spas**at**yelni p**o**-yas]
lifeguard (man/woman) спасатель
[spas**at**yel]
life jacket спасательный жилет
[spas**at**yelni Jil**yet**]
lift (in building) лифт [leeft]
could you give me a lift? вы не
могли бы меня подвезти? [viy
nyeh magl**ee**bi men**ya**
padvyest**ee**?]
would you like a lift? вас
подвезти? [vas padvyest**ee**?]

light (noun) свет [svyet]
(not heavy) лёгкий [lyoHkee]
do you have a light? (for cigarette) нет ли у вас огонька? [nyetlee oo vas aganka?]
light green светло-зелёный [svyetla-zyelyoni]
light bulb лампочка [lampachka]
I need a new light bulb мне нужна новая лампочка [mnyeh nooJna nova-ya lampachka]
lighter (cigarette) зажигалка [zaJigalka]
lightning молния [molnee-ya]
like: **I like it** мне это нравится [mnyeh eta nraveetsa]
I like going for walks я люблю гулять [ya lyooblyoo goolyat]
I like you вы мне нравитесь [viy mnyeh nraveetyes]
I don't like it мне это не нравится [mnyeh eta nyeh nraveetsa]
do you like ...? вам нравится ...? [vam nraveetsa ...?]
I'd like a beer (said by man/woman) я бы выпил/выпила кружку пива [ya biy viypeel/viypeela krooshkoo peeva]
I'd like to go swimming (said by man/woman) я бы хотел/хотела поплавать [ya biy Hatyel/Hatyela paplavat]
would you like a drink? не хотите что-нибудь выпить? [nyeh Hateetyeh shto-neeboot viypeet?]

would you like to go for a walk? не хотите прогуляться? [nyeh Hateetyeh pragoolyatsa?]
what's it like? на что это похоже? [na shto eta paHoJeh?]
I want one like this я такой же хочу [ya takoyJeh Hachoo]
lime лайм [lIm]
line линия [leenee-ya]
lips губы [goobi]
lip salve гигиеническая помада [geegee-yeneechyeska-ya pamada]
lipstick губная помада [goobna-ya pamada]
liqueur ликёр [leekyor]
listen слушать [slooshat]
litre литр [leetr]
a litre of milk литр молока [leetr malaka]
little маленький [malyenkee]
just a little, thanks чуть-чуть, спасибо [choot-choot, spaseeba]
a little milk немного молока [nyemnoga malaka]
a little bit more ещё немного [yesh-cho nyemnoga]
live (verb) жить [Jit]
we live together мы живём вместе [miy Jivyom vmyestyeh]

•••••• DIALOGUE ••••••
where do you live? где вы живёте? [gdyeh viy Jivyotyeh?]
I live in London я живу в Лондоне [ya Jivoo vlondanyeh]

lively оживлённый [aJivlyon-ni]
liver (in body, food) печень f

[p**ye**chyen]

loaf буханка [boo**Ha**nka]

lobby (in hotel) вестибюль m
[vyesteeb**yool**]

lobster омар [am**ar**]

local местный [m**ye**sni]
 **can you recommend a local
 restaurant?** вы можете
 порекомендовать местный
 ресторан? [viy m**o**Jetyeh
 paryekamyendav**at** m**ye**sni
 ryestar**an**?]

lock (noun) замок [zam**ok**]
 (verb) запирать/запереть
 [zapeer**at**/zapyer**yet**]
 it's locked это заперто [**e**ta
 z**a**pyerta]

lock in запирать/запереть
 [zapeer**at**/zapyer**yet**]

lock out: I've locked myself out
 (said by man/woman) я захлопнул/захлопнула дверь
 [ya slooch**I**na za**H**lopn**ool**/
 za**H**lopnoola dvyer]

locker шкафчик [shk**a**fcheek]
 (for luggage etc)
 автоматическая камера
 хранения [aftamat**ee**chyeska-ya
 k**a**myera **H**ran**ye**nee-ya]

lollipop леденец [lyedeen**ye**ts]

London Лондон [l**o**ndan]

long длинный [dl**ee**n-ni]
 how long will it take to fix it?
 сколько времени займёт
 починка? [sk**o**lka vr**ye**meenee
 z**I**my**ot** pach**ee**nka?]
 how long does it take?
 сколько времени это
 занимает? [sk**o**lka vr**ye**meenee

eta zan**ee**ma-yet?]
 a long time долго [d**o**lga]
 one day/two days longer ещё
 один день/два дня [yesh-ch**o**
 ad**ee**n dyen/dva dnya]

long-distance call
 междугородный разговор
 [myeJdoogar**o**dni razgav**or**]

look: I'm just looking, thanks я
 просто смотрю, спасибо [ya
 pr**o**sta smatr**yoo**, spas**ee**ba]
 you don't look well вы
 неважно выглядите [viy nyeh
 v**a**Jna v**i**yglyadeetyeh]
 look out! осторожно!
 [astar**o**Jna!]
 can I have a look? можно мне
 взглянуть? [m**o**Jna mnyeh
 vzglyan**oot**?]

look after ухаживать за
 [ooHa**Jivat** za]

look at смотреть/посмотреть
 на [smatr**yet**/pasmatr**yet** na]

look for искать/поискать
 [eesk**at**/pa-eesk**at**]
 I'm looking for ... я ищу ... [ya
 eesh-ch**oo** ...]

look forward to с нетерпением
 ждать [snyetyerp**ye**nee-yem
 J**dat**]
 I'm looking forward to it я с
 нетерпением жду этого [ya s
 nyetyerp**ye**nee-yem Jdoo **e**tava]

loose (handle etc) расшатанный
 [rasshat**an**-ni]

lorry грузовик [groozav**ee**k]

lose терять/потерять [tyer**yat**/
 patyer**yat**]
 I've lost my way (said by man/

woman) я заблудился/
заблудилась [ya zabloodeelsya/
zabloodeelas]
I'm lost, I want to get to ...
(said by man/woman) я
заблудился/заблудилась, мне
нужно добраться до ... [ya
zabloodeelsa/zabloodeelas,
mnyeh nooJna dabratsa da ...]
I've lost my bag (said by man/
woman) я потерял/потеряла
сумку [ya patyeryal/patyeryala
soomkoo]
lost property (**office**) бюро
находок [byooro naHodak]
lot: a lot, lots много [mnoga]
not a lot немного [nyemnoga]
a lot of people много народу
[mnoga narodoo]
a lot bigger намного больше
[namnoga bolsheh]
I like it a lot мне очень
нравится [mnyeh ochyen
nraveetsa]
lotion лосьон [lasyon]
loud громкий [gromkee]
lounge (in house) гостиная
[gasteena-ya]
(in hotel) фойе [fay-yeh]
(in airport) зал ожидания [zal
aJidanee-ya]
love (noun) любовь f [lyoobof]
(verb) любить [lyoobeet]
lovely замечательный
[zamyechatyelni]
low низкий [neeskee]
luck удача [oodacha]
good luck! желаю успеха!
[Jila-yoo oospyeHa!]

luggage багаж [bagash]
luggage trolley тележка для
багажа [tyelyeshka dlya
bagaJa]
lunch обед [abyet]
lungs лёгкие [lyoHkee-yeh]
luxurious (hotel, furnishings)
роскошный [raskoshni]
luxury роскошь f [roskash]

M

machine машина [mashiyna]
mad (insane) сумасшедший
[soomashetshi]
(angry) рассерженный
[rassyerJen-ni]
magazine журнал [Joornal]
maid (in hotel) горничная
[gorneechna-ya]
maiden name девичья
фамилия [dyeveechya
fameelee-ya]
mail (noun) почта [pochta]
(verb) отправлять/отправить
[atpravlyat/atpraveet]
is there any mail for me? есть
ли для меня почта? [yestlee
dlya myenya pochta?]
see **post office**
mailbox почтовый ящик
[pachtovi yash-cheek]
main главный [glavni]
main course основное блюдо
[asnavno-yeh blyooda]
main post office главпочтамт
[glafpachtamt]
main road (in town) главная
улица [glavna-ya ooleetsa]

(in country) главная дорога
[glavna-ya daroga]

make (brand name) марка [**ma**rka]
(verb) делать/сделать [**dye**lat/
s**dye**lat]
I make it 130,000 roubles по
моим расчётам, сто
тридцать тысяч рублей [pa
ma-**ee**m rash-ch**o**tam, sto
tr**ee**tsat t**iy**syach roobl**yay**]
what is it made of? из чего
это сделано? [ees chyev**o** eta
z**dye**lana?]

make-up косметика
[kasm**ye**teeka]

man мужчина [moosh-ch**ee**na]

manager (hotel: man/woman)
администратор
[admeeneestr**a**trar]
(company: man/woman) менеджер
[**me**nedjer]
can I see the manager?
позовите администратора,
пожалуйста [pazav**ee**tyeh
admeeneestr**a**tara, pa**ja**lsta]

manageress (in shop etc)
заведующая
[zav**ye**doosh-cha-ya]

manual (with manual gears) с
ручной коробкой передач
[sroochn**oy** kar**o**pkı pyeryed**a**ch]

many многие [mn**o**gee-yeh]
not many немногие
[nyemn**o**gee-yeh]

map (city plan) план [plan]
(road map, geographical) карта
[k**a**rta]
network map схема [s**н**y**e**ma]

March март [mart]

margarine маргарин
[margar**ee**n]

market рынок [**riy**nak]

Any self-respecting town has a market (**riy**nak) selling all kinds of fresh produce, where shoppers can sample morsels with no obligation to buy and haggling is very much the order of the day. Generally speaking, opening hours are 8am–8pm. The primitive form of capitalism currently flourishing is best illustrated by the ever multiplying number of street kiosks, selling everything from alcohol to shoes. Another product of Russia's economic chaos is the appearance of unofficial street vendors (pyeryek**oo**psh-cheekee) and flea markets (talk**oo**chkee), where the newly poor dispose of family possessions to make ends meet.
see **bargaining**

marmalade мармелад
[marmyel**a**t]

married: I'm married (said by a
man/woman) я женат/замужем
[ya Jen**a**t/**za**mooJem]
are you married? (to man/woman)
вы женаты/замужем? [viy
Jen**a**ti/**za**mooJem?]

mascara тушь для ресниц
[toosh dlya ryesn**ee**ts]

match (football etc) матч [match]

matches спички [sp**ee**chkee]

material (fabric) ткань f [tkan]

matter: it doesn't matter
неважно [nyevaJna]

what's the matter? в чём дело?
[fchom dyela?]

mattress матрас [matras]

may: may I have another one?
можно ещё один,
пожалуйста? [moJna yesh-cho
adeen, paJalsta?]

may I come in? можно войти?
[moJna vitee?]

may I see it? можно мне
взглянуть? [moJna mnyeh
vzglyanoot?]

may I sit here? здесь
свободно? [zdyes svabodna?]

May май m [mI]

maybe может быть [moJet biyt]

mayonnaise майонез [mI-anes]

me*: that's for me это для меня
[eta dlya myenya]

send it to me пошлите это
мне [pashleetyeh eta mnyeh]

me too я тоже [ya toJeh]

meal еда [yeda]

did you enjoy your meal?
понравилась ли вам еда?
[panraveelaslee vam yeda?]

it was excellent, thank you было
очень вкусно, спасибо [biyla
ochyen fkoosna, spaseeba]

mean (verb) значить [znacheet]

what do you mean? что вы
имеете в виду? [shto viy
eemyeh-yetyeh v-veedoo?]

what does this word mean? что
значит это слово? [shto znacheet
eta slova?]

it means ... это значит ... [eta
znacheet ...]

measles корь f [kor]

German measles краснуха
[krasnooHa]

meat мясо [myasa]

mechanic механик [myeHaneek]

medicine медицина
[myedeetsiyna]

medium (adj: size) средний
[sryednee]

medium-dry полусухой
[poloo-sooHoy]

medium-rare немного
недожаренный [nyemnoga
nyedaJaryen-ni]

medium-sized среднего
размера [sryednyeva
razmyera]

meet встречаться/встретиться
[fstryechatsa/fstryeteetsa]

nice to meet you приятно
познакомиться [pree-yatna
paznakomeetsa]

where shall I meet you? где
мы встретимся? [gdyeh miy
fstryeteemsa?]

meeting встреча [fstryecha]
(business, with more than one
person) совещание [savyesh-
chanee-yeh]
(gathering) собрание
[sabranee-yeh]

meeting place место для

встречи [m**y**esta dlya
fst**ry**echee]
melon дыня [d**i**ynya]
men мужчины [moosh-ch**ee**ni]
mend чинить/починить
[cheen**ee**t/pacheen**ee**t]
could you mend this for me?
вы не могли бы это
починить? [viy nyeh mag**lee**bi
eta pacheen**ee**t?]
mens' room мужской туалет
[mooshsk**oy** too-al**ye**t]
menswear мужская одежда
[m**oo**shska-ya ad**ye**Jda]
mention (verb) упоминать/
упомянуть [oopameen**a**t/
oopameen**oo**t]
don't mention it не за что
[n**ye**h-za-shta]
menu меню [myen**yoo**]
may I see the menu, please?
можно меню, пожалуйста?
[m**o**Jna myen**yoo**, paJ**a**lsta?]
see **menu reader** page 231
message сообщение
[sa-apsh-ch**ye**nee-yeh]
**are there any messages for
me?** мне что-нибудь
передавали? [mnyeh
sht**o**-neeboot pyeryedav**a**lee?]
**I want to leave a message
for ...** вы не могли бы
передать ... [viy nyeh mag**lee**bi
pyeryed**a**t ...?]
metal (noun) металл [m**ye**tal]
metre метр [m**ye**tr]
microwave oven
высокочастотная печь
[vis**o**ka-chast**o**tna-ya pyech]

midday полдень m [p**o**ldyen]
at midday в полдень
[fp**o**ldyen]
middle: in the middle в
середине [fsyereed**ee**nyeh]
in the middle of the night
посреди ночи [pasreed**ee**
n**o**chee]
the middle one средний
[sr**ye**dnee]
midnight полночь f [p**o**lnach]
at midnight в полночь
[fp**o**lnach]
**might: I might want to stay
another day** возможно я
захочу остаться ещё на один
день [vazm**o**Jna ya zaHach**oo**
ast**a**tsa yesh-ch**o** na ad**ee**n dyen]
migraine мигрень f [meegr**ye**n]
mild (weather) тёплый [t**yo**pli]
(taste) неострый [nyeh-**o**stri]
milk молоко [malak**o**]
milkshake молочный коктейль
m [mal**o**chni kakt**ya**yl]
millimetre миллиметр
[meeleem**ye**tr]
minced meat фарш [farsh]
mind: never mind не важно
[nyeh v**a**Jna]
I've changed my mind (said by
man/woman) я передумал/
передумала [ya pyeryed**oo**mal/
pyeryed**oo**mala]

•••••• D I A L O G U E ••••••
do you mind if I open the window?
вы не возражаете, если я открою
окно? [viy nyeh vazra**J**a-yetyeh,
yeslee ya atkr**o**-yoo akno?]

no, I don't mind нет, я не возражаю [nyet, ya nyeh vazraJa-yoo]

mine*: it's mine это моё [eta ma-**yo**]

mineral water минеральная вода [meenyer**al**na-ya vada]

mints мятные конфеты [**mya**tni-yeh kanf**ye**ti]

minute минута [meen**oo**ta]
  in a minute через минуту [ch**ye**ryez meen**oo**too]
  just a minute минуточку [meen**oo**tachkoo]

mirror зеркало [z**ye**rkala]

miss: I missed the bus (said by a man/woman) я опоздал/опоздала на автобус [ya apazd**al**/apazd**a**la na aft**o**boos]

Miss девушка [d**ye**vooshka]

missing: one of my ... is missing пропал один из моих ... [prap**al** ad**ee**n eez ma-**ee**н ...]
  there's a suitcase missing одного чемодана не хватает [adn**a**vo chyemad**a**na nyeh нv**a**ta-yet]

mist туман [too**ma**n]

mistake (noun) ошибка [ash**i**ypka]
  I think there's a mistake мне кажется, здесь ошибка [mnyeh ka**J**etsa, zdyes ash**i**ypka]
  sorry, I've made a mistake (said by a man/woman) извините, я ошибся/ошиблась [eezveen**ee**tyeh, ya ash**i**ypsya/ash**i**yblas]

mix-up: sorry, there's been a

mix-up извините, произошла путаница [eezveen**ee**tyeh, pra-eezashl**a** p**oo**taneetsa]

mobile phone мобильный телефон [mab**ee**lni tyelyef**o**n]

modern современный [savryem**ye**n-ni]

modern art gallery галерея современного искусства [galyer**yeh**-ya savryem**ye**n-nava eesk**oo**ostva]

moisturizer увлажняющий крем [oovlaJn**ya**-yoosh-chee kryem]

moment: I won't be a moment минутку [meen**oo**tkoo]

monastery монастырь m [manast**i**yr]

Monday понедельник [panyed**ye**lneek]

money деньги pl [d**ye**ngee]

The dual economy has become a permanent fixture in Russia, dividing the population into those with access to hard currency (val**yoo**ta) and therefore protection against inflation, and those who are stuck with roubles. As a foreigner, you will routinely be charged many times what the locals pay, either officially (as at museums) or unofficially (by street vendors). There's a large variety of denominations in circulation: 5, 10, 50 and 100 rouble coins and notes to the value of 100, 200, 500, 1,000, 5,000, 10,000, 50,000, 100,000 and 500,000 →

roubles. Higher denominations may be introduced in the future. Counterfeiting is a major problem and shops and bureaux de change therefore err on the side of caution, which makes it hard to change foreign banknotes that are worn or scribbled upon. All cash transactions in Russia must be carried out in roubles, and the use of foreign money is banned. At the many stores and agencies that still price goods or services in dollars (or Deutschmarks), you have to pay in roubles at a rate of exchange set by the management, usually to the customers' disadvantage. If it's way out of line with the bank rate, and if they accept credit cards, you'll save money by paying by credit card instead. But as many places still don't take plastic, you must either go armed with large sums of roubles or be sure that you have access to an exchange point (not so easy after 6pm).

month месяц [m**ye**syats]
monument памятник [p**a**myatneek]
moon луна [loon**a**]
more* больше [b**o**lsheh]
  can I have some more water, please? можно ещё воды, пожалуйста [m**o**Jna yesh-ch**o** vad**iy**, paJ**a**lsta]
  more expensive/interesting

более дорогой/интересный [b**o**lyeh-yeh darag**oy**/ eentyer**ye**sni]
  more than 50 больше пятидесяти [b**o**lsheh pyat**ee**dyestee]
  more than that более того [b**o**lyeh-yeh tav**o**]
  a lot more гораздо больше [gar**a**zda b**o**lsheh]

• • • • • • DIALOGUE • • • • • •
would you like some more? вы хотите ещё? [viy Hat**ee**tyeh yesh-ch**o**?]
no, no more for me, thanks нет, спасибо, мне больше не надо [nyet, spas**ee**ba, mnyeh b**o**lsheh nyeh n**a**da]
how about you? а вы? [a viy?]
I don't want any more, thanks спасибо, я больше не хочу [spas**ee**ba, ya b**o**lsheh nyeh Hach**oo**]

morning утро [**oo**tra]
  this morning сегодня утром [syev**o**dnya **oo**tram]
  in the morning утром [**oo**tram]
Moscow Москва [maskv**a**]
mosquito комар [kam**a**r]
mosquito repellent средство от комаров [sr**ye**tstva at kamar**o**f]
most: I like this one most of all мне больше всего нравится вот это [mnyeh b**o**lsheh fsyev**o** nr**a**veetsa vot **e**ta]
  most of the time большую часть времени [bolshoo-yoo chast vr**ye**myenee]

most tourists большинство туристов [balshinstvo tooreestaf]

mostly главным образом [glavnim obrazam]

mother мать [mat]

mother-in-law (wife's mother) тёща [tyosh-cha] (husband's mother) свекровь [svyekrof]

motorbike мотоцикл [matatsiykl]

motorboat моторная лодка [matorna-ya lotka]

motorway автострада [aftastrada]

mountain гора [gara]
in the mountains в горах [vgaraH]

mountaineering альпинизм [alpeeneezm]

mouse мышь f [miysh]

moustache усы pl [oosiy]

mouth рот [rot]

mouth ulcer язвочка во рту [yazvachka vartoo]

move (verb) двигать/подвинуть [dveegat/padveenoot]
he's moved to another room он перешёл в другую комнату [on pyeryeshol vdroogoo-yoo komnatoo]
could you move up a little? вы не могли бы подвинуться? [viy nyeh magleebi padveenootsa?]
where has it moved to? где это теперь находится? [gdyeh eta tyepyer naHodeetsa?]

movie кинофильм [keenafeelm]

movie theater кинотеатр [keenatyeh-atr]

Mr господин [gaspadeen]

Mrs/Ms госпожа [gaspaJa]

much много [mnoga]
much better/worse гораздо лучше/хуже [garazda loochsheh/HooJeh]
much hotter гораздо жарче [garazda Jarchyeh]
not much немного [nyemnoga]
not very much не очень много [nyeh ochyen mnoga]
I don't want very much я не хочу много [ya nyeh Hachoo mnoga]

mud грязь f [gryas]

mug (for drinking) кружка [krooshka]
I've been mugged меня ограбили [menya agrabeelee]

mum мама [mama]

mumps свинка [sveenka]

museum музей m [moozyay]

Opening hours for museums and galleries tend to be 9 or 10am to 5 or 6pm. You'll find that they are closed at least one day a week, which varies from place to place, and one further day in the month will be set aside as a **санитарный день** (cleaning day). Visitors are often required →

to put on **t**apachkee (felt over-
shoes) to protect the parquet
floors.

It's quite common for museums,
galleries, cafés, shops and
government buildings to be
closed 'for repair' (**закрыто на
ремонт**) or 'for technical
reasons' (**по техническим
причинам**). Given this fact,
it's a good idea to have alterna-
tive plans when visiting galleries and museums.

mushrooms грибы [greeb**iy**]
music музыка [m**oo**zika]
musician (man/woman)
музыкант/музыкантша
[moozik**a**nt/moozik**a**ntsha]
Muslim (adj) мусульманский
[moosoolm**a**nskee]
mussels мидии [m**ee**dee-ee]
must*: I must (said by a man/
woman) я должен/должна [ya
d**o**lJen/dalJ**na**]
I mustn't drink alcohol мне не
следует пить алкоголь
[mnyeh nyeh sl**ye**doo-yet peet
alkag**o**l]
mustard горчица [garch**ee**tsa]
my* мой [moy] m, моя [ma-**ya**] f,
моё [ma-**yo**] n, мои [ma-**ee**] pl
myself: I'll do it myself (said by a
man/woman) я сам/сама это
сделаю [ya sam/sam**a** **e**ta
zd**ye**la-yoo]
by myself (said by man/woman)
один/одна [ad**ee**n/adn**a**]

N

nail (finger) ноготь m [n**o**gat]
(metal) гвоздь m [gvost]
nailbrush щёточка для ногтей
[sh-ch**o**tachka dlya nakt**yay**]
nail varnish лак для ногтей [lak
dlya nakt**yay**]
name имя n [**ee**mya]
my name's ... меня зовут ...
[men**ya** zav**oo**t ...]
what's your name? как вас
зовут? [kak vas zav**oo**t?]
what is the name of this
street? как называется эта
улица [kak naziv**a**-yetsa **e**ta
ooleetsa?]

Besides their first name and
surname, every Russian has a
patronymic derived from their
father's name (such as
Konstanteenovich, son of
Konstanteen, or Ivanovna,
daughter of Ivan), which is used
in conjunction with their first
name as a polite form of address. This is the norm among
older Russians, who find American informality – 'Hi, I'm Bob'
– rather crass.

napkin салфетка [salf**ye**tka]
nappy пелёнка [pyel**yo**nka]
narrow узкий [**oo**skee]
nasty (weather, person) скверный
[skv**ye**rni]
(accident) тяжёлый [tya**J**oli]
national национальный

[natsi-analni]

nationality национальность
[natsi-analnast]

natural натуральный
[natooralni]

nausea тошнота [tashnata]

navy (blue) тёмно-синий
[tyomna-seenee]

near рядом [ryadam]
    is it near the city centre? это
    недалеко от центра города?
    [eta nyedalyeko at tsentra
    gorada?]
    **do you go near the Winter
    Palace?** вы не проезжаете
    Зимний дворец? [viy nyeh
    pra-yeJJa-yetyeh zeemnee
    dvaryets?]
    where is the nearest ...? где
    ближайший ...? [gdyeh
    bleeJIshi ...?]

nearby поблизости
[pableezastee]

nearly почти [pachtee]

necessary необходимый
[nyeh-apHadeemi]

neck шея [sheh-ya]

necklace ожерелье
[aJeryeh-lyeh]

necktie галстук [galstook]

need: I need ... мне надо ...
[mnyeh nada ...]
    do I need to pay? нужно ли
    мне заплатить? [nooJnalee
    mnyeh zaplateet]

needle иголка [eegolka]

negative (film) негатив
[nyegateef]

neither: neither (one) of them ни

один из них [nee adeen eez
neeH]

neither ... nor ... ни ... ни ...
[nee ... nee ...]

nephew племянник
[plyemyan-neek]

net (in tennis) сетка [syetka]
    (in football) ворота [varota]

Netherlands Нидерланды
[neederlandi]

never никогда [neekagda]

•••••• DIALOGUE ••••••

have you ever been to Pskov? вы
когда-нибудь были в Пскове? [viy
kagda-neeboot biylee fpskovyeh?]
no, never, I've never been there
(said by man/woman) нет, я там
никогда не был/не была [nyet, ya
tam neekagda nyebil/nyeh bila]

new новый [novi]

news (radio, TV etc) новости pl
[novastee]

newsagent's (kiosk) газетный
киоск [gazyetni kee-osk]

newspaper газета [gazyeta]

newspaper kiosk газетный
киоск [gazyetni kee-osk]

New Year Новый год [novi got]
    Happy New Year! с Новым
    годом! [snovim godam!]

New Year's Eve новогодняя
ночь f [navagodnya-ya noch]

New Zealand Новая Зеландия
[nova-ya zyelandee-ya]

**New Zealander: I'm a New
Zealander** (man/woman) я
новозеландец/новозеландка
[ya novazyelandyets/

novazyel**a**ntka]

next следующий
[sl**ye**doosh-chee]

the next turning on the left
следующий поворот налево
[sl**ye**doosh-chee pavar**o**t
nal**ye**va]

at the next stop на
следующей остановке [na
sl**ye**doosh-chyay astan**o**fkyeh]

next week на следующей
неделе [na sl**ye**doosh-chyay
nyed**ye**lyeh]

next to рядом с [**rya**dam s]

nice (food) вкусный [fk**oo**sni]
(looks, view etc) красивый
[kras**ee**vi]
(person) приятный [pree-
yatni]

niece племянница
[plyem**ya**n-neetsa]

night ночь f [noch]

at night ночью [n**o**chyoo]

good night спокойной ночи
[spak**oy**ni n**o**chee]

•••••• DIALOGUE ••••••

do you have a single room for one
night? у вас есть одноместный
номер на одни сутки? [oo vas yest
adnam**ye**stni n**o**myer na adn**ee**
s**oo**tkee?]

yes, madam да, есть [da, yest]

how much is it per night? сколько
это стоит в сутки? [sk**o**lka **e**ta
st**o**-eet fs**oo**tkee?]

it's 300,000 roubles for one night
триста тысяч рублей в сутки
[tr**ee**sta t**ii**ysyach roobl**yay** fs**oo**tkee]

OK, I'll take it хорошо, это меня
устраивает [Harash**o**, **e**ta myen**ya**
oostr**a**-eeva-yet]

nightclub ночной клуб
[nachn**oy** kloop]

nightdress ночная рубашка
[nachn**a**-ya roob**a**shka]

night porter ночной портье m
[nachn**oy** part**yeh**]

no нет [nyet]

I've no change у меня нет
мелочи [oo myen**ya** nyet
m**ye**lachee]

there's no ... left ... больше
нет [b**o**lsheh nyet]

no way! ни за что!
[nee-za-sht**o**!]

nobody никто [neekt**o**]

there's nobody there там
никого нет [tam neekav**o** nyet]

noise шум [shoom]

noisy: it's too noisy слишком
шумно [sl**ee**shkam sh**oo**mna]

non-alcoholic безалкогольный
[byezalkag**o**lni]

none ничего [neech**ye**v**o**]

nonsmoking compartment купе
для некурящих [koop**eh** dlya
nyekoor**ya**sh-cheen]

noon полдень m [p**o**ldyen]

at noon в полдень [fp**o**ldyen]

no-one никто [neekt**o**]

nor: nor do I я тоже нет [ya
t**o**Jeh nyet]

normal нормальный [narm**a**lni]

north север [s**ye**vyer]

in the north на севере [na
s**ye**vyeryeh]

to the north на север [na syevyer]

north of Moscow к северу от Москвы [ksyevyeroo at maskviy]

northeast северо-восточный [syevyera-vastochni]

northern северный [syevyerni]

Northern Ireland Северная Ирландия [syevyerna-ya eerlandee-ya]

northwest северо-западный [syevyera-zapadni]

Norway Норвегия [narvyegee-ya]

Norwegian (adj) норвежский [narvyeshskee]

nose нос [nos]

not* не [nyeh]

I'm not hungry (said by man/ woman) я не голоден/голодна [ya nyeh goladyen/galadna]

I don't want any, thank you я не хочу, спасибо [ya nyeh Hachoo, spaseeba]

it's not necessary в этом нет необходимости [vetam nyet nyeh-apHadeemastee]

I didn't know that (said by man/ woman) я этого не знал/знала [ya etava nyeh znal/znala]

not that one, this one не тот, а этот [nyeh tot, a etat]

note (banknote) банкнота [banknota]

notebook блокнот [blaknot]

notepaper (for letters) почтовая бумага [pachtova-ya boomaga]

nothing ничего [neechyevo]

nothing for me, thanks мне ничего, спасибо [mnyeh neechyevo, spaseeba]

nothing else больше ничего [bolsheh neechyevo]

novel роман [raman]

November ноябрь m [na-yabr]

now сейчас [seechas]

number (room, telephone etc) номер [nomyer]

(figure) число [cheeslo]

I've got the wrong number (said by man/woman) я не туда попал/попала [ya nyeh tooda papal/papala]

what is your phone number? какой ваш номер телефона? [kakoy vash nomyer tyelyefona?]

number plate номерной знак [namyernoy znak]

nurse (man/woman) медбрат/ медсестра [myedbrat/ myetsyestra]

nut (for bolt) гайка [gIka]

nuts орехи [aryeHee]

O

occupied (toilet/telephone) занято [zanyata]

o'clock*: it's 3 o'clock три часа [tree chasa]

October октябрь m [aktyabr]

odd (strange) странный [stran-ni]

of*

off (lights) выключено [viyklyoochyena]

it's just off Pushkin Square это рядом с Пушкинской площадью [eta **rya**dam sp**oo**shkeenski pl**o**sh-chadyoo]

we're off tomorrow мы уезжаем завтра [miy oo-ye**J**-**Ja**-yem z**a**ftra]

offensive (language, behaviour) оскорбительный [askarb**ee**tyelni]

office (place of work) офис [**o**fees]

often часто [ch**a**sta]

not often нечасто [nyech**a**sta]

how often are the buses? как часто ходят автобусы? [kak ch**a**sta **H**odyat aft**o**boosi?]

oil масло [m**a**sla]

ointment мазь f [maz]

OK хорошо [**H**arash**o**]

are you OK? с вами всё в порядке? [sv**a**mee fsyo fpar**ya**tkyeh?]

is that OK with you? вы не возражаете? [viy nyeh vazra**Ja**-yetyeh?]

is it OK to ...? можно ...? [m**o**Jna...?]

that's OK thanks ничего, спасибо [neech**e**vo, spas**ee**ba]

I'm OK мне ничего, спасибо [mnyeh neech**e**vo, spas**ee**ba] (I feel OK) со мной всё в порядке [sa mnoy fsyo fpar**ya**tkyeh]

is this train OK for ...? этот поезд идёт до ...? [**e**tat p**o**-yest eed**yo**t da ...?]

I said I'm sorry, OK? (said by man/ woman) я же уже извинился/

извинилась! [ya Jeh oo**J**eh eezveen**ee**lsya/eezveen**ee**las]

old старый [st**a**ri]

• • • • • • DIALOGUE • • • • • •

how old are you? сколько вам лет? [sk**o**lka vam lyet?]

I'm 25 мне двадцать пять [mnyeh dv**a**tsat pyat]

and you? а вам? [a vam?]

old-fashioned старомодный [staram**o**dni]

old town (old part of town) старая часть города [st**a**ra-ya chast g**o**rada]

in the old town в старой части города [fst**a**ri ch**a**stee g**o**rada]

omelette омлет [aml**ye**t]

on* на [na]

on the street/beach на улице/ пляже [na **oo**leetseh/pl**ya**Jeh]

is it on this road? это на этой дороге? [**e**ta na **e**tl dar**o**gyeh?]

on the plane на самолёте [na samal**yo**tyeh]

on Saturday в субботу [fsoob**o**too]

on television по телевизору [pa tyelyev**ee**zaroo]

I haven't got it on me у меня его нет с собой [oo men**ya** yevo nyet s-sab**oy**]

this one's on me (drink) этот за мой счёт [**e**tat za moy sh-chot]

the light wasn't on свет не горел [svyet nyeh gar**ye**l]

what's on tonight? что идёт сегодня? [shto eed**yo**t

syevodnya?]

once (one time) один раз [adeen ras]

   at once (immediately) сразу же [srazooJeh]

one* один [adeen]

   the white one белый [byeli]

one-way ticket билет в один конец [beelyet vadeen kanyets]

onion лук [look]

only только [tolka]

   only one только один [tolka adeen]

   it's only 6 o'clock сейчас только шесть часов [syechas tolka shest chasof]

   I've only just got here (said by man/woman) я только что пришёл/пришла [ya tolka shto preeshol/preeshla]

on/off switch выключатель m [viklyoochatyel]

open (adj) открытый [atkriyti]

   (verb: door) открывать/ открыть [atkrivat/atkriyt]

   when do you open? когда вы открываетесь? [kagda viy atkriva-yetyes?]

   I can't get it open я не могу это открыть [ya nyeh magoo eta atkriyt]

   in the open air на открытом воздухе [na atkriytam vozdooHyeh]

opening times время открытия [vryemya atkriytee-ya]

open ticket билет с открытой датой [beelyet satkriytı datı]

opera опера [opyera]

operation (medical) операция [apyeratsi-ya]

operator (telephone: man/woman) телефонист/телефонистка [tyelyefaneest/tyelyefaneestka]

opposite: in the opposite direction в противоположном направлении [fprateevapaloJnam napravlyenee-ee]

   the bar opposite бар напротив [bar naproteef]

   opposite my hotel напротив моей гостиницы [naproteef ma-yay gasteeneetsi]

optician оптика [opteeka]

or или [eelee]

orange (fruit) апельсин [apyelseen]

   (colour) оранжевый [aranJevi]

   fizzy orange газированный апельсиновый напиток [gazeerovan-ni apyelseenavi napeetak]

orange juice апельсиновый сок [apyelseenavi sok]

orchestra оркестр [arkyestr]

order: can we order now? (in restaurant) можно заказать сейчас? [moJna zakazat syechas?]

   I've already ordered, thanks (said by man/woman) я уже заказал/заказала, спасибо [ya ooJeh zakazal/zakazala, spaseeba]

   I didn't order this (said by man/ woman) я этого не заказывал/

заказывала [ya **e**tava nyeh
zak**a**zival/zak**a**zivala]
out of order не работает [nyeh
rab**o**ta-yet]
ordinary обычный [ab**iy**chni]
Orthodox православный
[pravasl**a**vni]
other другой [droog**oy**]
the other one другой
[droog**oy**]
the other day на днях [na
dnyaн]
I'm waiting for the others я
жду остальных [ya Jdoo
astaln**iy**н]
do you have any others? у вас
нет других? [oo vas nyet
droog**ee**н?]
otherwise иначе [een**a**chyeh]
our*/ours* наш [nash] m, наша
[n**a**sha] f, наше [n**a**sheh] n,
наши [n**a**shi] pl
out: he's out его нет [yev**o** nyet]
three kilometres out of town в
трёх километрах от города
[ftr**yo**н keelam**ye**traн at g**o**rada]
outdoors на открытом воздухе
[na atkr**iy**tam v**o**zdooнyeh]
outside снаружи [snar**oo**Ji]
can we sit outside? можно
сесть снаружи? [m**o**Jna syest
snar**oo**Ji?]
oven духовка [doon**o**fka]
over: over here вот здесь [vot
zdyes]
over there вон там [von tam]
over 500 свыше пятисот
[sv**iy**sheh pyatees**o**t]
our holidays are over наш

отпуск кончился [nash
otpoosk k**o**ncheelsa]
**overcharge: you've overcharged
me** вы с меня слишком
много взяли [viy smen**ya**
sl**ee**shkam mn**o**ga vz**ya**lee]
overcoat пальто [pal't**o**]
**overlooking: I'd like a room
overlooking the courtyard** (said
by man/woman) я хотел/хотела
бы номер с окнами во двор
[ya нat**ye**l/нat**ye**la biy n**o**myer
s **o**knamee va dvor]
overnight (travel) ночной
[nachn**oy**]
overtake обгонять/обгнать
[abgan**ya**t/abgn**a**t]
owe: how much do I owe you?
(said by man/woman) сколько я
вам должен/должна? [sk**o**lka
ya vam d**o**lJen/dalJn**a**?]
own: my own ... мой
собственный ... [moy
s**o**pstvyen-ni ...]
are you on your own? (to man/
woman) вы один/одна? [viy
ad**ee**n/adn**a**?]
I'm on my own (said by man/
woman) я один/одна [ya ad**ee**n/
adn**a**]
owner (man/woman) владелец/
владелица [vlad**ye**lyets/
vlad**ye**leetsa]

P

pack (verb) складывать/
сложить вещи [skl**a**divat/
slaJ**iy**t v**ye**sh-chee]

a pack of ... пачка ...
[**pa**chka]

package (parcel) посылка
[pas**iy**lka]

package holiday
организованный отдых
[arganeez**o**van-ni **o**ddiH]

packet: a packet of cigarettes
пачка сигарет [**pa**chka
seegar**ye**t]

padlock висячий замок
[vees**ya**chee zam**o**k]

page (of book) страница
[stran**ee**tsa]

could you page Mr ...?
вызовите, пожалуйста,
господина ... [v**iy**zaveetyeh,
pa**J**alsta gaspad**ee**na ...]

pain боль [bol]

I have a pain here у меня
здесь болит [oo myen**ya** zdyes
bal**ee**t]

painful болезненный
[bal**ye**znyen-ni]

painkillers болеутоляющие
[bolyeh-ootal**ya**-yoosh-chee-yeh]

paint (noun) краска [kr**a**ska]

painting (occupation) живопись f
[**J**iyvapees]

(picture) картина [kart**ee**na]

pair: a pair of ... пара ...
[p**a**ra ...]

Pakistani (adj) пакистанский
[pakeest**a**nskee]

palace дворец [dvar**ye**ts]

pale бледный [bl**ye**dni]

pale blue светло-голубой
[sv**ye**tla-galoob**oy**]

pan кастрюля [kastr**yoo**lya]

pancakes блины [bleen**iy**]

panties (women's) трусики
[tr**oo**seekee]

pants (underwear: men's) трусы
[troos**iy**]

(women's) трусики
[tr**oo**seekee]

(US: trousers) брюки
[br**yoo**kee]

pantyhose колготки pl
[kalg**o**tkee]

paper бумага [boom**a**ga]

(newspaper) газета [gaz**ye**ta]

a piece of paper листок
бумаги [leest**o**k boom**a**gee]

paper handkerchiefs бумажные
носовые платки
[boom**a**Jni-yeh nasav**iy**-yeh
plat**kee**]

parcel посылка [pas**iy**lka]

pardon (me)? (didn't understand/
hear) простите? [prast**ee**tyeh?]

parents родители [rad**ee**tyelee]

park (noun) парк [park]

(verb) парковаться/
припарковаться [parkav**a**tsa/
preeparkav**a**tsa]

can I park here? можно здесь
припарковаться? [m**o**Jna
zdyes preeparkav**a**tsa?]

parking lot стоянка [sta-**ya**nka]

part часть f [chast]

partner (boyfriend, girlfriend) друг/
подруга [drook/padr**oo**ga]

party (group) группа [gr**oo**p-pa]

(celebration) вечеринка
[vyechyer**ee**nka]

pass (in mountains) перевал
[pyeryev**a**l]

passenger (man/woman)
пассажир/пассажирка
[pasaJiyr/pasaJiyrka]

passport паспорт [paspart]

past*: in the past в прошлом
[fproshlam]

just past the post office сразу
за почтой [srazoo za pochtɪ]

path тропинка [trapeenka]

patronymic отчество [ochyestva]

pattern узор [oozor]

pavement тротуар [tratoo-ar]

on the pavement на тротуаре
[na tratoo-aryeh]

pay (verb) платить/заплатить
[plateet/zaplateet]

can I pay, please? можно
заплатить? [moJna zaplateet?]

it's already paid for это уже
оплачено [eta ooJeh
aplachyena]

• • • • • DIALOGUE • • • • •

who's paying? кто платит? [kto
plateet?]

I'll pay я заплачу [ya zaplachoo]

no, you paid last time, it's my turn
now нет, вы платили в прошлый
раз, теперь моя очередь [nyet, viy
plateelee fproshlɪ ras, tyepyer ma-ya
ochyeryet]

payphone телефон-автомат
[tyelyefon-aftamat]

peaceful мирный [meerni]

peach персик [pyerseek]

peanuts арахис [araHees]

pear груша [groosha]

peas горох [garoH]

peculiar странный [stran-ni]

pedestrian crossing
пешеходный переход
[pyesheHodni pyeryeHot]

peg (for washing) прищепка
[preesh-chyepka]

(for tent) колышек [kolishek]

pen ручка [roochka]

pencil карандаш [karandash]

penfriend (man/woman)
знакомый/знакомая по
переписке [znakomi/
znakoma-ya pa pyeryepeeskyeh]

penicillin пенициллин
[pyeneetsileen]

penknife перочинный ножик
[pyeracheen-ni noJik]

pensioner (man/woman)
пенсионер/пенсионерка
[pyensee-anyer/
pyensee-anyerka]

people люди [lyoodee]

the other people in the hotel
другие люди в гостинице
[droogee-yeh lyoodee
vgasteeneetse]

too many people слишком
много народу [sleeshkam
mnoga narodoo]

pepper (spice, vegetable) перец
[pyerets]

peppermint (sweet) мятная
конфета [myatna-ya kanfyeta]

perfect идеальный [eedee-alni]

perfume духи pl [dooHee]

perhaps может быть [moJet
biyt]

perhaps not может быть, нет
[moJet biyt, nyet]

period (of time) период

[pyere**e**-ot]
(menstruation) месячные pl
[m**ye**syachni-yeh]
perm перманент [pyerman**ye**nt]
permit (noun) разрешение
[razryesh**e**nee-yeh]
per: per night за ночь [z**a**nach]
how much per day? сколько
стоит в сутки? [sk**o**lka st**o**-eet
fs**oo**tkee?]
per cent процент [pr**a**tsent]
person человек [chyelav**ye**k]
personal stereo плейер
[pl**a**y-yer]
petrol бензин [byenz**ee**n]
petrol can канистра для
бензина [kan**ee**stra dlya
byenz**ee**na]
petrol station бензоколонка
[byenzakal**o**nka]
pharmacy аптека [apt**ye**ka]

For minor medical complaints,
it's easiest to go to a pharmacy
аптека (apt**ye**ka), many of
which now have a reasonable
selection of Western drugs.
Choice is more limited in pro-
vincial towns and cities, so if
you are on any prescribed medi-
cation, bring enough supplies
for your stay. This is particularly
true for diabetics.

phone (noun) телефон
[tyelyef**o**n]
(verb) звонить/позвонить
[zvan**ee**t/pazvan**ee**t]

Virtually all public phones
(taksaf**o**ni) now take brown
plastic tokens (Jet**o**ni) – though
you might still find the occa-
sional old-style phone, taking 1-
rouble coins (no longer legal
tender, but still valid for making calls). The 'Jet**o**ni', which
you can buy at most metro stations, must be placed in the slot
before dialling; when your call
connects, it will drop. A series
of beeps indicates that the
money is about to run out.
Ordinary public phones can
only be used for local calls, and
the few inter-city payphones
(myeɹdoogar**o**dni tyelyef**o**n) in
existence usually require special tokens that are impossible
to find.
There are various ways of making long-distance or international calls. If you are lucky
enough to have access to a private phone, it is now possible to
call just about anywhere direct,
from the main cities, and considerably cheaper than booking
calls through the international
operator. The cost varies, depending on the time of day: it's
cheapest to call between 10pm
and 8am or at weekends.
Another way of making international calls is to go to a communications centre (pyeryegav**o**rni
poonkt) – there's one in every →

district of large cities. You pay in advance at the **касса** (**kassa**) and are given the number of booth from which you can dial direct; it might take several attempts to get through. If you don't succeed you'll have to stand in line again at the same counter to reclaim your money. In Moscow it is also possible to use Comstar phones in the lobbies of major hotels, which take prepaid cards (sold on the spot) or Amex, Visa or JCB credit cards. These phones enable you to dial direct (but not call collect) at even steeper rates, but this still works out cheaper than calling through a hotel switchboard or business centre.

phone book телефонный справочник [tyelyef**on**-ni spr**a**vachneek]

phone box телефонная будка [tyelyef**on**-na-ya b**oo**tka]

phone call звонок [zvan**ok**]

phonecard карточка для телефона-автомата [k**a**rtachka dlya tyelyef**o**na-aftam**a**ta]

phone number номер телефона [n**o**myer tyelyef**o**na]

photo фотография [fatagr**a**fee-ya]

excuse me, could you take a photo of us? извините, пожалуйста, вы не могли бы

нас сфотографировать? [eezvin**ee**tyeh, pa**a**lsta, viy nyeh magl**ee**bi nas sfatagraf**ee**ravat?]

phrasebook разговорник [razgav**o**rneek]

piano пианино [pee-an**ee**na]

pickpocket (man/woman) вор/ воровка-карманник [vor/ var**o**fka-karm**a**n-neek]

pick up: will you pick me up? вы заедете за мной? [viy za-**ye**deetyeh za mnoy?]

picnic пикник [peekn**ee**k]

picture (painting) картина [kart**ee**na]
(photo) фотография [fatagr**a**fee-ya]

pie пирог [peer**ok**]

piece кусок [koos**ok**]
a piece of ... кусок ... [koos**ok** ...]

pill противозачаточные таблетки [proteeva-zach**a**tachni-yeh tabl**ye**tkee]
I'm on the pill я принимаю противозачаточные таблетки [ya preeneem**a**-yoo proteeva-zach**a**tachni-yeh tabl**ye**tkee]

pillow подушка [pad**oo**shka]

pillow case наволочка [n**a**valachka]

pin булавка [bool**a**fka]

pineapple ананас [anan**a**s]

pineapple juice ананасовый сок [anan**a**savi sok]

pink розовый [r**o**zavi]

pipe (for smoking) трубка [tr**oo**pka]
(for water) трубопровод [tr**oo**baprav**o**t]
pity: it's a pity жаль [Jal]
place (noun) место [m**ye**sta]
at your place у вас [oo vas]
at his place у него [oo ny**e**vo]
plain (not patterned) однотонный [adnat**o**n-ni]
plane самолёт [samal**yo**t]
by plane самолётом [samal**yo**tam]
plant растение [rast**ye**nee-yeh]
plasters пластыри [pl**a**stiree]
plastic пластмассовый [plasm**a**s-savi]
plastic bag пластиковый пакет [pl**a**steekavi pak**ye**t]
plate тарелка [tar**ye**lka]
platform платформа [platf**o**rma]
which platform is it for Sergiev Posad? с какой платформы идут поезда до Сергиева Посада? [skak**oy** platf**o**rmi eed**oo**t po-yezda da s**ye**rgee-yeva pas**a**da?]
play (verb) играть/сыграть [eegr**a**t/sigr**a**t]
(noun: in theatre) пьеса [p**ye**sa]
playground детская площадка [d**ye**tska-ya plosh-ch**a**tka]
pleasant приятный [pree-y**a**tni]
please пожалуйста [paJ**a**lsta]
yes please да, спасибо [da, spas**ee**ba]
could you please ...? вы не могли бы ...? [viy nyeh magl**ee**bi ...?]
please don't пожалуйста, не надо [paJ**a**lsta, nyeh n**a**da]
pleased: pleased to meet you очень приятно [**o**chyen pree-y**a**tna]
pleasure: my pleasure пожалуйста [paJ**a**lsta]
plenty: plenty of ... много ... [mn**o**ga ...]
we have plenty of time у нас много времени [oo nas mn**o**ga vr**ye**myenee]
that's plenty, thanks достаточно, спасибо [dast**a**tchna, spas**ee**ba]
pliers плоскогубцы [plaskag**oo**ptsi]
plug (electrical) штепсельная вилка [sht**e**psyelna-ya v**ee**lka]
(for car) свеча [svy**e**cha]
(in sink) пробка [pr**o**pka]
plumber сантехник [sant**ye**Hneek]
pm*: 2pm два часа дня [dva chas**a** dnya]
10pm десять часов вечера [d**ye**syat chas**o**f vy**e**chyera]
poached egg яйцо-пашот [yitso-pash**o**t]
pocket карман [karm**a**n]
point: two point five две целых пять десятых [dvyeh tsel**i**H pyat desy**a**tiH]
there's no point нет смысла [nyet sm**i**ysla]
poisonous ядовитый [yadav**ee**ti]
Poland Польша [p**o**lsha]

police милиция [meel**ee**tsi-ya]
call the police! вызовите
милицию! [v**iy**zaveetyeh
meel**ee**tsi-yoo!]

> The police (meel**ee**tsi-ya) are
> easily recognised by their
> blue-grey uniforms with red
> lapels and cap bands. Some
> of them now drive Western cars
> or police jeeps and, like the traf-
> fic police, they may well be
> armed.
> In theory, you're supposed to
> carry some form of identifica-
> tion at all times, and the police
> can stop you in the street and
> demand it. In practice, they're
> rarely bothered if you're clearly
> a foreigner and tend to confine
> themselves to activities such as
> traffic control and harassing
> gypsies.
> In an emergency dial 02 for the
> police.

policeman милиционер
[meel**ee**tsi-an**yer**]
police station отделение
милиции [add**yel**y**e**nee-yeh
meel**ee**tsee-ee]
policewoman женщина-
милиционер
[**J**ensh-cheena-meeleetsi-an**yer**]
polish (for shoes) крем для обуви
[kryem dlya **o**boovee]
Polish польский [**po**lskee]
polite вежливый [v**yè**Jleevi]
polluted загрязнённый

[zagryazn**yo**n-ni]
pool (for swimming) бассейн
[bas**yay**n]
poor (not rich) бедный [b**ye**dni]
(quality) низкокачественный
[n**ee**ska-k**a**chyestvyen-ni]
pop music поп-музыка [pop
m**oo**zika]
pop singer (man/woman) поп-
певец/певица [pop pyev**ye**ts/
pyev**ee**tsa]
popular популярный
[papool**ya**rni]
pork свинина [sveen**ee**na]
port (for boats) порт [port]
(drink) портвейн [partv**yay**n]
porter (in hotel) швейцар
[shvyayts**ar**]
portrait портрет [partr**ye**t]
posh шикарный [shik**a**rni]
possible возможный [vazm**o**Jni]
is it possible to ...? возможно
ли ...? [vazm**o**Jnalee]
as soon as possible как
можно быстрее [kak m**o**Jna
bistr**ye**h-yeh]
post (noun: mail) почта [p**o**chta]
(verb) отправлять/отправить
[atpravl**ya**t/atpr**a**veet]
could you post this for me? вы
не могли бы отправить это?
[viy nyeh magl**ee**bi atpr**a**veet eta]
postbox почтовый ящик
[pacht**o**vi **ya**sh-cheek]
postcard открытка [atkr**iy**tka]
postcode почтовый индекс
[pacht**o**vi **ee**ndeks]
poster плакат [plak**a**t]
poste restante до

востребования
[da vast**rye**bavanee-ya]
post office почта [p**o**chta]

The Russian postal system is
notoriously inefficient, with out-
bound international mail taking
on average a couple of weeks to
reach its destination and incoming mail up to three weeks to
arrive.

Most main post offices have post
restante до **востребования**
(da vast**rye**bavanee-ya) sections, while American Express
offices in Moscow and St.
Petersburg will hold mail for
Amex card or travellers' cheque
holders for up to a month.

Main post offices are open
Mon–Fri 8am–8pm; Sat 8am–
7pm; Sun 9am–7pm.)

Parcels must be taken to a main
or international post office un-
wrapped; there they'll be in-
spected and wrapped for you,
whereupon you can send them
from any post office, or by a courier (a very expensive option).
If you only want stamps, it's
easier to go to the postal couri-
ers in hotels, rather than queue
in a post office, though there's
a mark-up on the price.

---

potato картофель m [kart**o**fyel]
pots and pans кухонная посуда
[k**oo**Han-na-ya pas**oo**da]
pottery керамика [kyer**a**meeka]

pound (money) фунт стерлингов
[foont st**ye**rleengaf]
power cut отключение
электричества
[atklyooch**ye**nee-yeh
elyektr**ee**chyestva]
power point розетка [raz**ye**tka]
**practise: I want to practise my
Russian** я хочу
поупражняться в русском
языке [ya Hach**oo**
pa-oopraJn**ya**tsa vr**oo**skam
yazik**yeh**]
prawns креветки [kreev**ye**tkee]
prefer: I prefer ... я
предпочитаю ... [ya
pryetpacheet**a**-yoo ...]
pregnant беременная
[byer**ye**myen-na-ya]
prescription (for medicine) рецепт
[ryets**e**pt]
see **doctor** and **pharmacy**
present (gift) подарок [pad**a**rak]
president (of country) президент
[pryezeed**ye**nt]
pretty симпатичный
[seempat**ee**chni]
it's pretty expensive это
довольно дорого [**e**ta dav**o**lna
d**o**raga]
price цена [tsen**a**]
priest священник
[svyash-ch**ye**n-neek]
prime minister премьер-
министр [pryem**ye**r
meen**ee**str]
printed matter печатный
материал [pech**a**tni matyer**ya**l]
prison тюрьма [tyoorm**a**]

124

private частный [chasni]
private bathroom отдельная
ванная [addyelna-ya van-na-ya]
probably вероятно [vyera-yatna]
program(me) программа
[pragram-ma]
promise: I promise я обещаю
[ya abyesh-cha-yoo]
pronounce: how is this
pronounced? как это
произносится? [kak eta
pra-eeznoseetsa?]
properly (repaired, locked etc) как
следует [kak slyedoo-yet]
protection factor (of suntan lotion)
защитный фактор
[zash-cheetni faktar]
Protestant протестантский
[pratyestantskee]
public toilet туалет [too-alyet]
public holiday официальный
праздник [afeetsalni prazneek]

Public holidays are:
1 January (New Year's Day)
7 January (Orthodox Christmas)
23 February (Defender of the
Motherland Day)
8 March (International Wom-
en's Day)
Orthodox Easter
1 & 2 May (International Labour
Day/Spring Festival)
9 May (Victory Day)
12 June (Russian Independence
Day)
→

21 August (anniversary of the
1991 putsch)
7 November (formerly the anniversary of the Great October
Socialist Revolution)
12 December (Russian Consti-
tution Day)

pudding (dessert) десерт
[dyesyert]
pull тянуть/потянуть [tyanoot/
patyanoot]
pullover свитер [sveeter]
puncture (noun) прокол [prakol]
purple фиолетовый
[fee-alyetavi]
purse (for money) кошелёк
[kashelyok]
(US: handbag) сумочка
[soomachka]
push толкать/толкнуть [talkat/
talknoot]
pushchair детская коляска
[dyetska-ya kalyaska]
put класть/положить [klast/
palaJiyt]
where can I put ...? куда мне
положить ...? [kooda mnyeh
palaJiyt ...?]
could you put us up for the
night? нельзя ли нам
переночевать у вас?
[nyelzyalee nam
pyeryenacheevat oo vas?]
pyjamas пижама [peeJama]

Q

quality качество [**ka**chyestva]

quarantine карантин [karant**ee**n]

quarter четверть f [**chye**tvyert]

question вопрос [vap**ro**s]

queue (noun) очередь f [**o**chyeryet]

quick быстрый [**bi**ystri]
  what's the quickest way there?
  как туда побыстрее
  добраться? [kak too**da**
  pabistr**yeh**-yeh dab**ra**tsa?]
  fancy a quick drink? не хотите
  пропустить стаканчик? [nyeh
  Hat**ee**tyeh prap**oo**st**ee**t
  stak**a**ncheek?]

quickly быстро [**bi**ystra]

quiet (place, hotel) тихий [**tee**Hee]
  quiet! тише! [**tee**sheh!]

quite: that's quite right
  совершенно верно
  [savyersh**en**-na **vye**rna]
  quite a lot довольно много
  [dav**o**lna mn**o**ga]

R

rabbit кролик [k**ro**leek]

race (for cars) гонки pl [**go**nkee]
  (for runners) забег [zab**ye**k]
  (for horses) скачки pl [sk**a**chkee]

racket (tennis, squash) ракетка [rak**ye**tka]

radiator (in room) батарея [batar**yeh**-ya]
  (in car) радиатор [radee-**a**tar]

radio радио [**ra**dee-o]
  on the radio по радио [pa **ra**dee-o]

rail: by rail поездом [**po**-yezdam]

railway железная дорога [Jel**ye**zna-ya dar**o**ga]

rain (noun) дождь m [dosht]
  in the rain под дождём [pad daJd**yo**m]
  it's raining идёт дождь [eed**yo**t dosht]

raincoat плащ [plash-ch]

rape (noun) изнасилование [eeznas**ee**lavanee-yeh]

rare (uncommon) редкий [**rye**tkee]
  (steak) с кровью [sk**ro**vyoo]

rash (on skin) сыпь f [siyp]

raspberry малина [mal**ee**na]

rat крыса [k**ri**ysa]

rate (for changing money) курс [koors]

rather: it's rather good очень неплохо [**o**chyen nyepl**o**Ha]
  I'd rather ... (said by man/woman)
  я предпочёл/предпочла бы ...
  [ya pryetpach**o**l/pryetpachl**a** biy ...]

razor бритва [b**ree**tva]

razor blades лезвия бритвы [l**ye**zvee-ya b**ree**tvi]

read читать/прочесть [cheet**a**t/pr**a**chyest]

ready готовый [gat**o**vi]
  are you ready? вы готовы? [viy gat**o**vi?]
  I'm not ready yet (said by man/woman) я ещё не готов/готова [ya yesh-ch**o** nyeh gat**o**f/gat**o**va]

when will it be ready? когда это
будет готово? [kagda eta boodyet
gatova?]

**it should be ready in a couple of
days** это будет готово через пару
дней [eta boodyet gatova chyeryes
paroo dnyay]

real настоящий
[nasta-yash-chee]

really действительно
[dyestveetyelna]

I'm really sorry я очень
сожалею [ya ochyen
saJalyeh-yoo]

that's really great это
замечательно! [eta
zamyechatyelna!]

really? (doubt) серьёзно?
[syeryozna?]
(polite interest) да? [da?]

rear lights задние фары
[zadnee-ee fari]

rearview mirror зеркало заднего
вида [zyerkala zadnyeva
veeda]

reasonable (prices etc)
умеренный [oomyeryen-ni]

receipt квитанция
[kveetantsi-ya]

recently недавно [nyedavna]

reception (in hotel) служба
размещения [slooJba
razmyesh-chyenee-ya]
at reception в службе
размещения [fslooJbyeh
razmyesh-chyenee-ya]

reception desk конторка

дежурного администратора
[kantorka dyeJoornava
admeeneestratara]

receptionist дежурный
администратор [dyeJoorni
admeeneestratar]

recognize узнать [ooznat]

**recommend: could you
recommend ...?** вы можете
порекомендовать ...? [viy
moJetyeh paryekamyendavat ...?]

record (music) пластинка
[plasteenka]

red красный [krasni]

red wine красное вино
[krasna-yeh veeno]

refund возмещение
[vazmyesh-chyenee-yeh]
can I have a refund? могу я
получить обратно деньги?
[magoo ya paloocheet abratna
dyengee?]

region область f [oblast]

registered: by registered mail
заказной почтой [zakaznoy
pochti]

registration number номер
машины [nomyer mashiyni]

relative (man/woman)
родственник/родственница
[rotstvyen-neek/
rotstvyen-neetsa]

religion религия [ryeleegee-ya]

remember: I don't remember я
не помню [ya nyeh pomnyoo]
I remember я помню [ya
pomnyoo]
do you remember? вы
помните? [viy pomneetyeh?]

rent (noun: for apartment)
квартирная плата
[kvarteerna-ya plata]
(verb: car etc) брать/взять
напрокат [brat/vzyat naprakat]

•••••• D I A L O G U E ••••••

I'd like to rent a car (said by a man/
woman) я хотел/хотела бы взять
напрокат машину [ya Hatyel/
Hatyela biy vzyat naprakat
mashiynoo]

for how long? на какой срок? [na
kakoy srok?]

two days два дня [dva dnya]

this is our range вот перечень
наших машин [vot pyeryechyen
nashiH mashiyn]

I'll take the ... я возьму ... [ya
vazmoo ...]

is that with unlimited mileage? это
с неограниченным
километражем? [eta
snyeh-agraneechyen-nim
keelamyetragem?]

it is да [da]

can I see your licence please?
ваши водительские права,
пожалуйста [vashi
vadeetyelskee-yeh prava, paJalsta]

and your passport и ваш паспорт
[ee vash paspart]

is insurance included? включена
ли страховка? [fklyoochyenalee
straHofka?]

yes, but you pay the first 1,000,000
roubles да, но вы выплачиваете
первый миллион рублей [da, no
viy viplacheeva-yetyeh pyervi

meelee-on rooblyay]

you have to leave a deposit of
170,000 roubles вы должны
оставить задаток в размере ста
семидесяти тысяч рублей [viy
dalJniy astaveet zadatak
vrazmyeryeh sta syemeedyestee
tiysyach rooblyay]

rented car взятая напрокат
машина [vzyata-ya naprakat
mashiyna]

repair (verb) чинить/починить
[cheeneet/pacheeneet]

can you repair it? вы можете
это починить? [viy moJetyeh
eta pacheeneet?]

repeat повторять/повторить
[paftaryat/paftareet]

could you repeat that?
повторите, пожалуйста
[paftareetyeh, paJalsta]

reservation предварительный
заказ [pryedvareetyelni zakas]

I'd like to make a reservation
(at hotel/theatre: said by a man/
woman) я хотел/хотела бы
заказать номер/билет [ya
Hatyel/Hatyela biy zakazat
nomyer/beelyet]

•••••• D I A L O G U E ••••••

I have a reservation (at hotel/
theatre) у меня заказан номер/
билет [oo myenya zakazan nomyer/
beelyet]

what name please? ваше имя,
пожалуйста [vasheh eemya,
paJalsta]

reserve (verb) заказывать/
заказать заранее [zak**a**zivat/
zakaz**a**t zar**a**nyeh-yeh]

•••••• DIALOGUE ••••••

can I reserve a table for tonight?
могу я заказать столик на
сегодня вечером? [mag**oo** ya
zakaz**a**t st**o**leek na syev**o**dnya
v**ye**chyeram]

yes madam, for how many people?
да, пожалуйста, на сколько
человек? [da, paJ**a**lsta, na sk**o**lka
chyelav**ye**k?]

for two на двоих [na dva-**ee**H]

and for what time? на какое
время? [na kak**o**-yeh vr**ye**mya?]

for eight o'clock на восемь часов
[na v**o**syem chas**o**f]

**and could I have your name
please?** ваше имя, пожалуйста
[v**a**sheh **ee**mya, paJ**a**lsta]

see **alphabet** for spelling

rest: I need a rest мне нужно
отдохнуть [mnyeh n**oo**Jna
ad-daHn**oo**t]

the rest of the group
остальные члены группы
[astaln**iy**-yeh chl**ye**ni gr**oo**p-pi]

restaurant ресторан [ryestar**a**n]

Moscow and St Petersburg now
abound with private cafés and
restaurants offering everything
from pizza to Indian, French
and Chinese food. Prices are frequently astronomical. Although
more and more privately owned
→

eating places are opening up in
the outlying towns and cities
too, these are still relatively few
and far between. In the regional
centres, hotel restaurants generally offer a reasonable variety
and standard of dishes and are
relatively inexpensive.

For a full meal, you can go
anywhere from the most basic
self-service canteen **столовая**
(stal**o**va-ya) to a proper restaurant **ресторан** (ryestar**a**n). In
general restaurants open from
mid-morning to about 11pm or
midnight, usually with a break
of a couple of hours in the afternoon. Russians like to un-
wind of an evening, so loud
bands and energetic dancing are
very much the order of the day
in traditional Russian restaurants. Good affordable restaurants are usually full in the eve-
nings, so advance booking is
strongly advised.

restaurant car вагон-ресторан
[vag**o**n-ryestar**a**n]

rest room туалет [too-al**ye**t]

retired: I'm retired я на пенсии
[ya na p**ye**nsee-ee]

return: a return to ... туда и
обратно до ... [tood**a** ee
abr**a**tna da ...]

return ticket обратный билет
[abr**a**tni beel**ye**t]

see **ticket**

reverse charge call разговор, оплачиваемый вызываемым лицом [razgav**o**r, apl**a**cheeva-yemi viz**i**va-yemim leets**o**m]

reverse gear задний ход [z**a**dnee Hot]

revolting отвратительный [atvrat**ee**tyelni]

rib ребро [ryebr**o**]

rice рис [rees]

rich (person) богатый [bag**a**ti]
(food) жирный [J**i**yrni]

ridiculous нелепый [nyel**y**epi]

right (correct) правильный [pr**a**veelni]
(not left) правый [pr**a**vi]
you were right вы были правы [viy b**i**ylee pr**a**vi]
that's right правильно [pr**a**veelna]
this can't be right не может такого быть [nyeh m**o**Jet tak**o**va biyt]
right! хорошо [Harash**o**]
is this the right road for ...? я доеду по этой дороге до ...? [ya da-y**e**doo pa **e**ti dar**o**gyeh da ...?]
on the right справа [spr**a**va]
to the right направо [napr**a**va]
turn right поверните направо [pavern**ee**tyeh napr**a**va]

right-hand drive вождение по правой стороне [vaJd**ye**nee-yeh pa pr**a**vi staran**ye**h]

ring (on finger) кольцо [kalts**o**]
I'll ring you я вам позвоню [ya

vam pazvan**yoo**]

ring back перезвонить [pyeryezvan**ee**t]

rip-off: it's a rip-off это обдираловка [**e**ta abdeer**a**lofka]
rip-off prices грабительские цены [grab**ee**tyelskee-yeh ts**e**ni]

ripe (fruit) зрелый [zr**ye**li]

risky рискованный [reesk**o**van-ni]

river река [ryek**a**]

road дорога [dar**o**ga]
is this the road for ...? это дорога до ... [**e**ta dar**o**ga da ...?]
it's just down the road это совсем близко отсюда [**e**ta safs**y**em bl**ee**ska ats**yoo**da]

road accident дорожная катастрофа [dar**o**Jna-ya katastr**o**fa]

road map дорожная карта [dar**o**Jna-ya k**a**rta]

roadsign дорожный знак [dar**o**Jni znak]

rob: I've been robbed меня ограбили [men**ya** agr**a**beelee]

rock скала [skal**a**]
(music) рок [rok]
on the rocks (with ice) со льдом [sald**o**m]

roll (bread) булочка [b**oo**lachka]

Romania Румыния [room**i**ynee-ya]

roof крыша [kr**i**ysha]

room (in hotel) номер [n**o**myer]
(in house) комната [k**o**mnata]

in my room в моём номере [vma-**yo**m **no**myeryeh]

•••••• DIALOGUE ••••••

do you have any rooms? есть ли у вас свободные номера? [**ye**stlee oo vas svab**o**dni-yeh namyer**a**?]

for how many people? для скольких человек? [dlya sk**o**lkeeн chyelav**ye**k?]

for one/for two для одного/двух [dlya adnav**o**/dvooн]

yes, we have rooms free да, у нас есть свободные номера [da, oo nas yest svab**o**dni-yeh namyer**a**]

for how many nights will it be? на сколько ночей? [na sk**o**lka nach**ya**y?]

just for one night только на одну ночь [t**o**lka na adn**oo** noch]

how much is it? сколько это стоит? [sk**o**lka **e**ta st**o**-eet?]

... with bathroom and ... without bathroom ... с ванной и ... без ванной [... sv**a**n-nı ee ... byez v**a**n-nı]

can I see a room with bathroom? можно посмотреть номер с ванной? [m**o**Jna pasmat**rye**t **no**myer sv**a**n-nı?]

OK, I'll take it хорошо, это подойдёт [Harash**o**, **e**ta padıd**yo**t]

room service обслуживание в номере [apsl**oo**Jivanee-yeh vn**o**myeryeh]

rope канат [kan**a**t]

rosé (wine) розовое вино [**ro**zava-yeh veen**o**]

roughly (approximately) приблизительно

[preebleez**ee**tyelna]

round: it's my round моя очередь [**ma**-ya **o**chyeryet]

roundabout (for traffic) круговое движение [kroogav**o**-yeh dveeJ**e**nee-yeh]

route маршрут [marshr**oo**t]

what's the best route to ...? как лучше добраться до ...? [kak l**oo**chsheh dabr**a**tsa da ...?]

rubber (material) резина [ryez**ee**na]

(eraser) ластик [l**a**steek]

rubber band резинка [ryez**ee**nka]

rubbish (waste) мусор [m**oo**sar]

(poor quality goods) барахло [baraнl**o**]

rubbish! (nonsense) чепуха! [chyepoo**на**!]

rucksack рюкзак [ryookz**a**k]

rude грубый [gr**oo**bi]

ruins развалины [razv**a**leeni]

rum ром [rom]

rum and Coke® кока-кола с ромом [koka-k**o**la sr**o**mam]

run (verb: person) бежать/ побежать [byeJ**a**t/pabyeJ**a**t]

how often do the buses run? как часто ходят автобусы? [kak ch**a**sta н**o**dyat aft**o**boosi?]

I've run out of money у меня кончились деньги [oo men**ya** k**o**ncheelees d**ye**ngee]

Russia Россия [rass**ee**-ya]

Russian (adj, man) русский [r**oo**skee]

(woman) русская [r**oo**ska-ya]

(language) русский язык

[**roo**skee yaz**iy**k]
the Russians русские
[**roo**skee-yeh]

S

sad грустный [gr**oo**sni]
saddle (for bike, horse) седло
[syedl**o**]
safe (not in danger) в
безопасности
[vbyezap**a**snastee]
(not dangerous) безопасный
[byezap**a**sni]
safety pin английская булавка
[angl**ee**ska-ya bool**a**fka]
sail (verb) плавать/плыть
[pl**a**vat/pliyt]
sailing (sport) парусный спорт
[p**a**roosni sport]
salad салат [sal**a**t]
salad dressing заправка к
салату [zapr**a**fka ksal**a**too]
salami саляли f [sal**ya**mee]
sale: for sale продаётся [prada-
yotsa]
salmon лосось m [las**o**s]
salt соль f [sol]
same: the same то же самое
[t**o**Jeh s**a**ma-yeh]
the same as this такой же как
этот [tak**oy**Jeh kak **e**tat]
the same again, please то же
самое, пожалуйста [t**o**Jeh
s**a**ma-yeh, pa**J**alsta]
it's all the same to me мне всё
равно [mnyeh fsyo ravn**o**]
sand песок [pyes**o**k]
sandals сандали [sand**a**lee]

sandwich бутерброд
[**boo**terbrot]
sanitary napkins/towels
гигиенические прокладки
[geegee-yen**ee**chyeskee-yeh
prakl**a**tkee]
Saturday суббота [soob**o**ta]
sauce соус [s**o**-oos]
saucepan кастрюля
[kastr**yoo**lya]
saucer блюдце [bl**yoo**tseh]
sauna сауна [s**a**-oona]
sausage (salami) колбаса
[kalbas**a**]
(frankfurter) сосиска [sas**ee**ska]
say говорить/сказать
[gavar**ee**t/skaz**a**t]
how do you say ... in Russian?
как по-русски ...? [kak
pa-**roo**skee ...?]
what did he say? что он
сказал? [shto on skaz**a**l?]
she said ... она сказала ...
[an**a** skaz**a**la ...]
could you say that again?
повторите, пожалуйста
[paftar**ee**tyeh, pa**J**alsta]
scarf (for neck) шарф [sharf]
(for head) платок [plat**o**k]
scenery пейзаж [pyayz**a**sh]
schedule (US: timetable)
расписание [raspees**a**nee-yeh]
scheduled flight рейсовый
полёт [**ryay**savi pal**yo**t]
school школа [shk**o**la]
scissors: a pair of scissors
ножницы pl [n**o**Jneetsi]
scooter мотороллер
[matar**o**l-lyer]

scotch виски n [**vee**skee]

Scotch tape® клейкая лента
[kl**yay**ka-ya l**yen**ta]

Scotland Шотландия
[shatl**a**ndee-ya]

Scottish шотландский
[shatl**a**ntskee]

I'm Scottish (man/woman) я
шотландец/шотландка [ya
shatl**a**ndyets/shatl**a**ntka]

scrambled eggs яичница-
болтунья [ya-**ee**shneetsa-
balt**oo**nya]

scratch (noun) царапина
[tsar**a**peena]

screw (noun) винт [veent]

screwdriver отвёртка [atv**yor**tka]

sea море [**mo**ryeh]

by the sea у моря [oo **mo**rya]

seafood морские продукты
[marskee-yeh prad**oo**kti]

search (verb) искать [eesk**a**t]

seasick: I feel seasick меня
укачало [men**ya** ookach**a**la]

I get seasick меня укачивает
[men**ya** ook**a**cheeva-yet]

seaside: by the seaside на море
[na **mo**ryeh]

seat место [**mye**sta]

is this seat taken? это место
свободно? [eta m**ye**sta
svab**o**dna?]

seat belt ремень m [ryem**yen**]

secluded уединённый
[oo-yedeen**yon**-ni]

second (adj) второй [ftar**oy**]

(in time) секунда [syek**oo**nda]

just a second! секундочку!
[syek**oo**ndachkoo!]

second class (travel etc) второй
класс [ftar**oy** klas]

second floor третий этаж
[tr**ye**tee et**a**sh]

(US) второй этаж [ftar**oy**
et**a**sh]

second-hand подержанный
[pad**yer**Jan-ni]

second-hand bookshop
букинистический магазин
[bookeenees**tee**chyeskee
magaz**een**]

see видеть/увидеть [**vee**dyet/
oov**ee**dyet]

can I see? можно
посмотреть? [m**o**Jna
pasmatr**ye**t?]

have you seen ...? вы не
видели ...? [viy nyeh
v**ee**dyelee ...?]

I saw him this morning (said by
man/woman) я видел/видела
его сегодня утром [ya
v**ee**dyel/v**ee**dyela yev**o**
syev**o**dnya **oo**tram]

see you! пока! [pak**a**!]

I see (I understand) понятно
[pan**ya**tna]

self-service самообслуживание
[sama-apsl**oo**Jivanee-yeh]

sell продавать/продать
[pradav**a**t/prad**a**t]

do you sell ...? у вас
продаётся ...? [oo vas
prada-**yo**tsa ...?]

Sellotape® клейкая лента
[kl**yay**ka-ya l**yen**ta]

send посылать/послать
[pasil**a**t/pasl**a**t]

I want to send this to England
я хочу послать это в Англию
[ya Hach**oo** paslat **e**ta
v**a**nglee-yoo]

senior citizen (man/woman)
пожилой человек/пожилая
женщина [paжil**oy** chyelav**ye**k/
paжila-ya ж**e**nsh-cheena]

separate (adj) отдельный
[ad-d**ye**lni]

separated: we're separated мы
разошлись [miy razashl**ee**s]

separately (pay, travel) отдельно
[ad-d**ye**lna]

September сентябрь m
[syent**ya**br]

septic септический
[syept**ee**chyeskee]

serious серьёзный [syer**yo**zni]
(illness) опасный [ap**a**sni]

service charge плата за
обслуживание [pl**a**ta za
apsl**oo**жivanee-yeh]

service station (for repairs)
станция техобслуживания
[st**a**ntsi-ya
tyeнapsl**oo**жivanee-ya]
(for petrol) бензоколонка
[byenzakal**o**nka]

serviette салфетка [salf**ye**tka]

set menu комплексный обед
[k**o**mplyeksni ab**ye**t]

several несколько [n**ye**skolka]

sew шить/сшить [shiyt/s-shiyt]
could you sew this back on?
вы не могли бы пришить
это [viy nyeh magl**ee**bi
preeshiyt **e**ta]

sex секс [seks]

sexy привлекательный
[preevlyek**a**tyelni]

shade: in the shade в тени
[ftyen**ee**]

shake: to shake hands
пожимать/пожать руку
[paжim**a**t/paж**a**t r**oo**koo]

shallow мелкий [m**ye**lkee]

shame: what a shame! как
жаль! [kak ж**a**l!]

shampoo шампунь m
[shamp**oo**n]

shampoo and set мытьё и
укладка волос [mit**yo** ee
ookl**a**tka val**o**s]

share: to share a room жить в
одной комнате [жiyt vadn**oy**
k**o**mnatyeh]
to share a table сидеть за
одним столом [seed**ye**t za
adn**ee**m stal**o**m]

sharp острый [**o**stri]

shattered: I'm shattered я
совершенно без сил [ya
sav**ye**rsh**e**n-na byes seel]

shaver бритва [br**ee**tva]

shaving foam пена для бритья
[p**ye**na dlya breet**ya**]

shaving point розетка для
электробритвы [raz**ye**tka dlya
elyektrabr**ee**tvi]

shawl шаль f [shal]

she* она [an**a**]
is she here? она здесь? [an**a**
zdyes?]

sheet (for bed) простыня
[prastin**ya**]

shelf полка [p**o**lka]

shellfish моллюск [mal**yoo**sk]

sherry херес [н**ye**ryes]
ship корабль m [ka**ra**bl]
  by ship на корабле [na ka**ra**bl**yeh**]
shirt рубашка [roo**ba**shka]
shit! чёрт! [chort!]
shock шок [shok]
  I got an electric shock меня ударило током [men**ya** oo**da**reela **to**kam]
shocking ужасный [oo**J**asni]
shoe (man's/woman's) ботинок/туфля [bat**ee**nak/**too**flya]
  a pair of shoes ботинки/туфли [bat**ee**nkee/**too**flee]
shoelaces шнурки [shnoork**ee**]
shoe polish крем для обуви [kryem dlya **o**boovee]
shoe repairer's мастерская по ремонту обуви [mastyerska-ya pa ryem**o**ntoo **o**boovee]
shop магазин [magaz**ee**n]

The older-style, state-run stores tend to stock a fairly limited range of goods, although choice is improving all the time. At the other end of the scale, there are boutiques and supermarkets which cater for the new rich and where everything is imported and even foreigners reel at the prices (sometimes up to six times what you'd pay back home). In between are the countless private shops and street kiosks, given to cut-throat trading and selling goods past their sell-by-dates. →

In general, food stores are open Mon–Sat 8am–8pm with a break for lunch 1–2 pm. Other shops generally open 9, 10 or 11am to 7 or 8pm usually with a 2–3pm or 3–4pm lunch break. Sunday opening hours are less predictable, although an increasing number of shops open on Sundays, as do most bars and restaurants. Many street kiosks are open 24 hours every day.

In most state-owned shops you order and get the price at the counter before paying at the cash desk касса (ka-ss-a) and taking the receipt back to claim your goods – a system that entails queuing at least twice. Stores quite often have only one 'ka-ss-a' serving a number of counters, in which case you will need to specify which one the receipt is for. Look out for a number above the counter and refer to it when you go to pay at the cash desk (e.g. 'pyat **tiy**syach roobl**yay**, p**ye**rva-ya s**ye**ktsi-ya' – five thousand roubles, 1st Section).

Fortunately, shopping in the private sector is much easier as most places operate on a self-service, pay-as-you-leave basis. Here, however, the pitfall is pricing. Items are often priced in US dollars or deutschmarks, which the cashier converts into roubles →

at a rate (koors) set by the store (which should be posted). You may end up paying five to ten per cent more in real terms, unless you pay by credit card. Credit cards are fairly widely accepted in private shops, but haven't yet penetrated the state sector.

shopping: I'm going shopping я иду за покупками [ya eed**oo** za pak**oo**pkamee]

shopping centre торговый центр [t**a**rgovi tsentr]

shop window витрина [veetr**ee**na]

shore берег [b**ye**ryek]

short (person) невысокий [nyevis**o**kee]
(time, journey) короткий [kar**o**tkee]

shortcut кратчайший путь [kratch**i**shi poot]

shorts шорты [sh**o**rti]

should: what should I do? что мне делать? [shto mnyeh d**ye**lat?]
you should ... вам следует ... [vam sl**ye**doo-yet ...]
you shouldn't ... вам не следует ... [vam nyeh sl**ye**doo-yet ...]
he should be back soon он должен скоро вернутся [on d**o**lJen sk**o**ra vyern**oo**tsa]

shoulder плечо [pl**ye**cho]

shout (verb) кричать/крикнуть [kreech**a**t/kr**ee**knoot]

show (in theatre) представление [pryedstavl**ye**nee-yeh]
could you show me? покажите, пожалуйста [paka**J**iytyeh, pa**J**alsta]

shower (of rain) ливень m [l**ee**vyen]
(in bathroom) душ [doosh]
with shower с душем [sd**oo**shem]

shower gel гель для душа m [gyel dlya d**oo**sha]

shut (verb) закрывать/закрыть [zakriv**a**t/zakr**i**yt]
when do you shut? когда вы закрываетесь? [kagd**a** viy zakr**i**va-yetyes?]
they're shut они закрыты [an**ee** zakr**i**yti]
I've shut myself out я не могу попасть внутрь [ya nyeh mag**oo** pap**a**st vnootr]
shut up! замолчите! [zamalch**ee**tyeh!]

shutter (on camera) затвор [zatv**o**r]
(on window) ставень m [st**a**vyen]

shy застенчивый [zast**ye**ncheevi]

sick (ill) больной [baln**oy**]
I'm going to be sick (vomit) меня сейчас стошнит [myen**ya** syech**a**s stashn**ee**t]
I feel sick меня тошнит [men**ya** tashn**ee**t]

side сторона [stal**a**na]
on the other side of the street

на другой стороне улицы [na droogoy staranyeh ooleetsi]

side lights подфарники [patfarneekee]

side street переулок [pyeryeh-oolak]

sidewalk тротуар [tratoo-ar]
on the sidewalk на тротуаре [na tratoo-aryeh]

sight: the sights of ... достопримечательности ... [dastapreemyechatyelnastee ...]

sightseeing: we're going sightseeing мы идём осматривать достопримечательности [miy eedyom asmatreevat dastapreemyechatyelnastee]

sightseeing tour экскурсия [ekskoorsee-ya]

sign (roadsign etc) знак [znak]

signature подпись f [potpees]

signpost указатель m [ookazatyel]

silence тишина [teeshina]

silk шёлк [sholk]

silly глупый [gloopi]

silver серебро [syeryebro]

similar похожий [pahoji]

simple (easy) простой [prastoy]

since: since last week с прошлой недели [sproshli nyedyelee]
since I got here (said by man/woman) с тех пор, как я приехал/приехала [styeH por, kak ya pree-yeHal/pree-yeHala]

sing петь/спеть [pyet/spyet]

singer (man/woman) певец/

певица [pyevyets/pyeveetsa]

single: a single to ... билет в один конец до ... [beelyet vadeen kanyets da ...]
I'm single (said by man/woman) я не женат/замужем [ya nyeh Jenat/zamooJem]

single bed односпальная кровать [adnaspalna-ya kravat]

single room одноместный номер [adnamyesni nomyer]

single ticket билет в один конец [beelyet vadeen kanyets]

sink (in kitchen) раковина [rakaveena]

sister сестра [syestra]

sister-in-law (wife's sister) свояченица [sva-yachyeneetsa] (husband's sister) золовка [zalofka]

sit: can I sit here? можно здесь сесть? [moJna zdyes syest?]
is anyone sitting here? здесь кто-нибудь сидит? [zdyes kto-neeboot seedeet?]

sit down садится/сесть [sadeetsa/syest]
please, sit down садитесь, пожалуйста [sadeetyes, paJalsta]

size размер [razmyer]

skate (verb) кататься на коньках [katatsa na kankaH]

skates коньки [kankee]

skating rink каток [katok]

ski (verb) кататься на лыжах [katatsa na liyJaH]

skis лыжи [liyJi]

skin кожа [ko**J**a]

skinny тощий [**t**osh-chee]

skirt юбка [**yoo**pka]

sky небо [**ny**eba]

sleep (verb) спать/поспать [spat/pasp**a**t]

did you sleep well? вам хорошо спалось? [vam Harash**o** spalos?]

sleeper (on train) спальный вагон [sp**a**lni v**a**gon]

sleeping bag спальный мешок [sp**a**lni myesh**o**k]

sleeping car спальный вагон [sp**a**lni v**a**gon]

sleeping pills снотворные таблетки [snatv**o**rni-yeh tabl**ye**tkee]

sleepy: I'm feeling sleepy меня клонит ко сну [myen**ya** kl**o**neet ka snoo]

sleeve рукав [rook**a**f]

slide (photographic) слайд [slīd]

slippers тапочки [t**a**pachkee]

slippery скользкий [sk**o**lskee]

Slovakia Словакия [slav**a**kee-ya]

slow медленный [m**ye**dlyen-ni]

slow down! помедленнее, пожалуйста [pam**ye**dleen-nyeh-yeh, pa**J**alsta]

slowly медленно [m**ye**dlyen-na]

very slowly очень медленно [**o**chyen m**ye**dlyen-na]

could you speak more slowly? вы не могли бы говорить помедленнее? [viy nyeh magl**ee**bi gavar**ee**t pam**ye**dleenyeh-yeh?]

small маленький [m**a**lyenkee]

smell: it smells (smells bad) плохо пахнет [pl**o**Ha p**a**Hnyet]

smile (verb) улыбаться/улыбнуться [oolib**a**tsa/oolibn**oo**tsa]

smoke (noun) дым [diym]

do you mind if I smoke? вы не возражаете, если я закурю? [viy nyeh vazra**J**a-yetyeh, **ye**slee ya zakoor**yoo**?]

I don't smoke я не курю [ya nyeh koor**yoo**]

do you smoke? вы курите? [viy k**oo**reetyeh?]

snack: I'd just like a snack (said by man/woman) я хотел/хотела бы слегка перекусить [ya Hat**ye**l/Hat**ye**la biy sl**ye**Hka pyeryekoos**ee**t]

sneeze (verb) чихать/чихнуть [cheeH**a**t/cheeHn**oo**t]

snorkel дыхательная трубка [diH**a**tyelna-ya tr**oo**pka]

snow снег [snyek]

it's snowing снег идёт [snyek eed**yo**t]

snowstorm метель f [myet**ye**l]

so так [tak]

this wine is so good очень хорошее вино [**o**chyen Har**o**sheh-yeh v**ee**no]

it's so expensive это так дорого [eta tak d**o**raga]

not so much не так много [nyeh tak mn**o**ga]

not so bad не так уж плохо [nyeh tak oosh pl**o**Ha]

so am I, so do I я тоже [ya t**o**Jeh]

so-so так себе [tak seebyeh]

soaking solution (for contact lenses) раствор для линз [rastvor dlya leenz]

soap мыло [miyla]

soap powder стиральный порошок [steeralni parashok]

sober трезвый [tryezvi]

sock носок [nasok]

socket (electrical) розетка [razyetka]

soda (water) газированная вода [gazeerovan-na-ya vada]

sofa диван [deevan]

soft (material etc) мягкий [myaнkee]

soft-boiled egg яйцо всмятку [yıtso fsmyatkoo]

soft drink безалкогольный напиток [byezalkagolni napeetak]

soft lenses мягкие линзы [myaнkee-yeh leenzi]

soldier солдат [saldat]

sole (of foot) ступня [stoopnya]
(of shoe) подошва [padoshva]

could you put new soles on these? вы не могли бы поставить сюда новые подмётки? [viy nyeh magleebi pastaveet syooda novi-yeh padmyotkee?]

some: can I have some? дайте мне, пожалуйста [dityeh mnyeh, paлalsta]

can I have some water/bread? дайте мне, пожалуйста воды/ хлеба [dityeh mnyeh, paлalsta, vadiy/Hlyeba]

somebody, someone кто-то [kto-ta]

something что-нибудь [shto-neeboot]

something to eat что-нибудь поесть [shto-neeboot pa-yest]

sometimes иногда [eenagda]

somewhere где-нибудь [gdyeh-neeboot]

son сын [siyn]

son-in-law зять [zyat]

song песня [pyesnya]

soon скоро [skora]

I'll be back soon я скоро вернусь [ya skora vyernoos]

as soon as possible как можно скорее [kak moлna skaryeh-yeh]

sore: it's sore болит [baleet]

sore throat: I've got a sore throat у меня болит горло [oo myenya baleet gorla]

sorry: I'm sorry прошу прощения [prashoo prash-chyenee-ya]

sorry! извините! [eezveeneetyeh!]

sorry? (didn't understand) простите? [prasteet-yeh?]

sort: what sort of ...? какой ...? [kakoy ...?]

this sort такой [takoy]

soup суп [soop]

sour (taste) кислый [keesli]

soured cream сметана [smyetana]

south юг [yook]

in the south на юге [na yoogyeh]

South Africa Южная Африка
[**yoo**Jna-ya **a**freeka]
South African (adj)
южно-африканский
[**yoo**Jna-afreek**a**nskee]
I'm South African я из Южной
Африки [ya eez **yoo**Jni
afreekee]
southeast юго-восточный
[**yoo**ga-vast**o**chni]
southern южный [**yoo**Jni]
southwest юго-западный
[**yoo**ga-z**a**padni]
souvenir сувенир [soovyen**ee**r]
Soviet советский [sav**ye**tskee]
Soviet Union Советский Союз
[sav**ye**tskee sa-**yoo**s]
spade лопата [lap**a**ta]
Spain Испания [eesp**a**nee-ya]
Spanish (adj) испанский
[eesp**a**nskee]
spanner гаечный ключ
[g**a**-yechni kly**oo**ch]
spare part запчасть f [zapch**a**st]
spares запчасти [zapch**a**stee]
spare tyre запасная шина
[zapasn**a**-ya sh**i**yna]
speak: do you speak English? вы
говорите по-английски? [viy
gavar**ee**tyeh pa-angl**ee**skee?]
I don't speak Russian я не
говорю по-русски [ya nyeh
gavary**oo** pa-r**oo**skee]

• • • • • DIALOGUE • • • • •

can I speak to Nikolai? можно
Николая, пожалуйста? [m**o**Jna
neek**a**la-ya, paJ**a**lsta?]
who's calling? кто говорит? [kto

gavar**ee**t?]
it's Patricia это Патриша [**e**ta
patr**ee**sha]
I'm sorry, he's not in, can I take a
message? извините, его нет, вы
хотите что-нибудь передать?
[eezven**ee**tyeh, yev**o** nyet, viy
Hat**ee**tyeh shto-neeb**oo**t pyeryed**a**t?]
no thanks, I'll call back later нет,
спасибо, я перезвоню попозже
[nyet, spas**ee**ba, ya pyeryezvany**oo**
pap**o**J-Jeh]
please tell him I called
пожалуйста, передайте ему, что я
звонила [paJ**a**lsta, pyeryed**i**tyeh
yem**oo**, shto ya zvan**ee**la]

spectacles очки [ach**kee**]
speed (noun) скорость f
[sk**o**rast]
speed limit максимальная
скорость [makseem**a**lna-ya
sk**o**rast]
spell: how do you spell it? как
это пишется по буквам? [kak
eta p**ee**shetsa pa b**oo**kvam?]
see alphabet
spend тратить/потратить
[tr**a**teet/patr**a**teet]
spider паук [pa-**oo**k]
spin-dryer центробежная
сушилка [tsentrab**ye**Jna-ya
soosh**i**ylka]

spirits
Russia produces cognac (kan-
yak) as well as vodka. It can be
pretty rough compared with
the genuine article. The best
→

> cognac hails from Armenia and
> Moldova, for instance Белый
> Аист (byeli a-eest), 'white
> stork'.
> see **vodka**

spoon ложка [loshka]

sport спорт [sport]

sprain: I've sprained my ... (said
by man/woman) я растянул/
растянула ... [ya rastyanool/
rastyanoola ...]

spring (of car, seat) рессора
[ryes-sora]
(season) весна [vyesna]
in the spring весной [vyesnoy]

square (in town) площадь f
[plosh-chat]

stairs лестница [lyesneetsa]

stale несвежий [nyesvyeJi]

stalls партер [parter]

stamp (noun) марка [marka]

• • • • • • DIALOGUE • • • • • •

how much is a stamp for England?
сколько стоит марка для Англии?
[skolka sto-eet marka dlya
anglee-ee?]

what are you sending? что вы
посылаете? [shto viy pasila-yetyeh?]

this postcard эту открытку [etoo
atkriytkoo]

star звезда [zvyezda]

start (noun) начало [nachala]
(verb) начинать/начать
[nacheenat/nachat]
when does it start? когда
начало? [kagda nachala?]
my car won't start моя

машина не заводится [ma-ya
mashiyna nyeh zavodeetsa]

starter (food) закуска [zakooska]

starving: I'm starving я умираю
от голода [ya oomeera-yoo at
golada]

state (country) государство
[gasoodarstva]
(adj) государственный
[gasoodarstvyen-ni]
the States Штаты [shtati]

station (main, rail) вокзал
[vakzal]
(underground, bus) станция
[stantsi-ya]

stationery канцелярские
принадлежности
[kantselyarskee-yeh
preenadlyeJnastee]

statue статуя [statoo-ya]

stay: where are you staying? где
вы остановились? [gdyeh viy
astanaveelees?]
I'm staying at ... (said by man/
woman) я остановился/
остановилась в ... [ya
astanaveelsa/astanaveelas v ...]
**I'd like to stay another two
nights** (said by man/woman) я бы
хотел/хотела остаться ещё на
пару суток [yabi Hatyel/
Hatyela astatsa yesh-cho na
paroo sootak]

steak бифштекс [beefshteks]

steal красть/украсть [krast/
ookrast]
my bag has been stolen у
меня украли сумку [oo
menya ookralee soomkoo]

steep (hill) крутой [krootoy]

step: on the steps на ступеньках [na stoopyenkaн]

stereo стерео [styeryeh-o]

sterling фунт стерлингов [foont styerleengaf]

steward (on plane) стюард [styoo-art]

stewardess стюардесса [styoo-ardes-sa]

still: I'm still here я ещё здесь [ya yesh-cho zdyes]

is he still there? он ещё здесь? [on yesh-cho zdyes?]

keep still! не двигайтесь! [nyeh dveegɪtyes!]

sting: I've been stung by a wasp меня укусила оса [menya ookooseela asa]

stockings чулки [choolkee]

stomach желудок [Jeloodak]

stomach ache: I have stomach ache у меня болит живот [oo menya baleet Jivot]

stone (rock) камень m [kamyen]

stop (verb) останавливать/ остановить [astanavleevat/ astanaveet]

stop here, please (to taxi driver etc) пожалуйста, остановитесь здесь [paJalsta, astanaveetyes zdyes]

do you stop near ...? вы останавливаетесь у ...? [viy astanavleeva-yetyes oo ...?]

stop it! прекратите! [pryekrateetyeh!]

stopover остановка (в пути) [astanofka (fpootee)]

storm буря [boorya]

St Petersburg Санкт-Петербург [sankt-peetyerboork]

straight прямой [pryamoy]

(whisky etc) неразбавленный [nyerazbavlyen-ni]

it's straight ahead это прямо [eta pryama]

straightaway немедленно [nyemyedlyen-na]

strange (odd) странный [stran-ni]

stranger (man/woman) незнакомец/незнакомка [nyeznakomyets/nyeznakomka]

I'm a stranger here (said by man/ woman) я здесь чужой/чужая [ya zdyes chooJoy/chooJa-ya]

strap (on watch, suitcase) ремешок [ryemyeshok]

(on dress) бретелька [bryetelka]

strawberry клубника [kloobneeka]

stream ручей m [roochay]

street улица [ooleetsa]

on the street на улице [na ooleetseh]

streetmap план города [plan gorada]

string верёвка [vyeryofka]

strong (person, material, taste) сильный [seelni]

(drink) крепкий [kryepkee]

stuck: it's stuck застряло [zastryala]

student (male/female) студент/ студентка [stoodyent/ stoodyentka]

stupid глупый [gloopi]

suburb пригород [**pree**garat]

subway подземный переход [padz**ye**mni pyerye**H**ot]
(US: underground) метро [myet**ro**]

suede замша [**za**msha]

sugar сахар [s**a**Har]

suit (noun) костюм [kast**yoo**m]
it doesn't suit me (jacket etc)
мне это не идёт [mnyeh **e**ta nyeh eed**yo**t]
it suits you вам это идёт [vam **e**ta eed**yo**t]

suitcase чемодан [chyemad**a**n]

summer лето [l**ye**ta]
in the summer летом [l**ye**tam]

sun солнце [**so**ntseh]
in the sun на солнце [na s**o**ntseh]
out of the sun в тени [vtyen**ee**]

sunbathe загорать [zagar**a**t]

sunblock средство против загара [sr**ye**tstva pr**o**teef zag**a**ra]

sunburn солнечный ожог [s**o**lnyechni a**J**ok]

sunburnt (burnt) обгорелый [abgar**ye**li]

Sunday воскресенье [vaskrye**sye**nyeh]

sunglasses очки от солнца [achk**ee** at s**o**ntsa]

sunny: it's sunny солнечно [s**o**lnyechna]

sunset закат [zak**a**t]

sunshade зонтик от солнца [z**o**nteek at s**o**ntsa]

sunshine солнечный свет [s**o**lnyechni svyet]

sunstroke солнечный удар [s**o**lnyechni ood**a**r]

suntan загар [zag**a**r]

suntan lotion лосьон для загара [las**yo**n dlya zag**a**ra]

suntanned загорелый [zagar**ye**li]

suntan oil масло для загара [m**a**sla dlya zag**a**ra]

super замечательный [zamyech**a**tyelni]

supermarket универсам [ooneevyers**a**m], супермаркет [soopyerm**a**rkyet]

---

superstitions

Russians consider it bad luck to kiss or shake hands across a threshold or to go back home for something that's been forgotten. When offering flowers, make sure there's an odd number of blooms, as even-numbered bouquets are for funerals. Before going on a long journey, Russians gather all their luggage by the door and sit on it for a minute or two to bring themselves good luck.

---

supper ужин [**oo**Jin]

supplement (extra charge) доплата [dapl**a**ta]

sure: are you sure? вы уверены? [viy oov**ye**ryeni?]
I'm sure (said by man/woman) я уверен/уверена [ya oov**ye**ryen/oov**ye**ryena]
sure! конечно! [kan**ye**shna!]

surname фамилия
[fameelee-ya]

sweater свитер [sveeter]

sweatshirt спортивная майка
[sparteevna-ya mıka]

Sweden Швеция [shvyetsi-ya]

Swedish (adj) шведский
[shvyetskee]

sweet (taste) сладкий [slatkee]
(noun: dessert) десерт
[dyesyert]

sweets конфеты [kanfyeti]

swelling опухоль f [opooнal]

swim (verb) плавать/поплавать
[plavat/paplavat]
I'm going for a swim я иду
плавать [ya eedoo plavat]
let's go for a swim пойдём
поплаваем [pıdyom
paplava-yem]

swimming costume купальник
[koopalneek]

swimming pool бассейн
[basyayn]

swimming trunks плавки
[plafkee]

Swiss швейцарский
[shvyetsarskee]

switch (noun) выключатель m
[viklyoochatyel]

switch off выключать/
выключить [viklyoochat/
viyklyoocheet]

switch on включать/включить
[fklyoochat/fklyoocheet]

Switzerland Швейцария
[shvyetsaree-ya]

swollen распухший
[raspooнshi]

T

table стол [stol]
a table for two столик на
двоих [stoleek na dva-eeн]

tablecloth скатерть f [skatyert]

table tennis настольный
теннис [nastolni tenees]

table wine столовое вино
[stalova-yeh veeno]

tailor портной [partnoy]

take (verb: lead) брать/взять
[brat/vzyat]
(accept) принимать/принять
[preeneemat/preenyat]
can you take me to the ...? вы
можете отвезти меня в ...?
[viy moлetyeh atvyestee menya
v ...?]
do you take credit cards? вы
принимаете кредитные
карточки? [viy
preeneema-yetyeh
kryedeetni-yeh kartachkee]
fine, I'll take it хорошо, я
возьму это [Harasho, ya
vazmoo eta]
can I take this? (leaflet etc)
можно это взять? [moлna eta
vzyat?]
how long does it take?
сколько времени это займёт?
[skolka vryemyenee eta
zımyot?]
it takes three hours это
займёт три часа [eta zımyot
tree chasa]
is this seat taken? это место
свободно? [eta myesta

svabodna?]

hamburger to take away
гамбургер на вынос
[**ga**mboorgyer na v**iy**nas]

can you take a little off here?
(to hairdresser) вы можете
немного подстричь здесь [viy
mo**J**etyeh nyemn**o**ga patstr**ee**ch
zdyes?]

talcum powder тальк [tallk]

talk (verb) говорить/
поговорить [gavar**eet**/
pagavar**eet**]

tall высокий [vis**o**kee]

tampons тампоны [tamp**o**ni]

tan загар [zag**a**r]
  to get a tan загореть
  [zagar**ye**t]

tap кран [kran]

tape measure рулетка
[rool**ye**tka]

tape recorder магнитофон
[magneetaf**o**n]

taste (noun) вкус [fkoos]
  can I taste it? можно
  попробовать? [m**o**Jna
  papr**o**bavat?]

taxi такси n [taks**ee**]
  will you get me a taxi?
  вызовите для меня такси,
  пожалуйста [v**iy**zaveetyeh dlya
  myen**ya** taks**ee**, pa**J**alsta]
  where can I find a taxi? где
  можно поймать такси? [gdyeh
  m**o**Jna p**I**mat taks**ee**?]

•••••• DIALOGUE ••••••

to the airport/to the ... Hotel,
please в аэропорт/в

гостиницу ..., пожалуйста
[va-erap**o**rt/vgast**ee**neetsoo ...,
pa**J**alsta]

how much will it be? сколько это
будет стоить? [sk**o**lka eta b**oo**dyet
st**o**-eet?]

60,000 roubles шестьдесят тысяч
рублей [shezdyes**ya**t t**iy**syach
roobl**ya**y]

that's fine right here thanks я
выйду здесь, спасибо [ya v**iy**doo
zdyes, spas**ee**ba]

Taxis come in all shapes and
sizes. The official ones are
pale blue or yellow Volgas or
Moskveeches, with a chequered
logo on the door and a dome
light on the roof or green light
in the window. In practice,
though, you're more likely to
find yourself using an unme-
tered, unmarked private taxi.
Most Russians simply flag down
any vehicle, even ambulances
and trucks, and negotiate the
destination and fare. Try to es-
timate the length of taxi ride
beforehand and offer what you
think is an appropriate fare. You
should pay about $5 for short
journeys around the town centre and $10 or more (depending
on the distance) to go across
town. Taxi fares are considerably cheaper in the regions,
compared with Moscow and St
Petersburg. Rates are especially
→

high at airports where business is monopolised by a 'taxi Mafia'.
see **bus**

---

taxi driver таксист [tak**see**st]
taxi rank стоянка такси [sta-**ya**nka tak**see**]
tea (drink) чай m [ch**I**]
  one tea/two teas, please один чай/два чая, пожалуйста [ad**ee**n ch**I**/dva cha-ya, pa**J**alsta]
  tea with milk чай с молоком [ch**I** smalak**om**]
  tea with lemon чай с лимоном [ch**I** sleem**o**nam]

Russians traditionally prepare a strong leaf brew (zav**a**rka), topping it up with boiling water, from a samovar (a traditional ornate tea-urn). Note that tea is usually served with sugar already added, so you should make it clear when you order if you don't want sugar (byes s**a**Hara, pa**J**alsta). If you're offered tea in someone's home, it may well be 'travyan**oy**', a tisane made of herbs and leaves. Russians drink tea without milk; if you ask for milk it is likely to be condensed.

---

teabags чайные пакетики [ch**I**ni-yeh pak**ye**teekee]
teach: could you teach me? вы могли бы меня научить ...? [viy mag**lee**bi men**ya** na-ooch**ee**t ...?]
teacher (man/woman) учитель/ учительница [ooch**ee**tyel/ ooch**ee**tyelneetsa]
team команда [kam**a**nda]
teaspoon чайная ложка [ch**I**na-ya l**o**shka]
tea towel чайное полотенце [ch**I**na-yeh palat**ye**ntseh]
teenager подросток [padr**o**stak]
telegram телеграмма [tyelyegr**a**m-ma]
telephone телефон [tyelyef**o**n]
see **phone**
television (set) телевизор [tyelyev**ee**zar]
  (medium) телевидение [tyelyev**ee**dyenyeh]
tell: could you tell him ...? скажите ему, пожалуйста ... [ska**J**i**y**tyeh yemoo, pa**J**alsta ...]
  could you tell me where ...? вы не скажете, где ...? [viy nyeh ska**J**ityeh, gdyeh ...?]
temperature (weather) температура [tyempyerat**oo**ra]
tennis теннис [t**e**n-nees]
tent палатка [pal**a**tka]
term (at university, school) семестр [syem**ye**str]
terminus (rail, underground) конечная станция [kan**ye**chna-ya st**a**ntsi-ya]
  (bus, tram) конечная остановка [kan**ye**chna-ya astan**o**fka]
terrible ужасный [oo**J**asni]
terrific замечательный [zamyech**a**tyelni]

than* чем [chyem]
  smaller than ... меньше, чем ... [myensheh, chyem ...]
thank: thank you/thanks спасибо [spaseeba]
  thank you very much большое спасибо [balsho-yeh spaseeba]
  thanks for the lift спасибо, что подвезли [spaseeba, shto padvyezlee]
  no, thanks нет, спасибо [nyet, spaseeba]

•••••• DIALOGUE ••••••

  thanks спасибо [spaseeba]
  that's OK, don't mention it не за что [nyezashto]

that* тот m [tot], та f [ta], то n [to]
  that boy тот мальчик [tot malcheek]
  that girl та девочка [ta dyevachka]
  that one тот m [tot], та f [ta], то n [to]
  I hope that ... я надеюсь, что ... [ya nadyeh-yoos, shto ...]
  that's great отлично [atleechna]
  is that ...? это ...? [eta ...?]
  that's it (that's right) точно [tochna]
thaw (noun) оттепель f [ot-tyepyel]
the*
theatre театр [tyeh-atr]
their*/theirs* их [eeн]
them*: I'll tell them я им скажу [ya eem skaJoo]

I know them я их знаю [ya eeн zna-yoo]
  for them для них [dlya neeн]
  with them с ними [sneemee]
  to them им [eem]
  who? -- them кто? – они [kto? - anee]
then (at that time) тогда [tagda]
  (after that) потом [patom]
there там [tam]
  over there вон там [von tam]
  up there там, наверху [tam, navyerноo]
  is there/are there ...? есть ли ...? [yestlee ...?]
  there you are (giving something) вот, пожалуйста [vot, paJalsta]
thermometer термометр [tyermomyetr]
Thermos® flask термос [termas]
these* эти [etee]
  I'd like these (said by man/woman) я бы хотел/хотела вот эти [yabi Hatyel/Hatyela vot etee]
they* они [anee]
thick густой [goostoy]
  (stupid) тупой [toopoy]
thief (man/woman) вор/воровка [vor/varofka]
thigh бедро [byedro]
thin (person) худой [Hoodoy]
  (thing) тонкий [tonkee]
thing вещь f [vyesh-ch]
  my things мои вещи [ma-ee vyesh-chee]
think думать/подумать [doomat/padoomat]
  I think so думаю, да

[doo**ma**-yoo, da]
I don't think so я так не
думаю [ya tak nyeh d**oo**ma-yoo]
I'll think about it я подумаю
об этом [ya pad**oo**ma-yoo ab
etam]

third третий [t**ry**etee]

thirsty: **I'm thirsty** мне хочется
пить [mnyeh н**o**chyetsa peet]

this* этот m [etat], эта f [e**ta**],
это n [e**to**]
this boy этот мальчик [etat
malcheek]
this girl эта девочка [e**ta**
d**ye**vachka]
this one этот m [etat], эта f
[e**ta**], это n [e**ta**]
this is my wife это моя жена
[e**ta** ma-**ya** Jena]
is this ...? это ...? [e**ta** ...?]

those* те [tyeh]
which ones? – those какие? –
те [kak**ee**-yeh? – tyeh]

thread (noun) нитка [**nee**tka]

throat горло [**gor**la]

throat pastilles пастилки для
горла [past**ee**lka dlya g**or**la]

through через [ch**ye**ryes]
does it go through ...? (train,
bus) он проезжает через ...?
[on pra-ye**J**-J**a**-yet ch**ye**ryes ...?]

throw бросать/бросить [bras**at**/
br**o**seet]

throw away выбрасывать/
выбросить [vibr**a**sivat/
v**iy**braseet]

thumb большой палец [balsh**oy**
p**a**lyets]

thunderstorm гроза [graz**a**]

Thursday четверг [chyetv**ye**rk]

ticket билет [beel**ye**t]
(for bus) талон [tal**on**]

• • • • • DIALOGUE • • • • •

a return to Sergiev Posad
обратный билет до Сергиева
Посада [abr**a**tni beel**ye**t da s**ye**rgee-
yeva pas**a**da]
coming back when? когда
обратно? [kagd**a** abr**a**tna?]
today/next Tuesday сегодня/в
следующий вторник [syev**o**dnya/
fsl**ye**doosh-chee ft**or**neek]
that will be 10,000 roubles (это
будет) десять тысяч рублей [(e**ta**
b**oo**dyet) d**ye**syat t**iy**syach roobl**yay**]

ticket office билетная касса
[beel**ye**tna-ya k**a**s-sa]

ticket punch компостер
[kamp**o**styer]

tie (necktie) галстук [g**a**lstook]

tight (clothes etc) тесный [t**ye**sni]
it's too tight тесновато
[tyesnav**a**ta]

tights колготки [kalg**o**tkee]

till касса [k**a**s-sa]

time* время [v**ry**emya]
what's the time? который час?
[kat**o**ri chas?]
this time в этот раз [v**e**tat ras]
last time в прошлый раз
[fpr**o**shli ras]
next time в следующий раз
[fsl**ye**doosh-chee ras]
three times три раза [tree r**a**za]

timetable расписание
[raspees**a**nee-yeh]

tin (can) консервная банка

[kanservna-ya banka]

tinfoil оловянная фольга
[alavyan-na-ya falga]

tin-opener консервный нож
[kanservni nosh]

tiny крошечный [kroshechni]

tip (to waiter etc) чаевые pl
[cha-yeviy-yeh]

> In taxis the fare will be agreed
> in advance, so there's no need
> to tip. In restaurants it's consid-
> ered proper to leave an extra ten
> per cent or so, but it's not com-
> pulsory; check that it hasn't al-
> ready been included in the bill.
> It's also customary to give a
> small tip to the cloakroom at-
> tendant if he helps you on with
> your coat.

tired усталый [oostali]
  I'm tired (said by man/woman) я
  устал/устала [ya oostal/
  oostala]

tissues бумажные носовые
  платки [boomajni-yeh
  nasaviy-yeh platkee]

toast (bread) гренок [gryenok]

tobacco табак [tabak]

today сегодня [syevodnya]

toe палец ноги [palets nagee]

together вместе [vmyestyeh]
  we're together (in shop etc) мы
  вместе [miy vmyestyeh]

toilet туалет [too-alyet]
  where is the toilet? где туалет?
  [gdyeh too-alyet?]
  I have to go to the toilet мне

нужно в туалет [mnyeh
noojna ftoo-alyet]

> Public toilets are few and far
> between; toilet paper is unlikely
> to be provided and standards of
> hygiene are often low. Assuming
> you can get past the bouncers,
> the toilets in restaurants or ho-
> tels are preferable.

toilet paper туалетная бумага
  [too-alyetna-ya boomaga]

token жетон [Jeton]

tomato помидор [pameedor]

tomato juice томатный сок
  [tamatni sok]

tomato ketchup кетчуп
  [kyetchoop]

tomorrow завтра [zaftra]
  tomorrow morning завтра
  утром [zaftra ootram]
  the day after tomorrow
  послезавтра [poslyezaftra]

toner (cosmetic) тонизирующий
  лосьон [taneezeeroo-
  yoosh-chee lasyon]

tongue язык [yaziyk]

tonic (water) тоник [toneek]

tonight сегодня вечером
  [syevodnya vyechyeram]

tonsillitis тонзиллит [tanzeeleet]

too (excessively) слишком
  [sleeshkam]
  (also) тоже [toJeh]
  too hot слишком жарко
  [sleeshkam Jarka]
  too much слишком много
  [sleeshkam mnoga]

me too я тоже [ya to**J**eh]

tooth зуб [zoop]

toothache зубная боль f [zoobn**a**-ya bol]

toothbrush зубная щётка [zoobn**a**-ya sh-ch**o**tka]

toothpaste зубная паста [zoobn**a**-ya p**a**sta]

top: on top of ... на ... [na ...]

at the top наверху [navyer**H**oo]

top floor верхний этаж [v**y**er**H**nee et**a**sh]

topless с обнажённой грудью [sabna**J**on-n**I** gr**oo**dyoo]

torch фонарик [fan**a**reek]

total (noun) итог [eet**o**g]

to: to Moscow/London в Москву/в Лондон [v mask**voo**/vl**o**ndan]

to Russia/England в Россию/ Англию [vrass**ee**-yoo/v**a**nglee-yoo]

to the post office на почту [na p**o**chtoo]

tour (noun) экскурсия [eksk**oo**rsee-ya]

is there a tour of ...? есть ли экскурсия по ...? [**ye**stlee eksk**oo**rsee-ya pa ...?]

tour guide (man/woman) экскурсовод [ekskoorsav**o**t]

tourist (man/woman) турист/ туристка [toor**ee**st/toor**ee**stka]

---

tourist information
Moscow and St Petersburg have no centralized tourist information centre where you can walk →

in and get a map or an answer to any question. The main Intourist office can help with car rental, currency exchange, theatre bookings and other services. Most travellers use the information/service desks at major hotels which are usually willing to help out for a fee even if you're not staying there.

Useful sources for details of what's on in Moscow are the local English-language free newspapers, the Moscow Times and the Moscow Tribune. In St Petersburg, you might want to consult the St Petersburg Times (the St Petersburg equivalent of the Moscow Times) or the St Petersburg Yellow Pages.

---

tour operator бюро путешествий [byoor**o** pootyesh**e**stvee]

towards к [k]

towel полотенце [palat**ye**ntseh]

town город [g**o**rat]

in town в городе [vg**o**radyeh]

just out of town за городом [z**a**garadam]

town centre центр города [tsentr g**o**rada]

town hall мэрия [m**e**ree-ya]

toy игрушка [eegr**oo**shka]

track (US: platform) платформа [platf**o**rma]

tracksuit тренировочный костюм [tryeneer**o**vachni

kast**yoo**m]
traditional традиционный
[tradeetsi-**o**n-ni]
traffic движение [dvee**J**enee-yeh]
traffic jam пробка [**pro**pka]
traffic lights светофор
[svyeta**for**]
train поезд [**po**-yest]
  by train поездом [**po**-yezdam]

Buying tickets for long-distance
or international trains is rarely
easy. Aside from being unsure
which outlet currently handles
bookings for their destination,
foreigners are also subject to
constantly changing rules and
charged twice as much for tickets as Russians are. If you're in
Moscow you'll find it extremely
tempting to use the Travellers'
Guest House booking facility
which frequently offers dis-
counts on train tickets to Russian destinations, China or Europe, and charges only a mod-
est fee.

When travelling by overnight
train it's advisable to try and get
a place in a two-berth 'soft
class' compartment (es-veh).
Although more expensive, these
carriages are more comfortable
and generally have a higher degree of security. Alternatively,
there are the less expensive
four-berth soft 'koop**eh**' in
which the majority of Russians
→

try to travel. Shortly after departure, the sleeping-car attendant
will come around dispensing
sheets (for a surcharge) and offering tea. A train journey is a
good opportunity to socialize
with your Russian fellow passengers – don't be surprised if they
invite you to share a bottle of
vodka and some 'kalbas**a**' (sausage) even before you leave
the station. Sleeping arrange-
ments on Russian trains are
'mixed' – if you feel uncomfortable with this, ask to change
places with someone else (viy
nyeh mag**lee**bi pamyen**ya**tsa sa
mnoy myest**a**mee?).

Tourist attractions outside the
major towns and cities are generally accessible by suburban
train (pr**ee**garadni-yeh pa-
yezda, or elyektr**ee**chka). Most
mainline stations have a separate ticket office **пригородная
касса** (pr**ee**garadna-ya **ka**s-sa)
for suburban trains, which may
depart from an annexe to the
main building. To make it easier
to buy tickets and check time-
tables, get someone to write out
the name of your destination
in Cyrillic. Fares on these trains
are extremely cheap, as foreigners pay the same price as Russians do.

see **underground**

• • • • • DIALOGUE • • • • •

is this the train for Ufa? это поезд
до Уфы? [**e**ta po-yest da oof**iy**?]
sure да [da]
no, you want that platform there
нет, вам нужна та платформа
[nyet, vam n**oo**Jna ta platf**o**rma]

trainers (shoes) кроссовки
[kras**o**fkee]
train station железнодорожная
станция [Jelyeznadar**o**Jna-ya
st**a**ntsi-ya]
tram трамвай m [tramv**i**]
translate переводить/перевести
[pyeryevad**ee**t/pyeryeh-vyest**ee**]
would you translate that?
переведите это, пожалуйста
[pyeryeh-vyed**ee**tyeh **e**ta,
pa**л**a**l**sta]
translator (man/woman)
переводчик/переводчица
[pyeryev**o**tcheek/
pyeryev**o**tcheetsa]
trash мусор [m**oo**sar]
trash can мусорное ведро
[m**oo**sarna-yeh vyedr**o**]
travel путешествовать
[pootyesh**e**stvavat]
we're travelling around мы
путешествуем [miy
pootyesh**e**stvoo-yem]
travel agent's бюро
путешествий [by**oo**ro
pootyesh**e**stvee]
travellers' cheque дорожный
чек [dar**o**Jni chyek]

Travellers' cheques represent
the safest form of money available. US dollar cheques are
quite widely accepted now in
Moscow and St Petersburg, and
you should encounter few problems with Deutschmarks or sterling. Outside big cities, however,
it's more of a problem finding
somewhere to change travellers'
cheques, so you may have to
take a good proportion of your
money in dollar bills (low denominations are best). With op-
portunistic street crime generally on the increase, a well con-
cealed money-belt is a must for
the traveller in Russia. It should
also be noted that the only brand
of travellers' cheque that can be
easily replaced if lost or stolen
in Moscow is American Express.
Amex will cash travellers'
cheques into dollars, Deutschmarks or sterling, but it's better
to change them into roubles
somewhere else.

In the two big cities travellers'
cheques are accepted by most
hotels but few bureaux de
change accept them.

tray поднос [padn**o**s]
tree дерево [d**y**eryeva]
tremendous (large) огромный
[agr**o**mni]
(splendid) замечательный
[zamyech**a**tyelni]

trendy модный [**mo**dni]

trim: just a trim please (to hairdresser) немного подровняйте, пожалуйста [nyemn**o**ga padravn**yi**tyeh, paj**a**lsta]

trip (excursion) экскурсия [eksk**oo**rsee-ya]

I'd like to go on a trip to … я хочу съездить в …[ya nach**oo** sy**e**zdeet v …]

trolley тележка [tyel**ye**shka]

trolley bus троллейбус [tral**yay**boos]

trouble неприятность [nyepree-**ya**tnast]

I'm having trouble with … у меня проблемы с … [oo men**ya** prabl**ye**mi s …]

trousers брюки [br**yoo**kee]

true верно [v**ye**rna]

that's not true это неправда [eta nyepr**a**vda]

trunk (US: of car) багажник [bag**a**jneek]

trunks (swimming) плавки [pl**a**fkee]

try (verb) пробовать/ попробовать [pr**o**bavat/ papr**o**bavat]

can I try it? можно я попробую [m**o**jna ya papr**o**boo-yoo]

try on мерить/померить [m**ye**reet/pam**ye**reet]

can I try it on? можно померить? [m**o**jna pam**ye**reet?]

T-shirt футболка [footb**o**lka]

Tuesday вторник [ft**o**rneek]

tuna тунец [toon**ye**ts]

tunnel туннель m [t**oo**nel]

turning (in road) поворот [pavar**o**t]

turn: turn left/right повернуть налево/направо [pavvern**oo**t nal**ye**va/napr**a**va]

turn off: where do I turn off? где мне надо свернуть? [gdyeh mnyeh n**a**da svern**oo**t?]

can you turn the heating off? вы можете выключить отопление? [viy m**o**Jetyeh **viy**klyoocheet atapl**ye**nee-yeh?]

turn on: can you turn the heating on? вы можете включить отопление? [viy m**o**Jetyeh fklyooch**ee**t atapl**ye**nee-yeh?]

TV (set) телевизор [tyelyevee**ee**zar] (medium) телевидение [tyelyevee**ee**dyenyeh]

tweezers пинцет [peents**e**t]

twice дважды [dv**a**Jdi]

twice as much в два раза больше [vdva r**a**za b**o**lsheh]

twin beds две односпальные кровати [dvyeh adnasp**a**lni-yeh krav**a**tee]

twin room номер с двумя кроватями [n**o**myer sdvoom**ya** kpav**a**tyemee]

twist: I've twisted my ankle (said by man/woman) я подвернул/ подвернула ногу [ya padvyern**oo**l/padvyern**oo**la n**o**goo]

type (noun) тип [teep]

another type of … … другого

типа [... droogova **tee**pa]
typical типичный [teep**ee**chni]
tyre шина [sh**i**yna]

U

ugly некрасивый [nyekras**ee**vi]
UK Соединённое Королевство [sa-yedeen**yo**n-na-yeh karal**ye**fstva]
Ukraine Украина [ookra-**ee**na]
Ukrainian (adj) украинский [ookra-**ee**nskee]
ulcer язва [**ya**zva]
umbrella зонтик [z**o**nteek]
uncle дядя [d**ya**dya]
uncomfortable неудобный [nyeh-ood**o**bni]
unconscious без сознания [byes saznaneе-ya]
under (in position) под [pot]
(less than) меньше [m**ye**nsheh]
underdone (meat) недожаренный [nyedaJ**a**ryen-ni]
underground (railway) метро [myetr**o**]

Currently only Moscow and St Petersburg have major underground systems, although Novosibirsk and Ekaterinburg now also offer limited services. In Moscow the underground runs daily 5.30am–1am. In St Petersburg trains run from 5.30am to midnight. On major holidays like New Year and the →

Russian Orthodox Christmas and Easter, trains run until 2am.

Stations are marked with a large 'M' and have separate doors for incoming and outgoing passengers. Many have two or three exits, located 500-700 metres apart at street level, which can be disorienting if you pick the wrong one. Each exit is signposted with the appropriate street names (and even bus routes) at platform level. All signs and maps are in Russian only, so you'll have to learn to recognize the Cyrillic form of the words for 'entrance' **вход** (fнot), 'exit' **выход** (v**i**yнat) and 'passage to another line' **переход** (pyeryeн**o**t).

Since the platforms carry few signs indicating which station you're at, it's advisable to pay attention to tannoy announcements in the carriages. As the train pulls into each station, you'll hear its name, immediately followed by the words 'sl**ye**doosh-cha-ya st**a**ntsi-ya' – and then the name of the next station. Most importantly, be sure to heed the words 'astaro**J**na, dv**ye**ree zakriva-yootsa' – 'caution, doors closing'.

For the metro, passengers buy plastic tokens (Jet**o**ni) to slip →

into the seemingly barrier-less turnstiles. If you don't insert a token, or try to walk through before the light turns green, automatic barriers slam shut, with painful force. Providing you don't leave the metro you can travel any distance and change lines as many times as you like using a single token. In Moscow, magnetic cards have also now been introduced on a trial basis.

If you're using a lot of public transport, you can save money by buying a monthly pass (yedeeni beelyet), which goes on sale in metro stations and kiosks towards the end of the month, for a few days only. This covers all forms of transport, but it's also possible to buy a pass just for the metro or for surface transport. To use the pass on the metro, flash it as you walk by the barrier at the end of the line of turnstiles.

underpants трусы [troos**iy**]
understand: I understand я понимаю [ya paneem**a**-yoo]
I don't understand я не понимаю [ya nyeh paneem**a**-yoo]
do you understand? вы понимаете? [viy paneem**a**-yetyeh?]
unemployed безработный [byezrab**o**tni]

unfashionable немодный [nyem**o**dni]
United States Соединённые Штаты [sa-yedeen**yo**n-ni-yeh sht**a**ti]
university университет [ooneevyerseet**yet**]
unleaded petrol неэтилированный бензин [nyeh-eteel**ee**ravan-ni byenz**een**]
unlimited mileage неограниченный километраж [nyeh-agran**ee**chyen-ni keelamyetr**a**sh]
unlock открывать/открыть [atkriv**a**t/atrkr**iy**t]
unpack распаковывать/ распаковать [raspak**o**vivat/ raspakav**a**t]
until до [do]
unusual необыкновенный [nyeh-abiknav**yen**-ni]
up вверх [v-vyerH]
  up there там наверху [tam navyerH**oo**]
  he's not up yet он ещё не встал [on yesh-ch**o** nyeh fstal]
  what's up? в чём дело? [fchom d**ye**la?]
upmarket элитарный [eleet**a**rni]
upset stomach расстройство желудка [rastr**o**ystva Jel**oo**tka]
upside-down вверх дном [v-vyerH dnom]
upstairs наверху [navyerH**oo**]
up-to-date современный [savryem**yen**-ni]
urgent срочный [sr**o**chni]

us* мы [miy]
  with us с нами [snamee]
  for us для нас [dlya nas]
USA США [seh-sheh-**a**]
use (verb) пользоваться/
  воспользоваться [p**o**lzavatsa/
  vasp**o**lzavatsa]
  may I use your pen? можно
  воспользоваться вашей
  ручкой? [m**o**Jna vasp**o**lzavatsa
  v**a**shay r**oo**chkı?]
useful полезный [pal**ye**zni]
usual обыкновенный
  [abiknav**ye**n-ni]
  the usual (drink etc) то, что
  обычно [to, shto ab**i**ychna]
usually обычно [ab**i**ychna]

V

vacancy: do you have any
  vacancies? у вас есть
  свободные номера? [oo vas
  yest svab**o**dni-yeh namyer**a**?]
  see room
vacation отпуск [**o**tpoosk]
  on vacation в отпуске
  [v**o**tpooskyeh]
  see holiday
vaccination прививка
  [preev**ee**fka]
vacuum cleaner пылесос
  [pilyes**o**s]
valid (ticket etc)
  действительный
  [dyaystv**ee**tyelni]
  how long is it valid for? на
  сколько времени он
  действителен? [na sk**o**lka

vr**ye**myenee on
  dyaystv**ee**tyelyen?]
valley долина [dal**ee**na]
valuable (adj) ценный [ts**e**n-ni]
  can I leave my valuables here?
  можно оставить здесь
  ценные вещи? [m**o**Jna
  ast**a**veet zdyes ts**e**n-ni-yeh
  v**ye**sh-chee?]
value ценность f [ts**e**n-nast]
van фургон [foorg**o**n]
vanilla ваниль f [van**ee**l]
  a vanilla ice cream ванильное
  мороженое [van**ee**lna-yeh
  mar**o**Jena-yeh]
vase ваза [v**a**sa]
veal телятина [tyel**ya**teena]
vegetables овощи [**o**vash-chee]
vegetarian (noun: man/woman)
  вегетарианец/вегетарианка
  [vyegeetaree-**a**nyets/
  vyegeetaree-**a**nka]

Russia is no place for vegetarians: meat takes pride of place in the country's cuisine. Pancakes **блины** (bleen**iy**) are a good option (ask for them with sour cream), but the best dishes to look out for are mushrooms cooked with onions and sour cream known as **жульен** (Jool**ye**n), and **окрошка** (akr**o**shka), the cold summer soup.

In general the ethnic restaurants (Georgian, Armenian, Indian or Chinese) are better for vegetarians.

vending machine (торговый) автомат [(targ**o**vi) aftam**a**t]
very очень [**o**chyen]
  very little for me совсем чуть-чуть для меня [safs**ye**m choot-ch**oo**t dlya myen**ya**]
  I like it very much мне очень нравится [mnyeh **o**chyen nr**a**veetsa]
vest (under shirt) майка [m**ɪ**ka]
via через [ch**ye**ryes]
video (noun: film) видео [**vee**dee-o]
video recorder видеомагнитофон [**vee**dee-omagneetaf**o**n]
view вид [veet]
village деревня [dyer**ye**vnya]
vinegar уксус [**oo**ksoos]
visa виза [**vee**za]

All foreign nationals visiting Russia require a passport and a visa, which must be obtained in advance from a Russian embassy or consulate. Each embassy sets its own visa prices according on how quickly you need it. It's worth spending the extra money to have the entire business done through a visa agency or tour operator.

There are several types of visa: the most common one is a straight tourist visa, valid for a precise number of days up to a maximum of thirty. To get this, you must have proof of →

pre-booked accommodation. If you're going on a package tour, all the formalities can be sorted out for you by the travel agency, though they may charge extra for this.

A business visa is more flexible in that it is valid for up to sixty days (occasionally longer), and doesn't require you to book accommodation in advance. The procedure for obtaining a business visa is now quite bureaucratic. The host company in Russia has to apply to the Ministry of Foreign Affairs and it may take 2–3 weeks for you to receive an official invitation. Only then can you apply for a visa.

If you wish to stay with Russian friends, you'll need a private individual visa, which is the most difficult kind to obtain. This requires a personal invitation from your Russian host – cleared through OVIR (Visa and Foreign Citizen's Registration Department) guaranteeing to look after you for the duration of your stay. The whole process can take up to three or four months to complete.

If you are only planning to pass through Russia en route to another country, you must apply for a transit visa, which is valid for up to 48 hours, for air transit. Note that if you intend to →

leave Russia and enter any other republic of the former Soviet Union, you not only need a separate visa for each independent state, but also a multiple-entry visa to get back into Russia.

By law, all foreigners are supposed to register with the OVIR within three days of arrival and obtain a stamp on their exit visa to that effect. In practice, registration isn't as bad as it sounds, since anyone coming on a tour or staying at a hotel will have this done for them automatically, so it only applies to those staying in some kind of 'unofficial' accommodation. Visitors who do not get a registration stamp may be fined on leaving Russia.

OVIR is also responsible for issuing visa extensions, residence permits, and passports for Russian citizens. Its bureaucrats are notoriously unhelpful – so bring along a Russian to help out if possible.

visit (verb) посещать/посетить [pasyesh-chat/pasyeteet]
I'd like to visit ... (said by man/woman) я хотел/хотела бы посетить ... [ya Hatyel/Hatyela biy pasyeteet ...]
vital: it's vital that ... абсолютно необходимо, чтобы ... [apsalyootna nyeh-apHadeema,

shtobi ...]
vodka водка [votka]

Vodka is the Russian national drink – its name means something like 'a little drop of water'. Normally served chilled, it is drunk neat in one gulp, preceded by a toast and followed by a mouthful of food. Unlike most drinks, taste isn't a prime consideration; what counts is that the vodka is pure (cheesta-ya), since many well known brands like **Столичная** (staleechnaya) are now counterfeited by bootleggers.

In shops and bars, you will also see flavoured vodkas such as **Перцовка** (pyertsofka) – hot pepper vodka; **Лимонная** (leemon-na-ya) – lemon vodka; **Охотничья** (aHotneechya) – hunter's vodka, with juniper berries, ginger and cloves; **Старка** (starka) – apple and pear-leaf vodka; and **Зубровка** (zoobrofka) – bison-grass vodka.

voice голос [golas]
voltage напряжение [napreeJyenee-yeh]

Voltage is a standard continental 220 volts AC; most European appliances should work as long as you have an adapter for →

European-style two-pin round plugs. North Americans will need this plus a transformer. When using a computer in Russia, be wary of the fluctuations in the electricity current.

vomit тошнить/стошнить [tashn**ee**t/stashn**ee**t]

W

waist талия [t**a**lee-ya]

waistcoat жилет [Jil**ye**t]

wait ждать/подождать [Jdat/pada**J**d**a**t]
  wait for me подождите меня [pada**J**d**ee**tyeh men**ya**]
  don't wait for me не ждите меня [nyeh Jd**ee**tyeh myen**ya**]
  can I wait until my wife/my friend gets here? я могу подождать до прихода моей жены/моего друга? [ya mag**oo** pada**J**d**a**t da pree**H**oda ma-**yay** Jen**iy**/ma-yev**o** dr**oo**ga?]
  can you do it while I wait? вы можете это сделать при мне? [viy m**o**Jetyeh **e**ta zd**ye**lat pree mnyeh?]
  could you wait here for me? вы можете меня здесь подождать? [viy m**o**Jetyeh myen**ya** zdyes pada**J**d**a**t?]

waiter официант [afeetsi-**a**nt]
  waiter! официант! [afeetsi-**a**nt!]

waiting room (doctor's etc) приёмная [pree-**yo**mna-ya]

(station) зал ожидания [zal a**J**idanee-ya]

waitress официантка [afeetsi-**a**ntka]
  waitress! девушка! [d**ye**vooshka!]

wake: can you wake me up at 5.30? пожалуйста, разбудите меня в половине шестого [pa**J**alsta, razbood**ee**tyeh men**ya** fpalav**ee**nyeh shest**o**va]

wake-up call телефонный будильник [tyelyef**o**n-ni bood**ee**lneek]

Wales Уэльс [oo-**e**ls]

walk: is it a long walk? это далеко пешком? [**e**ta dalyek**o** pyeshk**o**m?]
  it's only a short walk это в нескольких шагах отсюда [**e**ta vn**ye**skalkeeн shaga**н** ats**yoo**da]
  I'll walk я пойду пешком [ya p**i**doo pyeshk**o**m]
  I'm going for a walk я иду прогуляться [ya eed**oo** pragool**ya**tsa]

Walkman® плейер [pl**ay**-yer]

wall стена [styen**a**]

wallet бумажник [boom**a**Jneek]

wander: I like just wandering around я люблю бродить [ya lyoobl**yoo** brad**ee**t]

want: I want ... я хочу ... [ya наch**oo** ...]
  I don't want any ... я не хочу ... [ya nyeh наch**oo** ...]
  I want to go home я хочу пойти домой [ya наch**oo**

pitee dam**oy**]

I don't want to я не хочу [ya nyeh Hach**oo**]

he wants to ... он хочет ... [on H**o**chyet ...]

what do you want? что вы хотите? [shto viy Hat**ee**tyeh?]

ward (in hospital) палата [pal**a**ta]

warm тёплый [t**yo**pli]

I'm so warm мне жарко [mnyeh J**a**rka]

was*: he was он был ... [on biyl ...]

she was она была ... [on**a** bil**a** ...]

it was это было ... [**e**ta b**i**yla ...]

wash (verb: hands etc) мыть/помыть [miyt/pam**i**yt] (clothes) стирать/постирать [steer**a**t/pasteer**a**t]

can you wash these? вы можете это постирать? [viy m**o**Jetyeh **e**ta pasteer**a**t?]

washhand basin раковина [r**a**kaveena]

washing (clothes) бельё [byel**yo**]

washing machine стиральная машина [steer**a**lna-ya mash**i**yna]

washing powder стиральный порошок [steer**a**lni parash**o**k]

washing-up: to do the washing-up мыть/помыть посуду [miyt/pam**i**yt pas**oo**doo]

washing-up liquid жидкость для мытья посуды f [J**i**ytkast dlya mit**ya** pas**oo**di]

wasp оса [as**a**]

watch (wristwatch) часы pl [chas**iy**]

will you watch my things for me? присмотрите, пожалуйста, за моими вещами [preesmatr**ee**tyeh, paJ**a**lsta, za ma-**ee**mee vyesh-ch**a**mee]

watch strap ремешок для часов [ryemyesh**o**k dlya chas**o**f]

water вода [vad**a**]

may I have some water? можно мне воды, пожалуйста? [m**o**Jna mnyeh vad**iy**, paJ**a**lsta?]

Tap water is suspect in some Russian cities and should very definitely be avoided in St Petersburg. You must either use bottled water, or ensure that the water has been boiled for fifteen minutes.

Local fizzy mineral water is all right, if a bit too salty and sulphurous for most Westerners; Нарзан (narz**a**n) and Боржоми (barJ**o**mee) from the Caucasus are the best-known brands. Imported mineral waters are also widely available, as is local bottled spring water such as 'Saint Springs', which is produced by a Russian-American joint venture.

waterproof (adj) непромокаемый [nyepramak**a**-yemi]

water-skiing воднолыжный
спорт [vadna-**liy**Jni sport]

way: it's this way в эту сторону
[**ve**too st**o**ranoo]

it's that way в ту сторону [ftoo
st**o**ranoo]

is it a long way to ...? далеко
ли до ... [dalyek**o**lee da ...?]

no way! ни в коем случае!
[nee fk**o**-yem sl**oo**cha-yeh!]

• • • • • DIALOGUE • • • • •

could you tell me the way to ...?
скажите, пожалуйста, как дойти
до ...? [ska**J**iytyeh, pa**J**alsta, kak
d**i**tee da ...?]

**go straight on until you reach the
traffic lights** идите прямо, до
светофора [eed**ee**tyeh pr**ya**ma, da
svyetaf**o**ra]

turn left сверните налево
[svyern**ee**tyeh nal**ye**va]

take the first turn on the right
первый поворот направа [p**ye**rvi
pavar**o**t napr**a**va]

see where

we* мы [miy]

weak слабый [sl**a**bi]

weather погода [pag**o**da]

• • • • • DIALOGUE • • • • •

what's the weather forecast? какой
прогноз погоды? [kak**o**y pragn**o**s
pag**o**di?]

it's going to be fine будет хорошая
погода [b**oo**dyet Har**o**sha-ya pag**o**da]

it's going to rain будет дождливо
[b**oo**dyet da**J**dl**ee**va]

it'll brighten up later обещают

просветление позже
[abyesh-ch**a**-yoot prasvyetl**ye**nee-yeh
p**oJ**-Jeh]

wedding свадьба [sv**a**dba]

wedding ring обручальное
кольцо [abroch**a**lna-yeh
kalts**o**]

Wednesday среда [sryed**a**]

week неделя [nyed**ye**lya]

a week (from) today ровно
через неделю [r**o**vna ch**ye**ryes
nyed**ye**lyoo]

a week (from) tomorrow через
неделю, считая с
завтрашнего дня [ch**ye**ryes
nyed**ye**lyoo, sh-cheet**a**-ya
z-z**a**ftrashnyeva dnya]

weekend конец недели
[kan**ye**ts nyed**ye**lee]

at the weekend в
субботу-воскресенье [v
soob-b**o**too-vaskryes**ye**nyeh]

weight вес [vyes]

weird странный [str**a**n-ni]

welcome: welcome to ... добро
пожаловать [dabr**o** pa**J**alavat]

you're welcome (don't mention
it) не за что [**nye**zashta]

well: I don't feel well мне
нехорошо [mnyeh nyeHar**o**sh**o**]

she's not well ей нехорошо
[yay nyeHar**o**sh**o**]

you speak English very well вы
очень хорошо говорите
по-английски [viy **o**chyen
Har**o**sh**o** gavar**ee**tyeh
pa-angl**ee**skee]

well done! молодец!

[maladyets]
this one as well этот тоже
[etat toJeh]
well well! ну и ну! [noo ee noo!]

•••••• D I A L O G U E ••••••

how are you? как вы поживаете?
[kak viy paJiva-yetyeh?]
very well, thanks, and you?
спасибо, хорошо, а вы?
[spaseeba, Harasho, a viy?]

well-done (meat) хорошо
прожаренный [harasho
praJaryen-ni]
Welsh уэльский [oo-elskee]
I'm Welsh я из Уэльса [ya eez
oo-elsa]
were*: we were мы были ...
[miy biylee ...]
you were вы были ... [viy
biylee ...]
they were они были ... [anee
biylee ...]
west запад [zapat]
in the west на западе [na
zapadyeh]
West: the West Запад [zapat]
western западный [zapadni]
West Indian (adj) вест-индский
[vyest-eentskee]
wet мокрый [mokri]
what? что? [shto?]
what's that? что это?
[shto-eta?]
what should I do? что мне
делать? [shto mnyeh dyelat?]
what a view! вот это вид!
[voteta veet!]
what bus do I take? на какой

автобус мне надо сесть? [na
kakoy aftoboos mnyeh nada
syest?]
wheel колесо [kalyeso]
wheelchair инвалидная
коляска [eenvaleedna-ya
kalyaska]
when? когда? [kagda?]
when we get back когда мы
вернёмся [kagda miy
vyernyomsya]
when's the train? когда поезд?
[kagda po-yest?]
where? где? [gdyeh?]
I don't know where it is я не
знаю, где это [ya nyeh zna-yoo,
gdyeh-eta]

•••••• D I A L O G U E ••••••

where is the cathedral? где собор?
[gdyeh sabor?]
it's over there вон там [von tam]
**could you show me where it is on
the map?** вы можете показать это
на карте? [viy moJetyeh pakazat eta
na kartyeh?]
it's just here вот здесь [vot zdyes]
see **way**

which: which bus? какой
автобус? [kakoy aftoboos?]

•••••• D I A L O G U E ••••••

which one? какой из них? [kakoy
eez neeH?]
that one тот [tot]
this one? этот? [etat?]
no, that one нет, тот [nyet, tot]

while: while I'm here пока я
здесь [paka ya zdyes]

whisky виски n [**vee**skee]

white белый [b**ye**li]

white wine белое вино
[b**ye**la-yeh veen**o**]

who? кто? [kto?]
  who is it? кто там? [kto tam?]
  the man who ... человек,
  который ... [chyela**vye**k,
  kat**o**ri ...]

whole: the whole week всю
неделю [vsyoo nyed**ye**lyoo]
  the whole lot всё [fsyo]

whose: whose is this? чьё это?
[chyo **e**ta?]

why? почему? [pacheem**oo**?]
  why not? почему бы нет?
  [pacheem**oo**bi nyet?]

wide широкий [shi**ro**kee]

wife жена [Jen**a**]

will*: will you do it for me? вы
это сделаете для меня? [viy
eta sd**ye**la-yetyeh dlya myen**ya**?]

wind (noun) ветер [**vye**tyer]

window окно [akn**o**]
  near the window у окна [oo
  akn**a**]
  in the window (of shop) в
  витрине [v-veetr**ee**nyeh]

window seat место у окна
[m**ye**sta oo akn**a**]

windscreen ветровое стекло
[vyetrav**o**-yeh styekl**o**]

windscreen wipers
стеклоочистители
[styekla-acheest**ee**tyelee],
дворники [d**vo**rneekee]

windsurfing виндсёрфинг
[veents**yo**rfeenk]

windy ветреный [**vye**tryen-ni]

wine вино [veen**o**]
  can we have some more wine?
  можно ещё вина,
  пожалуйста [m**o**Jna yesh-ch**o**
  veen**a**, paJ**a**lsta]

The wine on sale in Russia
comes mostly from Moldova,
Georgia and the Crimea, though
some of the Georgian wine has
been subject to counterfeiting.
The ones to look out for are
the Georgian reds Мукузани
(mookooz**a**nee) and Саперави (sapyer**a**vee), which are
both dry and drinkable, or
the sweeter Киндзмараули
(keendzmara-**oo**lee) and Акашени (akash**e**nee). Georgia
also produces some of the
best white wines, like the dry
Гурджани (goordJ**a**nee) and
Цинандали (tsinand**a**lee)
(traditionally served at room
temperature). The best fortified
wines, such as Массандра
(mass**a**ndra), come from the
Crimea. Avoid what the Russians call 'baramat**oo**на' or
'babbling juice'.

---

wine list карта вин
[k**a**rta veen]

winter зима [zeem**a**]
  in the winter зимой [zeem**oy**]

winter holiday зимний отпуск
[**zee**mnee **o**tpoosk]

wire проволока [pr**o**valaka]
  (electric) провод [pr**o**vat]

wish: best wishes с наилучшими пожеланиями [sna-eel**oo**chshimee paJil**a**nee-yamee]
with с [s]
  I'm staying with ... я живу у ... [ya Jiv**oo** oo ...] .
without без [byes]
witness (man/woman) свидетель/ свидетельница [sveed**ye**tyel/ sveed**ye**tyelneetsa]
  will you be a witness for me? (to man/woman) вы можете быть моим свидетелем/моей свидетельницей? [viy m**o**Jetyeh biyt ma-**ee**m sveed**ye**tyel-yem/ma-**yay** sveed**ye**tyelneetsay?]
woman женщина [J**e**nsh-cheena]

---

women
As a visitor to Moscow, you will find that Russian men veer between extreme gallantry and crude chauvinism. Attitudes in Moscow and St Petersburg are much more liberal than in the countryside, where women travelling alone can still expect to encounter stares and comments. Single women should avoid going to certain nightclubs and bars, where their presence may be misconstrued by the local pimps and prostitutes. Although you'll see plenty of Russian women flagging down cars
→

as potential taxis, unaccompanied foreign women would be ill-advised to do likewise.
Most hotels and nightclubs have their quota of prostitutes, run by whichever Mafia gang has struck a deal with the management. This causes problems for Russian women not involved in prostitution, who fear to enter such places alone lest they be mistaken for a freelance prostitute. If you should arrange to meet a Russian woman, respect any doubts she might express about the venue, and rendezvous outside so that you can go in together.

---

wonderful замечательный [zamyech**a**tyelni]
won't*: it won't start не заводится [nyeh zav**o**deetsa]
wood (material) дерево [d**ye**ryeva]
  (forest) лес [lyes]
wool шерсть f [sherst]
word слово [sl**o**va]
work (noun) работа [rab**o**ta]
  (verb) работать [rab**o**tat]
  it's not working это не работает [**e**ta nyeh rab**o**ta-yet]
  I work in ... я работаю в ... [ya rab**o**ta-yoo v ...]
world мир [meer]
worry: I'm worried я беспокоюсь [ya byespak**o**-yoos]
worse: it's worse это хуже [**e**ta

HooJeh]

worst самый плохой [sami plahoy]

worth: is it worth a visit? стоит ли туда ехать? [sto-eetlee tooda yeHat?]

would: would you give this to ...? передайте это, пожалуйста ... [pyeryedItyeh eta, paJalsta ...]

wrap: could you wrap it up? заверните, пожалуйста [zavyerneetyeh, paJalsta]

wrapping paper обёрточная бумага [abyortachna-ya boomaga]

wrist запястье [zapyastyeh]

write писать/написать [peesat/ napeesat]

could you write it down? запишите, пожалуйста [zapeeshiytyeh, paJalsta]

how do you write it? как это пишется? [kak eta peeshetsa?]

writing paper почтовая бумага [pachtova-ya boomaga]

wrong неправильно [nyepraveelna]

it's the wrong key это не тот ключ [eta nyeh tot klyooch]

this is the wrong train вы не на том поезде [viy nyeh na tom po-yezdyeh]

the bill's wrong счёт ошибочный [sh-chot ashiybachni]

sorry, wrong number (said by man/woman) извините, я не туда попал/попала

[eezveeneetyeh, ya nyeh tooda papal/papala]

sorry, wrong room (said by man/woman) извините, я ошибся/ ошиблась номером

[eezveeneetyeh, ya ashiypsya/ ashiyblas nomyeram]

there's something wrong with ... что-то не так с ... [shto-ta nyeh tak s ...]

what's wrong? в чём дело? [fchom dyela?]

X

X-ray рентгеновский снимок [ryentgyenafskee sneemak]

Y

yacht яхта [yaHta]

yard двор [dvor]

year год [got]

yellow жёлтый [Jolti]

yes да [da]

yesterday вчера [fchyera]

yesterday morning вчера утром [fchyera ootram]

the day before yesterday позавчера [pazafchyera]

yet ещё [yesh-cho]

•••••• DIALOGUE ••••••

is it here yet? оно ещё не пришло? [ano yesh-cho nyeh preeshlo?]

no, not yet нет ещё [nyet yesh-cho]

you'll have to wait a little longer yet вам придётся ещё немного подождать [vam preedyotsa yesh-cho nyemnoga padaJdat]

yoghurt йогурт [y**o**goort]
you* (sing pol or pl) вы [viy]
  (sing, fam) ты [tiy]
  this is for you это для вас [eta
  dlya vas]
  with you с вами [sv**a**mee]

Russian has two words for 'you':
вы (viy) and **ты** (tiy). **Вы** (viy)
is the polite form used when you
are addressing someone you do
not know at all or do not know
well enough to consider a friend;
it's also used as a sign of respect
to an older person. It is also the
plural form, used for addressing
more than one person. **Ты** is the
singular, familiar form used
when addressing a child or a
friend. If you feel it is appropriate to start addressing someone
in the **ты** form, but are unsure,
just ask '**mo**лna pyery**ay**tee na
tiy?'.

---

young молодой [malad**oy**]
your* (sing pol or pl) ваш [vash]
  (sing, fam) твой [tvoy]
  is this yours? это ваше? [eta
  v**a**sheh?]
your*/yours* (sing pol or pl) ваш
  m [vash], ваша f [v**a**sha], ваше
  n [v**a**sheh], ваши pl [vash**ee**]
  (sing, fam) твой m [tvoy], твоя f
  [tva-**ya**], твоё n [tva-**yo**], твои
  pl [tva-**ee**]
youth hostel молодёжная
  гостиница [malad**yo**лna-ya
  gast**ee**neetsa]

Z

zero нуль m [nool]
  below zero ниже нуля
  [n**ee**лeh nool**ya**]
zip молния [m**o**lnee-ya]
  could you put a new zip on?
  вставьте, пожалуйста, новую
  молнию [fst**a**ftyeh, paлalsta,
  n**o**voo-yoo m**o**lnee-yoo]
zip code почтовый индекс
  [pacht**o**vi **ee**ndeks]
zoo зоопарк [zo-op**a**rk]

Russian-English

COLLOQUIALISMS

The following are words you may well hear. You shouldn't be tempted to use any of the stronger ones unless you are sure of your audience.

алкаш [alkash] wino, boozer

баксы [baksi] dollars

безобразие! [byezabrazee-yeh!] it's disgraceful!

блин! [bleen!] damn!

выпивка [viypeefka] bevvy, drink

деревянные [dyeryevyan-ni-yeh] roubles

дура/дурак [doora/doorak] idiot, thickhead

ёлки-палки! [yolkee-palkee!] bloody hell!

ерунда! [eroonda!] nonsense!

здорово! [zdorava!] great!

иди к чёрту! [eedee kchortoo!] go to hell!

козёл! [kazyol!] idiot!

какого чёрта ...? [kakova chorta ...?] what the hell ...?

какой ужас! [kakoy ooJas!] that's awful!

класс! [klass!] great!, brilliant!

клёвый! [klyovi!] knockout!, brill!, fantastic!

кретин [kryeteen] twit

к черту! [kchortoo!] to hell with it!

лимон [leemon] a million

молодец! [maladyets!] well done!

ничего себе! [neechyevo syebyeh!] not bad!

отвяжись! [atvyaJiys!] get lost!

парень [paryen] bloke

пошёл ты! [pashol tiy!] get lost!

псих [pseeн] nutter

ребята [ryebyata] (the) lads, (the) guys

сволочь [svolach] bastard

с приветом [spreevyetam] crackers, nuts

хреновый [Hryenovi] rotten, lousy

хрен с ним! [Hryen sneem!] to hell with it!

чёрт! [chort!] damn!, shit!

чёрт знает что [chort zna-yet shto] God only knows

чёрт с тобой! [chort staboy!] to hell with you!

чокнутый [choknooti] barmy

ужасно! [ooJasna!] it's awful!, it's ghastly!

штука [shtooka] a thousand

это обдираловка [eta abdeeralafka] it's a rip-off

A

A bus stop

авария [av**a**ree-ya] accident;
breakdown

август [**a**vgoost] August

авиакомпания
[avee-a-kamp**a**nee-ya] airline

авиапочта [avee-a-p**o**chta]
airmail
авиапочтой [**a**vee-a-p**o**cht**ı**] by
airmail

Австралия [afstr**a**lee-ya]
Australia

Австрия [**a**fstree-ya] Austria

автобус [aft**o**boos] bus

автовокзал [aftavakz**a**l] bus
station

автоматический
[aftamat**ee**chyeskee] automatic

автомобилист [aftamabeel**ee**st]
car driver

автомобиль m [aftamab**ee**l] car

автоответчик [afta-atv**ye**tcheek]
answering machine

автостоянка [aftasta-y**a**nka] car
park, parking lot

автострада [aftastr**a**da]
motorway, freeway, highway

агентство [ag**ye**nstva] agency

адвокат [advak**a**t] lawyer

администратор
[admeeneestr**a**tar] manager

адрес [**a**dryes] address

адресат [adryes**a**t] addressee

адресная книга [**a**dryesna-ya
kn**ee**ga] address book

Азербайджан [azyerb**ı**dj**a**n]
Azerbaijan

аккумулятор [ak-koomool**ya**tar]
battery (for car)

акселератор [aksyelyer**a**tar]
accelerator

акцент [akts**e**nt] accent

алкоголь m [alkag**o**l] alcohol

аллергия [al-lyerg**ee**-ya] allergy

алмаз [alm**a**s] diamond

Америка [am**ye**reeka] America

американский [amyereek**a**nskee]
American

амперный: 13-и амперный
[amp**ye**rni] 13-amp

английская булавка
[angl**ee**ska-ya bool**a**fka] safety
pin

английский [angl**ee**skee]
English

английский язык [angl**ee**skee
yaz**ı**yk] English (language)

англичане [angleech**a**nyeh] the
English

англичанин [angleech**a**neen]
Englishman

англичанка [angleech**a**nka]
English woman

Англия [**a**nglee-ya] England

антигистамин
[anteegeestam**ee**n]
antihistamine

антикварная вещь
[anteekv**a**rna-ya vyesh-ch]
antique

антикварный [anteekv**a**rni]
antiquarian; antique

антикварный магазин
[anteekv**a**rni magaz**ee**n] antique
shop

аппендицит [ap-pyendeets**ı**yt]

appendicitis
аппетит [ap-pyeteet] appetite
апрель m [apryel] April
аптека [aptyeka] chemist,
  pharmacy
арестовать [aryestavat] to arrest
Армения [armyenee-ya]
  Armenia
аромат [aramat] flavour
Архангельск [arнangyelsk]
  Archangel
аспирин [aspeereen] aspirin
Афганистан [afganeestan]
  Afghanistan
афиша [afeesha] poster
аэропорт [a-eraport] airport
Аэрофлот [a-eraflot] Aeroflot

Б

бабушка [babooshka]
  grandmother
багаж [bagash] luggage,
  baggage
багажник [bagaлneek] boot (of
  car), (US) trunk
бак [bak] tank
бакалея [bakalyeh-ya] groceries
балалайка [balalıka] balalaika
балкон [balkon] balcony
Балтийское море [balteeska-yeh
  moryeh] Baltic Sea
бальзам для волос [balzam dlya
  valos] conditioner
бампер [bampyer] bumper, (US)
  fender
банк [bank] bank
банкнота [banknota] banknote,
  (US) bill

банкомат [bankamat] cash
  dispenser, ATM
баня [banya] bathhouse
бар [bar] bar
бармен [barmyen] barman
бассейн [basyayn] swimming
  pool
батарейка [bataryayka] battery
батарея [bataryeh-ya] radiator
башня [bashnya] tower
бегать/бежать [byegat/byeJat]
  to run
  бегать/бежать трусцой
  [byegat/byeJat troostsoy] to jog
беда [byeda] trouble;
  misfortune
бедный [byedni] poor
бедро [byedro] thigh; hip
бежать [byeJat] to run
бежевый [byeJevi] beige
без [byez] without
  без двадцати два [byez
  dvatsatee dva] twenty to two
безопасность [byezapasnast]
  safety
  в безопасности [f
  byezapasnastee] safe
безработный [byezrabotni]
  unemployed
белокурый [byelakoori] blond
Белорусь [byelaroos] Belarus
белый [byeli] white
Бельгия [byelgee-ya] Belgium
бельё [byelyo] washing;
  underwear
бензин [byenzeen] petrol,
  gasoline
берег [byeryek] coast; shore
  на берегу моря [na byeryegoo

morya] at the seaside
берегись ... [byeryegees ...]
beware of ...
беременная [byeryemyen-na-ya]
pregnant
бесплатный [byesplatni] free of
charge
беспокоиться [byespako-eetsa]
to worry about
бесполезный [byespalyezni]
useless
беспорядок [byesparyadak]
mess
беспошлинный
[byesposhleen-ni] duty-free
библиотека [beeblee-atyeka]
library
бизнес [beeznes] business
билет [beelyet] ticket
билет в один конец [beelyet
vadeen kanyets] single ticket,
one-way ticket
билетная касса [beelyetna-ya
kas-sa] ticket office
билеты [beelyeti] tickets
бить/побить [beet/pabeet] to
hit, to beat
благодарить/поблагодарить
[blagadareet/pablagadareet] to
thank
благодарный [blagadarni]
grateful
бланк [blank] form
ближайший [bleeлshi] nearest
ближе [bleeJeh] nearer
близкий [bleeskee] near, close
близнецы [bleeznyetsiy] twins
близорукий [bleezarookee]
shortsighted

блокнот [blaknot] notebook
блоха [blaHa] flea
блузка [blooska] blouse
блюдо [blyooda] dish
блюдце [blyoodtseh] saucer
бог [boH] God
богатый [bagati] rich
Болгария [balgaree-ya] Bulgaria
более [bolyeh-yeh] more
болезнь f [balyezn] disease;
illness
болеть/заболеть [balyet/
zabalyet] to be ill; to fall ill; to
be sore, to ache, to hurt
болеутоляющее средство
[bolyeh-ootalyayoosh-chyeh
sryetstva] painkiller
боль f [bol] ache; pain
боль в желудке [bol v
Jelootkyeh] stomach ache
больница [balneetsa] hospital
больной [balnoy] ill, (US) sick;
sore; patient
больше [bolsheh] more
большинство [balshinstvo]
most (of); majority
большой [balshoy] big, large
бомж [bomJ] homeless person
борода [barada] beard
борт-проводник
[bort-pravadneek] steward
боюсь: я боюсь [ya bayoos] I'm
afraid
бояться [ba-yatsa] to be afraid
(of)
браслет [braslyet] bracelet
брат [brat] brother
бриллиант [breel-lee-ant]
diamond

британский [breetanskee] British

бритва [breetva] razor

бритвенное лезвие [breetvyen-na-yeh lyezvee-yeh] razor blade

бриться/побриться [breetsa/ pabreetsa] to shave

бровь f [brof] eyebrow

бросать/бросить [brasat/ broseet] to throw

брошь f [brosh] brooch

брошюра [brashoora] brochure; leaflet

брюки [bryookee] trousers, (US) pants

будет [boodyet] he will; she will; it will; he will be; she will be; it will be

будете [boodyetyeh] you will; you will be

будешь [boodyesh] you will; you will be

будильник [boodeelneek] alarm clock

будить/разбудить [boodeet/ razboodeet] to wake

буду [boodoo] I will; I will be

будут [boodoot] they will; they will be

будущее [boodoosh-chyeh-yeh] future

будьте здоровы! [boodtyeh zdarovi!] bless you!

буква [bookva] letter (of alphabet)

букинист [bookeeneest] secondhand bookseller

букинистический магазин [bookeeneesteechyeskee magazeen] secondhand bookshop/bookstore

булавка [boolafka] pin

булочная [boolachna-ya] bakery

бульвар [boolvar] boulevard

бумага [boomaga] paper

бумажник [boomajneek] wallet

бумажные носовые платки [boomajni-yeh nasaviy-yeh platkee] tissues, Kleenex®

буря [boorya] storm

бутылка [bootiylka] bottle

буфет [boofyet] snack bar, café

бы: я хотел бы ... [ya Hatyel biy ...] I would like ...

бывать/побывать [bivat/ pabivat] to be; to frequent

бывший [biyfshi] former

был [biyl], была [biyla] was; were

были [biylee] were

было [biyla] was

быстрее! [bistryeh-yeh!] hurry up!

быстро [biystra] quickly, fast

быстрый [biystri] quick, fast

бытовая химия [bitava-ya неemee-ya] household cleaning materials

быть [biyt] to be

бюро [byooro] office

бюро находок [byooro naнodak] lost property office

бюро обслуживания [byooro apsloojivanee-ya] service bureau

бюро путешествий [byooro pootyeshestvee] travel agent's

бюстгальтер [byoostgaltyer] bra

В

в [v] in
вагон [vagon] carriage
вагон-ресторан [vagon-ryestaran] dining car
важный [vaJni] important
ваза [vaza] vase
валюта [valyoota] foreign currency
вам [vam] (to) you
вами [vamee] (by) you
ванна [van-na] bath
ванная [van-na-ya] bath; bathroom
вас [vas] you; of you
вата [vata] cotton wool, absorbent cotton
ваш [vash], ваша [vasha], ваше [vasheh] your; yours
вашего [vasheva] (of) your; (of) yours
ваше здоровье! [vasheh zdarovyeh!] cheers!
вашей [vashay] your; yours; of your; of yours; to your; to yours; by your; by yours
вашем [vashem] your; yours
вашему [vashemoo] (to) your; (to) yours
ваши [vashi] your; yours
вашим [vashim] your; yours; by your; by yours; to your; to yours
вашими [vashimee] (by) your; (by) yours
ваших [vashiн] (of) your; (of) yours
вашу [vashoo] your; yours

в воскресенья и праздничные дни [v vaskryesyenya ee prazneechni-yeh dnee] Sundays and public holidays
вдова [vdava] widow
вдовец [vdavyets] widower
вдруг [vdrook] suddenly
вегетарианец [vyegetaree-anyets] vegetarian
ведро [vyedro] bucket
вежливый [vyeЛeevi] polite
везде [vyezdyeh] everywhere
век [vyek] century
вёл [vyol], вела [vyela] led; was leading
вели [vyelee] led; were leading
Великобритания [vyeleekabreetanee-ya] Britain
великолепный [vyeleekalyepni] terrific, magnificent, splendid
велосипед [vyelaseepyet] bicycle
велосипедная трасса [vyelaseepyedna-ya tras-sa] cycle path
Венгрия [vyengree-ya] Hungary
веник [vyeneek] bunch of birch twigs; broom
вентилятор [vyenteelyatar] fan
верёвка [vyeryofka] string; rope
верить/поверить [vyereet/pavyereet] to believe
вернуть [vyernoot] to give back, to return
вернуться [vyernootsa] to get back, to come back, to return
верный [vyerni] true

А Б В Г Д Е Ё Ж З И Й К Л М Н О П Р С Т У Ф Х Ц Ч Ш Щ Ъ Ы Ь Э Ю Я

Ве

вероятно [vyera-yatna] probably

верхний этаж [vyerнnee etash] upper floor

верховая езда [vyerнava-ya yezda] horse riding

вес [vyes] weight

веселиться: веселитесь! [vyesyeleetyes!] have fun!

весёлый [vyesyoli] cheerful

весна [vyesna] spring
весной [vyesnoy] in spring

вести [vyestee] to drive; to lead

весь [vyes] all; the whole
весь день [vyes dyen] all day

ветер [vyetyer] wind

вечер [vyechyer] evening
добрый вечер [dobri vyechyer] good evening
11 часов вечера [chasof vyechyera] 11 p.m.

вешалка [vyeshalka] peg; rack; stand; coathanger

вещи [vyesh-chee] things, belongings

вещь f [vyesh-ch] thing

взбешённый [vzbyeshon-ni] furious

вздор [vzdor] rubbish, nonsense

взлёт [vzlyot] take-off

взрослые [vzrosli-yeh] adults

взрослый [vzrosli] adult

взять [vzyat] to take

взять напрокат [vzyat naprakat] to rent

вид [veet] view; appearance; form

видео [veedyeh-o] video

видеомагнитофон [veedyeh-omagneetafon] video recorder

видеть/увидеть [veedyet/ ooveedyet] to see

видоискатель m [veeda-eeskatyel] viewfinder

виза [veeza] visa

визит [veezeet] visit

визитка [veezeetka], визитная карточка [veezeetna-ya kartachka] business card

вилка [veelka] fork

Вильнюс [veelnyoos] Vilnius

винный магазин [veen-ni magazeen] wine and spirits shop

вираж [veerash] bend

витамины [veetameeni] vitamins

витрина [veetreena] shop window

включать/включить [fklyoochat/fklyoocheet] to switch on

включён [fklyoochon] on, switched on; included

включено в цену [fklyoochyeno f tsenoo] included in the price

включить [fklyoocheet] to switch on

вкус [fkoos] taste

вкусный [fkoosni] nice; delicious, tasty

владелец [vladyelyets] owner

Владивосток [vladeevastok] Vladivostok

вместе [vmyestyeh] together

вместо [vmyesta] instead of

внешний [vnyeshnee] outward;

external; foreign
вниз [vnees] down, downwards
внизу [vneezoo] downstairs
внимание [vneemanee-yeh] attention
внутренние рейсы [vnootryen-nee-yeh ryaysi] domestic flights
внутренний [vnootryen-nee] inner; inside; internal; domestic; inland
внутри [vnootree] inside
во время [va vryemya] during
вовремя [vovryemya] on time
вода [vada] water
водитель [vadeetyel] driver
водительские права [vadeetyelskee-yeh prava] driving licence
водить/вести [vadeet/vyestee] to drive; to lead
водопад [vadapat] waterfall
возвращать/вернуть [vazvrash-chat/vyernoot] to give back, to return
возвращаться/вернуться [vazvrash-chatsa/vyernootsa] to get back, to come back, to return
воздух [vozdooH] air
воздушный шар [vazdooshni shar] balloon
возместить [vazmyesteet] to refund
возможно [vazmoJna] possible; perhaps
возражать: вы не возражаете если я ...? [viy nyeh vazraJa-yetyeh yeslee ya ...?] do you

mind if I ...?
возраст [vozrast] age
возьмите тележку/корзину [vazmeetyeh tyelyeshkoo/karzeenoo] please take a trolley/basket
войдите! [vIdeetyeh!] come in!
война [vIna] war
войти [vItee] to enter, to go in
вокзал [vakzal] station (main-line railway)
Волгоград [valgagrat] Volgograd
волосы [volasi] hair
вон: вон! [von!] get out!
вон там [von tam] over there
вонь [von] stink
вообще [va-apsh-chyeh] at all; on the whole, generally
вопрос [vapros] question
вор [vor] thief
вор-карманник [var-karman-neek] pickpocket
ворота [varota] gate
воротник [varatneek] collar
восемнадцатый [vasyemnatsati] eighteenth
восемнадцать [vasyemnatsat] eighteen
восемь [vosyem] eight
восемьдесят [vosyemdyesyat] eighty
восемьсот [vasyemsot] eight hundred
воскресенье [vaskryesyenyeh] Sunday
восток [vastok] east
к востоку от [k vastokoo ot] east of

восьмой [vasmoy] eighth
вот [vot] here is; that's
вот и всё [vot ee fsyo] that's all
вот, пожалуйста [vot, paJalsta]
here is, here are; here you
are
вот эти [vot etee] these
вот этот [vot etat] this one
вперёд [vpyeryot] forwards; in
future; in advance
впереди [fpyeryedee] in front,
ahead; in front of; before; in
future
врач [vrach] doctor
вредить/повредить [vryedeet/
pavryedeet] to damage
время [vryemya] time
время года [vryemya goda]
season
время отправления [vryemya
atpravlyenee-ya] departure
time
все [fsyeh] everyone; all
всё [fsyo] everything; all
всё вместе [fsyo vmyestyeh]
altogether
всегда [fsyegda] always
всего [fsyevo] in all, only
всё-таки [vsyo-takee] anyway
вспомнить [fspomneet] to
remember, to recall
вспышка [fspiyshka] flash
вставать/встать [fstavat/fstat] to
get up
встретить [fstryeteet] to meet
встреча [fstryecha]
appointment; meeting
встречать/встретить
[fstryechat/fstryeteet] to meet

всякий [fsyakee] any
вторник [ftorneek] Tuesday
второй [ftaroy] second
второй этаж [ftaroy etash] first
floor, (US) second floor
вход [fHot] entrance, way in
вход бесплатный [fHot
byesplatni] admission free
вход воспрещён [fHot
vaspryesh-chon] no admittance
вход свободный [fHot svabodni]
admission free
входите [fHadeetyeh] come in
входить/войти [fHadeet/vItee]
to enter, to go in
вчера [fchyera] yesterday
вчера вечером [fchyera
vyechyeram] last night (before
midnight)
вчера днём [fchyera dnyom]
yesterday afternoon
вчера ночью [fchyera nochyoo]
last night (after midnight)
вы [viy] you
выбирать/выбрать [vibeerat/
viybrat] to choose
выбросить [viybraseet] to
throw away
выглядеть [viyglyadyet] to look;
to seem
выдача багажа [viydacha
bagaJa] baggage claim
выдача покупок [viydacha
pakoopak] purchase
collection point
выиграть [viy-eegrat] to win
выйти [viytee] to go out; to get
off
выключатель m [viklyoochatyel]

switch
выключать/выключить
[viklyoochat/**viy**klyoocheet] to
switch off
выключен [**viy**klyoochyen] off,
switched off
выключить [**viy**klyoocheet] to
switch off
вылет [**viy**lyet] departure
вылетать/вылететь [vilyetat/
viylyetyet] to take off
выпить [**viy**peet] to drink
высокий [vis**o**kee] tall; high
высота [vis**a**ta] height, altitude
выставка [**viy**stafka] exhibition
выставочный зал [**viy**stavachni
zal] exhibition hall
высший [**viy**s-shee] higher;
highest
выхлопная труба [vi**H**lapn**a**-ya
troob**a**] exhaust pipe
выход [**viy**Hat] way out, exit;
gate (at airport)
выход в город [**viy**Hat v g**o**rat]
exit
выходить/выйти [vi**H**ad**ee**t/
viytee] to go out; to get off
выход на посадку [**viy**Hat na
pas**a**tkoo] gate
выходной день ... [viHadn**oy**
dyen ...] closed on ...
выходные [viHadn**iy**-yeh]
weekend
выше [**viy**sheh] higher ·
вьюга [vy**oo**ga] snowstorm

Г

г. town/city
газ [gas] gas
газета [gaz**ye**ta] newspaper
газетный киоск [gaz**ye**tni
kee-**o**sk] newsagent
газон [gaz**o**n] lawn
галантерея [galantyer**yeh**-ya]
haberdashery
галерея [galyer**yay**-a] gallery
галстук [**ga**lstook] tie, necktie
гараж [gar**a**sh] garage
гарантия [gar**a**ntee-ya]
guarantee, warranty
гардероб [gardyer**o**p]
cloakroom
гастроном [gastran**o**m] food
store
гвоздь m [gvost] nail (in wall)
где? [gdyeh?] where?
где-нибудь [gd**yeh**-neeboot]
somewhere; anywhere
где-то [gd**yeh**-ta] somewhere
г-жа [gaspaj**a**] Mrs; Ms
гигиеническая прокладка
[geegee-yen**ee**chyeska-ya
prakl**a**tka] sanitary towel/
napkin
гид [geet] guide
главный [**gla**vni] main,
principal
гладить/погладить [gl**a**deet/
pagl**a**deet] to iron
глаз [glas] eye
глубокий [gloob**o**kee] deep
глупый [gl**oo**pi] stupid
глухой [glooH**oy**] deaf
г-н [gaspad**ee**n] Mr

гнилой [gneel**oy**] rotten

говорить/сказать [gavar**ee**t/ skaz**a**t] to say; to speak

вы говорите по-... [vi gavar**ee**tyeh pa-...] do you speak ...?

год [got] year

годовщина [gadafsh-ch**ee**na] anniversary

Голландия [gal-l**a**ndee-ya] Holland

голова [galav**a**] head

головная боль [galavn**a**-ya bol] headache

голодный [gal**o**dni] hungry

голос [g**o**las] voice

голый [g**o**li] naked

гомосексуалист [gomaseksoo- al**ee**st] gay, homosexual

гора [gar**a**] mountain

гораздо [gar**a**zda] much more

гордый [g**o**rdi] proud

гореть/сгореть [gar**ye**t/zgar**ye**t] to burn

горло [g**o**rla] throat

горничная [g**o**rneechna-ya] maid; cleaner

город [g**o**rat] town; city

городской [garadsk**oy**] town, city, urban

горький [g**o**rkee] bitter

горячий [gar**ya**chee] hot

господин [gaspad**ee**n] Mr; Sir

госпожа [gaspaj**a**] Miss; Mrs; Madam

гостеприимство [gastyepree- **ee**mstva] hospitality

гостиная [gast**ee**na-ya] lounge, living room

гостиница [gast**ee**neetsa] hotel

гость [gost]/гостья [g**o**stya] guest (male/female)

государство [gasood**a**rstva] state

готовить/приготовить [gat**o**veet/preegat**o**veet] to cook; to prepare

готовый [gat**o**vi] ready

град [grat] hail

градус [gr**a**doos] degree

грамматика [gram-m**a**teeka] grammar

грампластинки [gramplast**ee**nkee] records

граница [gran**ee**tsa] border

за границей [za gran**ee**tsay] abroad

гребная шлюпка [gryebn**a**-ya shly**oo**pka] rowing boat

Греция [gr**ye**tsi-ya] Greece

грипп [greep] flu

гроза [graz**a**] thunderstorm

гром [grom] thunder

громкий [gr**o**mkee] loud

громче [gr**o**mchyeh] louder

грубый [gr**oo**bi] rude; coarse

грудная клетка [groodn**a**-ya kl**ye**tka] chest

грудь f [groot] breast; chest

грузинский [grooz**ee**nskee] Georgian

Грузия [gr**oo**zee-ya] Georgia

грузовик [groozav**ee**k] lorry, truck

группа [gr**oo**pa] group

группа крови [gr**oo**pa kr**o**vee] blood group

грустный [gr**oo**stni] sad

грязное бельё [gr**ya**zna-yeh

byel**yo**] dirty laundry, washing

гря́зный [gr**ya**zni] dirty

губа́ [g**oo**ba] lip

губна́я пома́да [g**oo**bna-ya pam**a**da] lipstick

гуля́ть/погуля́ть [g**oo**l**ya**t/ pag**oo**l**ya**t] to go for a walk

густо́й [g**oo**st**oy**] thick

Д

д. house

да [da] yes

дава́й(те) ... [dav**i**(tyeh) ...] let's ...

дава́ть/дать [dav**a**t/dat] to give

давле́ние в ши́нах [davl**ye**nee-yeh fsh**i**naн] tyre pressure

давно́ [davn**o**] long ago; for a long time; long since

дади́м [dad**ee**m] we will give

дади́те [dad**ee**tyeh] you will give

даду́т [dad**oo**t] they will give

да́же [d**a**ɹeh] even

да́же е́сли [d**a**ɹeh y**e**slee] even if

далёкий [dal**yo**kee] far, far away

далеко́ [dal**ye**ko] far, far away

да́льше [d**a**lsheh] further

дам [dam] I will give

да́ма [d**a**ma] lady

Да́ния [d**a**nee-ya] Denmark

дари́ть/подари́ть [dar**ee**t/ padar**ee**t] to give (present)

даст [dast] he will give; she will give; it will give

дать [dat] to give

да́ча [d**a**cha] house/cottage in the country

дашь [dash] you will give

два [dva] two

двадца́тый [dv**a**tsati] twentieth

два́дцать [dv**a**tsat] twenty

две [dveh] two

две неде́ли [dveh nyed**ye**lee] fortnight, two weeks

двена́дцатый [dvyen**a**tsati] twelfth

двена́дцать [dvyen**a**tsat] twelve

дверь f [dvyer] door

две́сти [dv**ye**stee] two hundred

двойно́й [dvin**oy**] double

дворе́ц [dvar**ye**ts] palace

дво́рник [dv**o**rneek] windscreen wiper; janitor; street cleaner

двухме́стный но́мер [dvooн-m**ye**sni n**o**myer] double room

двухра́зовое пита́ние [dvooнraz**a**va-yeh peet**a**nee-yeh] half board

дебюта́нт [dyebyoot**a**nt] beginner

де́верь [d**ye**vyer] brother-in-law (husband's brother)

деви́чья фами́лия [d**ye**veechya fam**ee**lee-ya] maiden name

де́вочка [d**ye**vachka] girl (child)

де́вушка [d**ye**vooshka] girl (young woman)

девяно́сто [dyevyan**o**sta] ninety

девятна́дцатый [dyevyatn**a**tsati] nineteenth

девятна́дцать [dyevyatn**a**tsat] nineteen

девятый [dyevyati] ninth

девять [dyevyat] nine

девятьсот [dyevyatsot] nine hundred

дедушка [dyedooshka] grandfather

дежурная [dyeжoorna-ya] concierge

дежурная аптека [dyeжoorna-ya aptyeka] duty pharmacist

дезинфицирующее средство [dyezeenfeetseeroo-yoosh-chyeh sryetstva] antiseptic; disinfectant

дезодорант [dyezadarant] deodorant

действительно [dyaystveetyelna] really, indeed

действительный [dyaystveetyelni] valid

декабрь m [dyekabr] December

делать/сделать [dyelat/zdyelat] to do; to make

делиться/поделиться [dyeleetsa/padyeleetsa] to share

дело [dyela] matter, business
в самом деле [f samam dyelyeh] really
как дела? [kak dyela?] how are you?, how are things?

день m [dyen] day

деньги [dyengee] money

день рождения [dyen rajdyenee-ya] birthday

деревня [dyeryevnya] countryside; village

дерево [dyeryeva] tree; wood
из дерева [eez dyeryeva]

wooden

держать [dyerжat] to hold; to keep; to support

держитесь левой стороны [dyerжeetyes lyevı staraniy] keep to the left

десятый [dyesyati] tenth

десять [dyesyat] ten

дети [dyetee] children

детская коляска [dyetska-ya kalyaska] pram, baby carriage

детская кроватка [dyetska-ya kravatka] cot

детская порция [dyetska-ya portsi-ya] childrens' portion

дешевле [dyeshevlyeh] cheaper

дешёвый [dyeshovi] cheap

джинсы [dJeensi] jeans

диабетик [dee-abyeteek] diabetic

диета [dee-yeta] diet

дизель m [deezyel] diesel

дикий [deekee] wild

директор [deeryektar] director

дискотека [deeskatyeka] disco

длина [dleena] length

длинный [dleen-ni] long

для [dlya] for
для вас/меня [dlya vas/myenya] for you/me

для некурящих [dlya nyekooryash-cheeн] non-smoking

дневник [dnyevneek] diary

днём [dnyom] in the afternoon; p.m.

дно [dno] bottom
на дне [na dnyeh] at the

bottom of

до [do] up to, as far as; before; until

доброе утро [dobra-yeh ootra] good morning

добрый [dobri] good; kind

добрый вечер [dobri vyechyer] good evening

добрый день [dobri dyen] good afternoon

довольно [davolna] quite; fairly

довольно хорошо [davolna Harasho] pretty good

довольный [davolni] pleased

до востребования [da vastryebavanee-ya] poste restante, general delivery

договор [dagavor] contract

дождик [doJdeek] shower

дождливый [daJdleevi] rainy

дождь m [dosht] rain

идёт дождь [eedyot dosht] it's raining

документ [dakoomyent] document

долго [dolga] a long time

должен: я/он должен [ya/on dolJen] I/he must

должна: я/она должна [ya/ana dalJna] I/she must

долина [daleena] valley

дом [dom] house; home

дома [doma] at home

он дома? [on doma?] is he in?

доплата [daplata] supplement

дорога [daroga] road

дорогой [daragoy] expensive, dear

дороже [daroJeh] dearer

дорожные работы [daroJni-yeh raboti] roadworks

дорожный чек [daroJni chyek] travellers' cheque/check

досадно [dasadna] annoying

до свидания [da sveedanya] goodbye

доставать/достать [dastavat/dastat] to get, to obtain

достаточно [dastatachna] enough

достать [dastat] to get, to obtain

дочь [doch] daughter

драка [draka] fight

древний [dryevnee] ancient

друг [drook] friend; boyfriend

другой [droogoy] other; another, a different

в другом месте [v droogom myestyeh] elsewhere

что-то другое [shto-ta droogoy-yeh] something else

думать/подумать [doomat/padoomat] to think

я думаю, что ... [ya dooma-yoo, shto ...] I think that ...

духи [dooHee] perfume

духовка [dooHofka] oven

душ [doosh] shower

дым [diym] smoke

дыра [dira] hole

дышать [dishat] to breathe

дядя [dyadya] uncle

Е

еврейский [yevryayskee] Jewish

Европа [yevropa] Europe

европейский [yevrapyayskee] European

его [yevo] him; it; of him; of it; his; its

еда [yeda] food; meal

едим [yedeem] we eat

единый билет [yedeeni beelyet] monthly season ticket

едите [yedeetyeh] you eat

едят [yedyat] they eat

её [yeh-yo] her; it; of her; of it; hers; its

ездить [yezdeet] to go (by transport); to ride; to drive; to travel

ей [yay] her; to her; by her

ем [yem] I eat

ему [yemoo] him; it; to him; to it

если [yeslee] if

ест [yest] he eats; she eats; it eats

естественный [yestyestvyen-ni] natural

есть [yest] there is; there are
здесь есть ...? [zdyes yest ...?] is there ... here?
у меня есть ...? [oo myenya yest ...] I have ...

есть/съесть [yest/syest] to eat

ехать/ездить [yeнat/yezdeet] to go (by transport); to ride; to drive; to travel

ешь [yesh] you eat; eat

ешьте [yeshtyeh] eat

ещё [yesh-cho] still; another; another one; more
ещё более ... [yesh-cho bolyeh-yeh ...] even more ...
ещё не [yesh-cho nyeh] not yet
ещё одно пиво [yesh-cho adno peeva] another beer

Ж

Ж ladies' toilets, ladies' room

жаловаться [Jalavatsa] to complain

жаль [Jal] pity; it's a pity
как жаль [kak Jal] what a pity

жара [Jara] heat

жарить [Jareet] to fry; to grill

жвачка [Jvachka] chewing gum

ждать/подождать [Jdat/padaJdat] to wait
подождите меня! [padaJdeetyeh myenya!] wait for me!

железная дорога [Jelyezna-ya daroga] railway

железо [Jelyeza] iron (metal)

жёлтый [Jolti] yellow

желудок [Jeloodak] stomach

жена [Jena] wife

женат [Jenat] married (man)
не женат [nyeh Jenat] single

жених [Jeneeн] fiancé; bridegroom

женская одежда [Jenska-ya adyeJda] ladies' clothing

женский зал [Jenskee zal] ladies' hairdresser

женский отдел [Jenskee

ad-d**ye**l] ladies' department

женский туалет [**J**enskee too-al**ye**t] ladies' toilet, ladies' room

женщина [**J**ensh-cheena] woman

жетон [**J**et**o**n] token

живой [**J**iv**oy**] alive; living

живот [**J**iv**o**t] stomach; belly

животное [**J**ivotna-yeh] animal

жидкость для снятия лака [**J**eetkast dlya sn**ya**tee-ya l**a**ka] nail polish remover

жизнь f [**J**iyzn] life

жильё [**J**il**yo**] accommodation

жир [**J**iyr] grease, fat

жирный [**J**iyrni] greasy, fatty; rich

жить [**J**iyt] to live

жить в палатках [**J**iyt f pal**a**tkaн] to camp

журнал [**J**oorn**a**l] magazine

З

за [za] behind

забавный [zab**a**vni] funny, amusing

заблудиться [zablood**ee**tsa] to lose one's way

заболеть [zabal**ye**t] to be ill; to fall ill; to be sore

забор [zab**o**r] fence

забота [zab**o**ta] worry; bother

заботиться/позаботиться о [zabot**ee**tsa/pazabot**ee**tsa o] to take care of

забывать/забыть [zabiv**a**t/ zab**iy**t] to forget

заведующий [zav**ye**dooyoosh-chee] manager

завернуть [zavyern**oo**t] to wrap

зависеть: это зависит [eta zav**ee**seet] it depends

завод [zav**o**t] factory, plant

завтра [z**a**ftra] tomorrow

до завтра [da z**a**ftra] see you tomorrow

завтра вечером [z**a**ftra v**ye**chyeram] tomorrow night

завтра утром [z**a**ftra **oo**tram] tomorrow morning

завтрак [z**a**ftrak] breakfast

загар [zag**a**r] suntan

загорать/загореть [zagar**a**t/ zagar**ye**t] to get sunburnt, to tan

загораться/загореться [zagar**a**tsa/zagar**ye**tsa] to catch fire

загрязнённый [zagryazn**yo**n-ni] polluted

зад [zat] bottom (of body)

задержка [zad**ye**rshka] delay

задние фары [z**a**dnee-yeh f**a**ri] rear lights

задний [z**a**dnee] back; reverse

задний ход [z**a**dnee Hot] reverse gear

задняя часть [z**a**dnya-ya chast] back, back part

зажечь [zaJ**e**ch] to light

зажигалка [zaJig**a**lka] lighter

зажигание [zaJig**a**nee-yeh] ignition

зажигать/зажечь [zaJig**a**t/ zaJ**e**ch] to light

заказ [zak**a**s] order;

reservation

заказано [zakazana] reserved

заказное письмо [zakazno-yeh peesmo] registered mail

заказывать/заказать [zakazivat/ zakazat] to order; to book

закат [zakat] sunset

закон [zakon] law

закричать [zakreechat] to shout

закрывать/закрыть [zakrivat/ zakriyt] to close

закрыто [zakriyta] closed

закрыто на ремонт [zakriyta na ryemont] closed for repairs

закрыто на учёт [zakriyta na oochot] closed for stocktaking

закрыть [zakriyt] to close

закурить [zakooreet] to smoke

закуска [zakooska] snack; hors d'oeuvre, appetizer

зал ожидания [zal aJidanee-ya] waiting room; departure lounge

замечательный [zamyechatyelni] remarkable, wonderful

замок [zamok] lock

замок [zamak] castle

замороженный [zamaroJen-ni] frozen

замужем [zamooJem] married (woman)

не замужем [nyeh zamooJem] single

замшевый [zamshevi] suede

занавеска [zanavyeska] curtain

занимать/занять [zaneemat/ zanyat] to borrow; to occupy; to take up

заниматься/заняться [zaneematsa/zanyatsa] to occupy oneself with; to study; to begin to

занято [zanyata], **занятый** [zanyati] engaged, occupied; engaged, busy

занять [zanyat] to borrow

запад [zapat] west

к западу от [k zapadoo at] west of

запасной выход [zapasnoy viyHat] emergency exit

запах [zapaH] smell

запирать/запереть [zapeerat/ zapyeryet] to lock

записная книжка-календарь [zapeesna-ya kneeshka-kalyendar] diary; planner

заплатить [zaplateet] to pay

заполнить [zapolneet] to fill in

запор [zapor] bar; bolt; lock; constipation

заправочная станция [zapravachna-ya stantsi-ya] petrol/gas station; garage

запрещено [zapryesh-chyeno] prohibited, forbidden

запчасти [zapchastee] spare parts

запястье [zapyastyeh] wrist

зарабатывать/заработать [zarabativat/zarabotat] to earn

заработок [zarabatak] salary

заражение [zaraJenee-yeh] infection; contamination

заранее [zaranyeh-yeh] in advance

засмеяться [zasmyeh-**ya**tsa] to laugh

засоренный [zas**o**ryen-ni] blocked

застегните привязные ремни [zastyegn**ee**tyeh preevyazn**i**y-yeh ryemn**ee**] fasten seatbelts

застёжка-молния [zast**yo**shka-m**o**lnee-ya] zip

застенчивый [zast**ye**ncheevi] shy

затвор объектива [zatv**o**r abyekt**ee**va] shutter (on camera)

затормозить [zatarmaz**ee**t] to brake

защищать/защитить [zash-cheesh-ch**a**t/zash-cheet**ee**t] to protect, to defend

звать/позвать [zvat/pazv**a**t] to call

  как вас зовут? [kak vas zav**oo**t?] what's your name?

  меня зовут ... [myen**ya** zav**oo**t ...] my name is ...

звезда [zvyezd**a**] star

звонить/позвонить [zvan**ee**t/ pazvan**ee**t] to ring; to phone

звонок [zvan**o**k] bell; phone call

здание [zd**a**nee-yeh] building

здесь [zdyes] here

здоровый [zdar**o**vi] healthy; huge

здоровье [zdar**o**vyeh] health

  за ваше здоровье! [za v**a**sheh zdar**o**vyeh!] your health!, cheers!

здравствуйте [zdr**a**stvooytyeh] hello; how do you do?

зелёный [zyel**yo**ni] green

земля [zyeml**ya**] earth; world; ground

зеркало [z**ye**rkala] mirror

зима [zeem**a**] winter

  зимой [zeem**oy**] in winter

змея [zmyeh-**ya**] snake

знакомить/познакомить [znak**o**meet/paznak**o**meet] to introduce

знакомиться/познакомиться [znak**o**meetsa/paznak**o**meetsa] to get to know, to become acquainted with, to meet

знать [znat] to know

  я не знаю [ya nyeh zn**a**-yoo] I don't know

значить [zn**a**cheet] to mean

  что это значит? [shto eta zn**a**cheet?] what does it mean?

золовка [zal**o**fka] sister-in-law (husband's sister)

золото [z**o**lata] gold

зонтик [z**o**nteek] umbrella

зоопарк [za-ap**a**rk] zoo

зрелый [zr**ye**li] ripe

зуб [zoop] tooth

зубная боль [zoobn**a**-ya bol] toothache

зубная паста [zoobn**a**-ya p**a**sta] toothpaste

зубная щётка [zoobn**a**-ya sh-ch**o**tka] toothbrush

зубной врач [zoobn**oy** vrach] dentist

зубной протез [zoobn**oy** pr**a**tes] dentures

зуд [zoot] itch

зять [zyat] son-in-law

И

и [ee] and

иголка [eegolka] needle

игра [eegra] game

играть/сыграть [eegrat/sigrat] to play

игрушка [eegrooshka] toy

идея [eedyeh-ya] idea

идти/ходить [eet-tee/Hadeet] to go (on foot), to walk; to suit

известный [eezvyesni] famous

извините! [eezveeneetyeh!] excuse me!, sorry!

извините, пожалуйста [eezveeneetyeh, paJalsta] excuse me

извиняться/извиниться [eezveenyatsa/eezveeneetsa] to apologize

я очень извиняюсь [ya ochyen eezveenya-yoos] I'm really sorry

из-за [eez-za] because of

изнасиловать [eeznaseelavat] to rape

икона [eekona] icon

или [eelee] or

или ... или ... [eelee ... eelee ...] either ... or ...

им [eem] him; it; by him; by it; them; to them

имеется ... [eemyeh-yetsa ...] there is ...

иметь [eemyet] to have

имеются ... [eemyeh-yootsa ...] there are ...

ими [eemee] (by) them

имя [eemya] name, first name

иначе [eenachyeh] otherwise

инвалид [eenvaleet] disabled

иногда [eenagda] sometimes

иностранец [eenastranyets]/ иностранка [eenastranka] foreigner (man/woman)

иностранный [eenastran-ni] foreign

институт иностранных языков [eensteetoot eenastran-niH yazikov] language school

инструктор [eenstrooktar] instructor

инструмент [eenstroomyent] tool; instrument

интересный [eentyeryesni] interesting

Интернет [eenternet] Internet

Интурист [eentooreest] Intourist

информация [eenfarmatsi-ya] information

Ирландия [eerlandee-ya] Ireland

искать [eeskat] to look for

искренний [eeskryen-nee] sincere

искупаться [eeskoopatsa] to go swimming

искусственный [eeskoostvyen-ni] artificial

искусство [eeskoostva] art

Испания [eespanee-ya] Spain

исполнитель [eespalneetyel] executive; performer

использовать [eespolzavat] to use

испорченный [eesporchyen-ni]

faulty; rotten

исторический [eestar**ee**chyeskee] historical

история [eest**o**ree-ya] history

исчезать/исчезнуть [eeschyez**at**/eeschy**e**znoot] to disappear

Италия [eet**a**lee-ya] Italy

итог [eet**o**k] total; result

их [eeH] their; theirs; them; of them

июль m [ee-**yoo**l] July

июнь m [ee-**yoo**n] June

К

к [k] to; towards

к. block

кабинет врача [kabeeny**et** vr**a**cha] doctor's surgery

каблук [kabl**oo**k] heel

каждый [k**a**Jdi] each; every

каждый день [k**a**Jdi dyen] every day

каждый раз [k**a**Jdi ras] every time

Казак [kaz**a**k] Cossack

Казахстан [kazaнst**a**n] Kazakhstan

казачий [kaz**a**chee] Cossack

как [kak] like, as

как? [kak?] how?

как дела? [kak dyel**a**?] how are you?, how are things?

календарь m [kalyend**a**r] calendar

камень m [k**a**myen] stone

камера хранения [k**a**myera нran**ye**nee-ya] left luggage

office, baggage check room

Канада [kan**a**da] Canada

канал [kan**a**l] canal; channel

канат [kan**a**t] rope

каникулы [kan**ee**kooli] school holidays

канун Нового года [kan**oo**n n**o**vava g**o**da] New Year's Eve

канцтовары [kantstav**a**ri] stationery

капля [k**a**plya] drop

капот [kap**o**t] bonnet, (US) hood

карандаш [karand**a**sh] pencil

карий [k**a**ree] brown (eyes)

карман [karm**a**n] pocket

карта [k**a**rta] map; playing card

картина [kart**ee**na] painting

картинная галерея [kart**ee**n-na-ya galyer**yeh**-ya] art gallery

картон [kart**o**n] cardboard

карточка (биснесмена) [k**a**rtachka (beeznyesm**ye**na)] business card

Каспийское море [kasp**ee**ska-yeh m**o**ryeh] Caspian Sea

касса [k**a**s-sa] cash desk; booking office; box office

кассета [kas-s**ye**ta] cassette

кассетный магнитофон [kas-s**ye**tni magneetaf**o**n] cassette recorder

кастрюля [kastry**oo**lya] saucepan

катастрофа [katastr**o**fa] disaster

кататься на коньках [kat**a**tsa na kank**a**н] to skate

кататься на лыжах [katatsa na liyлан] to ski
католик [katoleek] Catholic
кафе [kafeh] café
кафетерий [kafyeteree] cafeteria
качество [kachyestva] quality
кашель m [kashel] cough
кашлять [kashlyat] to cough
каштановый [kashtanavi] brown, chestnut (hair)
каюта [ka-yoota] cabin
кв., квартира [kvarteera] flat, apartment
квартирная плата [kvarteerna-ya plata], квартплата [kvartplata] rent
квитанция [kveetantsi-ya] receipt; ticket
кеды [kyedi] trainers
кем [kem] who; (by) whom
кемпинг [kempeenk] campsite
Киев [kee-yev] Kiev
кило [keelo] kilo
километр [keelamyetr] kilometre
кино(театр) [keeno(-tyeh-atr)] cinema, movie theater
кинокамера [keenakamyera] camcorder
кинофильм [keenafeelm] film, movie
кислый [keesli] sour
кисть f [keest] paintbrush
Китай [keeti] China
кладбище [kladbeesh-chyeh] cemetery
класс [klas] class
классика [klaseeka] classical

music or literature
классическая музыка [klaseechyeska-ya moozika] classical music
классический [klas-seechyeskee] classical
класть/положить [klast/palaJeet] to put; to lay
клей [klyay] glue
клейкая лента [klyayka-ya lyenta] Sellotape®, Scotch tape®
клиент [klee-yent] client
климат [kleemat] climate
клиника [kleeneeka] clinic
клуб [kloop] club
ключ [klyooch] key
книга [kneega] book
книжечка [kneeJechka] book of 10 tickets
книжный магазин [kneeJni magazeen] bookshop, bookstore
ковёр [kavyor] carpet; rug
когда? [kagda?] when?
когда-нибудь [kagda-neeboot] at some time; ever; one day вы когда-нибудь ...? [vi kagda-neeboot ...?] have you ever ...?
когда-то [kagda-ta] one day; some time
кого [kavo] who; (of) whom
код [kot] code
кожа [koJa] skin; leather
кожаный [koJani] leather
койка [koyka] bunk bed
колготки [kalgotkee], колготы [kalgoti] tights, pantyhose

колено [kal**ye**na] knee
колесо [kal**ye**so] wheel
количество [kal**ee**chyestva]
  quantity
коллекция [kal-l**ye**ktsi-ya]
  collection
колокол [k**o**lakal] bell
кольцо [kal**tso**] ring; circle
ком [kom] who; whom
команда [kam**a**nda] team
командировка [kamande**e**rofka]
  business trip
комар [kam**a**r] mosquito
комиссионный (магазин)
  [kamees-see-**o**n-ni (magaz**ee**n)]
  secondhand shop
Коммунистическая партия
  [kam-moonee**stee**chyeska-ya
  p**a**rtee-ya] Communist Party
комната [k**o**mnata] room
компания [kamp**a**nee-ya]
  company
компостер [kamp**o**styer] ticket
  punch
компьютер [kamp**yoo**tyer]
  computer
кому [kam**oo**] who; (to) whom
конверт [kanv**ye**rt] envelope
кондитерская [kand**ee**tyerska-ya]
  confectioner's
кондиционирование воздуха
  [kandeetsi-an**ee**ravanee-yeh
  v**o**zdoo**н**a] air-conditioning
конец [kan**ye**ts] end
конечно [kan**ye**shna] of course
конечный пункт [kan**ye**chni
  poonkt] terminus
консервный нож [kans**ye**rvni
  nosh] tin-opener

консульство [k**o**nsoolstva]
  consulate
контактные линзы [kant**a**ktni-
  yeh l**ee**nzi] contact lenses
контролёр [kantral**yo**r] ticket
  inspector
конфета [kanf**ye**ta] sweet,
  candy
концерт [kants**e**rt] concert
концертный зал [kants**e**rtni zal]
  concert hall
кончать/кончить [kanch**a**t/
  k**o**ncheet] to finish
коньки [kank**ee**] skates
кооператив [ka-apyerat**ee**f]
  co-operative
копейка [kap**ya**yka] kopeck
у меня ни копейки денег [oo
  myen**ya** nee kap**ya**ykee
  d**ye**nyek] I'm broke
корабль m [kar**a**bl] ship
корзина [karz**ee**na] basket
коридор [kar**ee**dor] corridor
коричневый [kar**ee**chnyevi]
  brown
коробка [kar**o**pka] box
коробка передач [kar**o**pka
  pyeryed**a**ch] gearbox
королева [karal**ye**va] queen
король [kar**o**l] king
короткий [kar**o**tkee] short
короткий путь [kar**o**tkee poot]
  shortcut
корп., корпус [k**o**rpoos] block
корь f [kor] measles
косметика [kasm**ye**teeka]
  make-up; cosmetics
костыли [kastil**ee**] crutches
кость f [kost] bone

костюм [kastyoom] suit

который [katori] which
который час? [katori chas?]
what time is it?

кофта [kofta] cardigan

кошелёк [kashelyok] purse,
coin purse

кошка [koshka] cat

кошмар [kashmar] nightmare

к перронам [k per-ronam] to the
platforms/tracks

к поездам [k pa-yezdam] to the
trains

кража [kraJa] theft

край [krı] edge

крайний: по крайней мере [pa
krınyay myeryeh] at least

кран [kran] tap, faucet

красивый [kraseevi] nice;
beautiful; handsome

красить/покрасить [kraseet/
pakraseet] to paint

Красная Площадь [krasna-ya
plosh-chat] Red Square

краснуха [krasnooHa] German
measles

красный [krasni] red

красть/украсть [krast/ookrast]
to steal

кредитная карточка
[kryedeetna-ya kartachka] credit
card

крем [kryem] cream; butter
cream

крем для бритья [kryem dlya
breetya] shaving foam

крем для обуви [kryem dlya
oboovee] shoe polish

крем для снятия косметики

[kryem dlya snyatee-ya
kasmyeteekee] cleansing
cream

Кремль m [kryeml] Kremlin

крепость f [kryepast] fortress;
strength

кресло-каталка [kryesla-katalka]
wheelchair

критическое положение
[kreeteechyeska-yeh palaJenee-
yeh] emergency

кричать/закричать [kreechat/
zakreechat] to shout

кровать f [kravat] bed

кровь f [krof] blood

кроме [kromyeh] except

кроме воскресений [kromyeh
vaskryesyenee] except
Sundays

круглый [kroogli] round

круиз [kroo-eez] cruise

крутой [krootoy] steep

крыло [krilo] wing

Крым [kriym] Crimea

крыша [kriysha] roof

крышка [kriyshka] lid

к себе [ksyebyeh] pull

ксерокс [ksyeraks] photocopy;
photocopier

кто? [kto?] who?

кто-нибудь [kto-neeboot],
кто-то [kto-ta] someone;
anyone

кувшин [koofshiyn] jug

кузен [koozen], кузина
[koozeena] cousin (male/female)

кукла [kookla] doll

кулинария [kooleenaree-ya]
delicatessen

купальная шапочка
[koopalna-ya shapachka]
bathing cap

купальник [koopalneek]
swimming costume

купаться/искупаться [koopatsa/
eeskoopatsa] to go swimming

купе [koopeh] compartment

купить [koopeet] to buy

купол [koopal] cupola, dome

курить/закурить [kooreet/
zakooreet] to smoke

курс (валюты) [koors (valyooti)]
exchange rate

куртка [koortka] jacket; anorak

кусок [koosok] piece

кухня [kooHnya] kitchen;
cooking, cuisine

кухонная посуда [kooHan-na-ya
pasooda] cooking utensils

кухонное полотенце
[kooHan-na-yeh palatyentseh]
tea towel

Л

ладно [ladna] all right, OK

лак для волос [lak dlya valos]
hair spray

лак для ногтей [lak dlya
naktyay] nail polish

лампа [lampa] lamp

лампочка [lampachka] light
bulb

ластик [lasteek] rubber, eraser

Латвия [latvee-ya] Latvia

лгать/солгать [lgat/salgat] to lie,
to tell a lie

левша [lyefsha] left-handed

левый [lyevi] left

лёгкие [lyoHkee-yeh] lungs

лёгкий [lyoHkee] light (not
heavy); easy

лёд [lyot] ice

леденец [lyedyenyets] lollipop

лезбиянка [lyezbee-yanka]
lesbian

лезвие бритвы [lyezvee-yeh
breetvi] razor blade

лейкопластырь [lyaykaplastir]
plaster, Bandaid®

лекарство [lyekarstva]
medicine, drug

ленивый [lyeneevi] lazy

лес [lyes] forest, wood

лестница [lyesneetsa] stairs;
ladder

летать/лететь [lyetat/lyetyet] to
fly

лето [lyeta] summer

летом [lyetam] in summer

лечь [lyech] to lie down

ли [lee] question particle

ливень m [leevyen] downpour

лист [leest] leaf

Литва [leetva] Lithuania

литр [leetr] litre

лифт [lift] lift, elevator

лихорадка [leeHaratka] fever

лицо [leetso] face

лишний [leeshnee] spare

лишний вес багажа [leeshnee
vyes bagaja] excess baggage

лоб [lop] forehead

ловить/поймать [laveet/plmat]
to catch

лодка [lotka] boat

лодыжка [ladiyshka] ankle

А
Б
В
Г
Д
Е
Ё
Ж
З
И
Й
К
Л
М
Н
О
П
Р
С
Т
У
Ф
Х
Ц
Ч
Ш
Щ
Ъ
Ы
Ь
Э
Ю
Я

|До

ложиться/лечь [laЈeetsa/lyech]
  to lie down
ложка [loshka] spoon
ложный [loЈni] false
локоть m [lokat] elbow
ломать/сломать [lamat/slamat]
  to break
ломтик [lomteek] slice
Лондон [londan] London
лосьон для загара [lasyon dlya
  zagara] suntan lotion
лосьон для снятия косметики
  [lasyon dlya snyatee-ya
  kasmyeteekee] make-up
  remover
лошадь f [loshat] horse
луна [loona] moon
лучше [looch-sheh] better
лучший [looch-shi] better; best
  самый лучший [sami looch-
  shi] the best
лыжи [liyЈi] skis
лыжные ботинки [liyЈni-yeh
  bateenkee] ski boots
лыжный спорт [liyЈni sport]
  skiing
любезный [lyoobyezni] kind,
  obliging
любимый [lyoobeemi] favourite
любить [lyoobeet] to love
любовь f [lyoobof] love
люди [lyoodee] people

M

M gents' toilet, men's room;
  underground, metro, (US)
  subway
магазин [magazeen] shop

магазин беспошлинной
  торговли [magazeen
  byesposhleen-nı targovlee]
  duty-free shop
магнитофонная кассета
  [magneetafon-na-ya kasyeta]
  tape, cassette
мазь f [mas] ointment
май [mı] May
маленький [malyenkee] small;
  little; short
мало [mala] not much; not
  many
  мало времени [mala
  vryemyenee] not much time
мальчик [malcheek] boy
мама [mama] mum
марка [marka] stamp; make (of
  car etc)
марки [markee] stamps
март [mart] March
маршрут [marshroot] route,
  itinerary
маршрутное такси
  [marshrootna-yeh taksee]
  minibus
масло [masla] oil
масло для загара [masla dlya
  zagara] suntan oil
мастер [mastyer] foreman;
  expert; hair stylist
матрас [matras] mattress
матрёшка [matryoshka] Russian
  doll
мать f [mat] mother
машина [mashıyna] car; vehicle
мебель f [myebyel] furniture
медленно [myedlyen-na] slowly
медленный [myedlyen-ni] slow

медовый месяц [myedovi myesyats] honeymoon

медсестра [myetsyestra] nurse

между [myeJdoo] between

междугородный автобус [myeJdoogarodni aftoboos] coach, long-distance bus

междугородный звонок [myeJdoo-garodni zvanok] long-distance call

междугородный телефон [myeJdoo-garodni tyelyefon] long-distance phone

международные рейсы [myeJdoonarodni-yeh ryaysi] international flights

международный [myeJdoonarodni] international

международный звонок [myeJdoonarodni zvanok] international call

международный телефон [myeJdoonarodni tyelyefon] international telephone

мелочь f [myelach] small change

менеджер [menedjer] manager

менее [myenyeh-yeh] less

меньше [myensheh] smaller; less

меня [myenya] me; of me

у меня [oo myenya] I have

менять/поменять [myenyat/pamyenyat] to change

мёртвый [myortvi] dead

мест нет [myest nyet] full

места [myesta] seats

местное время [myesna-yeh vryemya] local time

местность f [myesnast] area

местный звонок [myesni zvanok] local call

место [myesta] place; seat

на месте [na myestyeh] on the spot

место для курения [myesta dlya kooryenee-ya] smoking area

месяц [myesyats] month

месячные [myesyachni-yeh] period

металл [myetal] metal

метр [myetr] metre

метро [myetro] underground, metro, (US) subway

мех [myeн] fur

меха [myeна] fur shop

механик [myeнaneek] mechanic

меховая шапка [myeнava-ya shapka] fur hat

мешать [myeshat] to disturb; to stir; to mix; to prevent

милиционер [meeleetsi-anyer] policeman

милиция [meeleetsi-ya] police

миллион [mee-lee-on] million

Минск [meensk] Minsk

минута [meenoota] minute

мир [meer] world; peace

мне [mnyeh] me; to me

многие [mnogee-yeh] many; many people

много [mnoga] a lot (of); many; much

мной [mnoy] (by) me

могу: я могу [ya magoo] I can

мода [moda] fashion

модный [modni] fashionable

моё [mayo] my; mine

А
Б
В
Г
Д
Е
Ё
Ж
З
И
Й
К
Л
М
Н
О
П
Р
С
Т
У
Ф
Х
Ц
Ч
Ш
Щ
Ъ
Ы
Ь
Э
Ю
Я

Мо

моего [ma-yevo] (of) my; (of)
mine

моей [ma-yay] my; mine; of
my; of mine; to my; to mine;
by my; by mine

моём [ma-yom] my; mine

моему [ma-yemoo] (to) my;
(to) mine

может быть [moJet biyt] maybe

можно [moJna] one can, one
may; it is possible
можно ...? [moJna ...?] can I ...?

мои [ma-ee] my; mine; of my;
of mine

моим [ma-eem] (by) my; (by)
mine; (to) my; (to) mine

моими [mo-eemee] (by) mine

моих [ma-eeн], мой [moy] my;
mine

мокрый [mokri] wet

Молдова [maldova] Moldova

молния [molnee-ya] lightning;
zip, zipper

молодой [maladoy] young
молодые люди [maladiy-eh
lyoodee] young people

моложе [maloJeh] younger

море [moryeh] sea

мороженое [maroJena-yeh] ice
cream

мороз [maros] frost

морозилка [marazeelka] freezer

Москва [maskva] Moscow

мост [mosst] bridge

мотор [mator] engine

моторная лодка [matorna-ya
lotka] motorboat

мотоцикл [matatseekl]
motorbike

мочь/смочь [moch/smoch] can,
to be able to

мою [ma-yoo] my; mine

моя [ma-ya] my; mine

муж [moosh] husband

мужская одежда [mooshska-ya
adyeJda] menswear

мужской зал [mooshskoy zal]
men's hairdresser

мужской туалет [mooshskoy
too-alyet] gents' toilet, men's
room

мужчина m [moosh-cheena]
man

музей [moozyay] museum

музыка [moozika] music

музыкальный [moozikalni]
musical

мусор [moosar] rubbish, trash

мусорный ящик [moosarni
yash-cheek] dustbin, trashcan

муха [mooнa] fly (insect)

мы [miy] we

мыло [miyla] soap

мыть/помыть [miyt/pamiyt] to
wash

мыть/помыть посуду [miyt/
pamiyt pasoodoo] to do the
washing-up

мышь f [miysh] mouse

мягкие контактные линзы
[myaнkee-yeh kantaktni-yeh
leenzi] soft lenses

мягкий [myaнkee] soft

мясной магазин [myasnoy
magazeen] butcher's

мясо [myasa] meat

мяч [myach] ball

Н

на [na] on; at

наберите номер [nabyereetyeh nomyer] dial the number

наб., набережная [nabyeryeJna-ya] embankment

на вынос [na viynas] to take away, (US) to go

на себя [na syebya] pull

наверху [navyerHoo] at the top; upstairs
   там наверху [tam navyerHoo] up there

над [nat] over; above
   над головой [nad galavoy] overhead

надеяться [nadyeh-yatsa] to hope

надо [nada] it is necessary; one must; need
   мне надо ... [mnyeh nada ...] I need ...

надоесть: мне надоело ... [mnyeh nada-yela ...] I'm fed up with ...

назад [nazat] back; backwards; ago
   три дня назад [tree dnya nazat] three days ago

название [nazvanee-yeh] name; title

наиболее [na-eebolyeh-yeh] the most

найти [nItee] to find

накладная [nakladna-ya] invoice

наконец [nakanyets] at last

налево [nalyeva] to the left

наличные: платить наличными [plateet naleechnimee] to pay cash

налог [nalok] tax

нам [nam] (to) us

нами [namee] (by) us

нападать/напасть [napadat/napast] to attack

напасть [napast] to attack

написать [napeesat] to write

напиток [napeetak] drink

наполнять/наполнить [napalnyat/napolneet] to fill

направление [napravlyenee-yeh] direction

направо [naprava] to the right

например [napreemyer] for example

напрокат [naprakat] for hire, to rent

напротив [naproteef] opposite

народ [narot] people; nation

народная музыка [narodna-ya moozika] folk music

нарочно [narochna] deliberately

наружное [narooJna-yeh] for external use only

наружный [narooJni] external; outdoor

нас [nas] us; of us
   у нас [oo nas] we have

насекомое [nasyekoma-yeh] insect

насморк [nasmark] cold

настольный теннис [nastolni ten-nees] table tennis

настоящий [nasta-yash-chee] genuine, real

настроение [nastra-**ye**nee-yeh] mood

натощак [natash-ch**a**k] on an empty stomach

наука [na-**oo**ka] science

научить [na-ooch**ee**t] to teach

нахальный [na**h**alni] cheeky, impertinent

находить/найти [na**h**ad**ee**t/ n**ee**t**ee**] to find

национальность f [natsi-an**a**lnast] nationality

начало [nach**a**la] beginning

начальник [nach**a**lneek] head, chief, boss

начинать/начать [nacheen**a**t/ nach**a**t] to begin, to start

наш [nash], **наша** [n**a**sha] , **наше** [n**a**sheh] our; ours

нашего [n**a**sheva] (of) our; (of) ours

нашей [n**a**shay] our; ours; of our; of ours; to our; to ours; by our; by ours

нашем [n**a**shem] our; ours

нашему [n**a**shemoo] (to) our; (to) ours

наши [n**a**shi] our; ours

нашим [n**a**shim] (by) our; (by) ours; (to) our; (to) ours

нашими [n**a**shi**y**mee] (by) our; (by) ours

наших [n**a**shi**h**] (of) our; (of) ours

нашу [n**a**shoo] our; ours

не [nyeh] not

небо [n**ye**ba] sky

неважно [nyeva**J**na] it doesn't matter

невероятный [nyevyera-**ya**tni] incredible

невеста [nyev**ye**sta] fiancée; bride

невозможно [nyevazm**o**Jna] it's impossible

не высовываться из окон [nyeh vis**o**vivatsa eez **o**kan] do not lean out of the windows

него [nyev**o**] his; its

у него [oo nyev**o**] he has; it has

недалеко (от) [nyedalyek**o** (at)] not far (from)

неделя [nyed**ye**lya] week

в неделю [v nyed**ye**lyoo] per week

на этой неделе [na **e**ti nyed**ye**lyeh] this week

две недели [dvyeh nyed**ye**lee] fortnight, two weeks

недоразумение [nyedarazoom**ye**nee-yeh] misunderstanding

неё [nyeh-**yo**] her; hers; it; its

у неё [oo nyeh-**yo**] she has; it has

независимый [nyezav**ee**seemi] independent

не за что [ny**eh** za shta] you're welcome, don't mention it

ней [nyay] her; it

некоторые [n**ye**katari-yeh] some; a few

не курить [nyeh koor**ee**t] no smoking

нелепый [nyel**ye**pi] ridiculous

нём [nyom] him; it

немедленно [nyem**ye**dlyen-na] immediately

немецкий [nyem**ye**tskee] German

немецкий язык [nyem**ye**tskee yaz**iy**k] German (language)

немного [nyem**no**ga] a little bit

ненавидеть [nyenav**ee**dyet] to hate

не нырять [nyeh nir**ya**t] no diving

необходимо [nyeh-ар**нa**d**ee**ma] it's necessary

не останавливается в ... [nyeh astan**a**vleeva-yetsa v ...] does not stop at ...

неправильный [nyepr**a**veelni] wrong, incorrect

не прислоняться [nyeh preeslan**ya**tsa] do not lean against the door

неприятный [nyepree-**ya**tni] unpleasant

не работает [nyeh rab**o**ta-yet] out of order

не разрешается ... [nyeh razryesha-yetsa ...] do not ...

нервный [n**ye**rvni] nervous

нёс [nyos] carried; were carrying

несколько [n**ye**skolka] several; a few

несла [nyesl**a**] carried; was carrying; were carrying

несли [nyesl**ee**] carried; were carrying

несносный [nyesn**o**sni] intolerable

нести [nyest**ee**] to carry

нет [nyet] no

нет, спасибо [nyet, spas**ee**ba]

no, thank you

нет входа [nyet f**no**da] no entry

нет выхода [nyet v**iy**нada] no exit

не трогать [nyeh tr**o**gat] do not touch

неустойчивый [nyeh-oost**oy**cheevi] changeable; unstable

ни ... ни ... [nee ... nee ...] neither ... nor ...

нигде [neegd**ye**h] nowhere

нижнее бельё [n**ee**лnyeh-yeh byel**yo**] underwear

низкий [n**ee**skee] low

никогда [neek**a**gd**a**] never

никто [neekt**o**] nobody

ними: с ними [s n**ee**mee] with them

нитка [n**ee**tka] thread

них [neeн] their; theirs; them

у них [oo neeн] they have

ничего [neech**ye**v**o**], ничто [neesht**o**] nothing

но [no] but

Новая Зеландия [n**o**va-ya zyel**a**ndee-ya] New Zealand

новогодняя ночь [navag**o**dnya-ya noch] New Year's Eve

новости [n**o**vastee] news

новый [n**o**vi] new

новый год [n**o**vi got] New Year

с Новым годом! [sn**o**vim g**o**dam!] happy New Year!

нога [nag**a**] leg; foot

ноготь m [n**o**gat] fingernail; toenail

нож [nosh] knife

ножницы [noЈneetsi] scissors

ноль m [nol] zero

номер [nomyer] number; hotel room

номер на двоих [nomyer na dva-eeн] double room

номер с двумя кроватями [nomyer zdvoomya kravatyamee] twin room

номерной знак [namyernoy znak] number plate

Норвегия [narvyegee-ya] Norway

нормально [narmalna] not bad, OK

нормальный [narmalni] normal

нос [nos] nose

носить/нести [naseet/nyestee] to carry

носки [naskee] socks

носовой платок [nasavoy platok] handkerchief

ночная рубашка [nachna-ya roobashka] nightdress

ночь f [noch] night
    спокойной ночи [spakoynı nochee] good night

ноябрь m [na-yabr] November

нравиться [nraveetsa] to like
    мне нравится ... [mnyeh nraveetsa ...] I like ...

нуль [nool] zero

нырять/нырнуть [niryat/ nirnoot] to dive

O

o [o] about

оба/обе [oba/obyeh] both

обед [abyet] lunch

обёрточная бумага [abyortachna-ya boomaga] wrapping paper

обещать [abyesh-chat] to promise

обижать/обидеть [abeeЈat/ abeedyet] to offend

облако [oblaka] cloud

область f [oblast] administrative region

облачный [oblachni] cloudy

обмен валюты [abmyen valyooti] currency exchange

обогреватель m [abagryevatyel] heater

обратный адрес [abratni adryes] sender's address

обратный билет [abratni beelyet] return ticket, round-trip ticket

обручён/обручена [abroochon/ abroochyena] engaged (man/ woman: to be married)

обслуживание [apslooЈivanee-yeh] service

обслуживать/обслужить [apslooЈivat/apslooЈit] to serve

обувь f [oboof] footwear

общежитие [apsh-chyeЈeetee-yeh] hostel

общество [opsh-chyestva] society

объектив [abyekteef] lens

объяснение [abyasnyenee-yeh]

explanation

объяснять/объяснить [abyasnyat/abyasneet] to explain

обыкновенный [abiknavyen-ni] usual

обычай [abiychı] custom

обычно [abiychna] usually

овощи [ovash-chee] vegetables

овощной магазин [avash-chnoy magazeen] greengrocer's

огонь m [agon] fire

ограничение скорости [agraneechyenee-yeh skorastee] speed limit

одеваться/одеться [adyevatsa/adyetsa] to get dressed

одежда [adyeJda] clothes

одеколон после бритья [adyekalon poslyeh breetya] aftershave

Одесса [adyesa] Odessa

одеться [adyetsa] to get dressed

одеяло [adyeh-yala] blanket

один [adeen] alone; one

одиннадцатый [adeenatsati] eleventh

одиннадцать [adeenatsat] eleven

одна [adna] alone; one

одно [adno] one

одноместный номер [adna-myesni nomyer] single room

одолжить [adalJeet] to lend

ожерелье [aJeryelyeh] necklace

ожог [aJok] burn

озеро [ozyera] lake

окно [akno] window

около [okala] near; about

октябрь m [aktyabr] October

окулист [akooleest] optician

он [on] he; it

она [ana] she; it

они [anee] they

оно [ano] it

опаздывать/опоздать (на) [apazdivat/apazdat (na)] to arrive/be late; to miss

опасность f [apasnast] danger

опасный [apasni] dangerous

опера [opyera] opera

операция [apyeratsi-ya] operation

опоздать (на) [apazdat (na)] to arrive/be late; to miss

опрокинуть [aprakeenoot] to knock over

оптика [opteeka] optician's

опухший [apooнshi] swollen

оранжевый [aranJevi] orange (colour)

организация [arganeezatsi-ya] organization

организовать [arganeezavat] to organize

оркестр [arkyestr] orchestra

оса [asa] wasp

осень f [osyen] autumn, (US) fall

осенью [osyenyoo] in the autumn, in the fall

осмотр [asmotr] check-up

особенно [asobyen-na] especially

особняк [asabnyak] detached house

house

особый [asobi] special

оставаться/остаться [astavatsa/astatsa] to stay; to remain

оставить [astaveet] to leave behind; to forget

остановиться [astanaveetsa] to stop

остановитесь! [astanaveetyes!] stop!

остановка [astanofka] stop

остановка автобуса [astanofka aftoboosa] bus stop

остаток [astatak] rest

остаться [astatsa] to stay; to remain

осторожно! [astaroJna!] be careful!; look out!

осторожно, двери закрываются! [astaroJna, dvyeree zakriva-yootsa!] caution, the doors are closing!

осторожно, окрашено [astaroJna, akrashena] wet paint

осторожный [astaroJni] careful

остров [ostraf] island

острый [ostri] hot, spicy; sharp

от [ot] from

ответ [atvyet] answer

ответить [atvyeteet] to answer

ответственный [atvyetstvyen-ni] responsible

отвечать/ответить [atvyechat/atvyeteet] to answer

отвратительный [atvrateetyelni] disgusting

отдел [ad-dyel], отделение [ad-dyelyenee-yeh] department

отделение милиции [ad-dyelyenee-yeh meeleetsi-ee] police station

отдельно [ad-dyelna] separately

отдельный [ad-dyelni] separate

отдельный номер [ad-dyelni nomyer] single room

отдохнуть [ad-daHnoot] to take a rest

отдых [od-diH] holiday, vacation; rest

отдыхать/отдохнуть [ad-diHat/ad-daHnoot] to take a rest

отец [atyets] father

открывалка [atkrivalka] bottle-opener

открывать/открыть [atkrivat/atkrit] to open

открытка [atkritka] card; postcard

открыто [atkriyta] open

открытый [atkriyti] open

открыть [atkriyt] to open

отлично! [atleechna!] excellent!

отличный [atleechni] excellent

отменять/отменить [atmyenyat/atmyeneet] to cancel

отоларинголог [atalareengolak] ear, nose and throat specialist

отопление [ataplyenee-yeh] heating

отправитель [atpraveetyel] sender

отправить [atpraveet] to send

отправление [atpravl**ye**nee-yeh]
  departure
отправлять/отправить
  [atpravl**ya**t/atpr**a**veet] to send
от себя [at syeb**ya**] push
отъезд [at**ye**st] departure
офис [**o**fees] waiter
официант [afeetsi-**a**nt] waiter
официантка [afeetsi-**a**ntka]
  waitress; barmaid
очаровательный
  [acharav**a**tyelni] lovely,
  charming
очевидец [achyev**ee**dyets]
  witness
очевидно [achyev**ee**dna]
  obviously
очень [**o**chyen] very; very much
  очень приятно! [**o**chyen
  pree-**ya**tna!] pleased to meet
  you!
очередь f [**o**chyeryet] queue,
  (US) line
  стоять в очереди [sta-y**a**t v
  ochyeryedee] to queue, to line
  up
очки [achk**ee**] glasses,
  eyeglasses
очки от солнца [achk**ee** at
  s**o**ntsa] sunglasses
ошибиться [ashib**ee**tsa] to be
  mistaken
  я ошибся/ошиблась [ya
  ash**i**psa/ash**i**blas] I've made
  a mistake (said by man/woman)
ошибка [ash**i**pka] mistake,
  error

П

падать/упасть [**pa**dat/oop**a**st] to
  fall
падать/упасть в обморок
  [**pa**dat/oop**a**st v **o**bmarak] to
  faint
пакет [pak**ye**t] packet; parcel;
  paper bag
палатка [pal**a**tka] tent
палец [**pa**lyets] finger
палец ноги [**pa**lyets nag**ee**] toe
палуба [**pa**looba] deck
пальто [palt**o**] coat
памятник [**pa**myatneek]
  monument
папа [**pa**pa] dad
папироса [papeer**o**sa] Russian
  non-filter cigarette
пара [**pa**ra] pair; couple
парикмахер [pareekma**h**yer]
  hairdresser
парикмахерская
  [pareekma**h**yerska-ya] barber,
  hairdresser's
парилка [par**ee**lka] steam room
парк [park] park
паром [par**o**m] ferry
пароход [para**h**ot] steamer
партер [part**e**r] stalls
партия [**pa**rtee-ya] party
парус [**pa**roos] sail
парусная лодка [**pa**roosna-ya
  l**o**tka] sailing boat
парусник [**pa**roosneek] sailing
  boat
парусный спорт [**pa**roosni sport]
  sailing
паспорт [**pa**spart] passport

А
Б
В
Г
Д
Е
Ё
Ж
З
И
Й
К
Л
М
Н
О
П
Р
С
Т
У
Ф
Х
Ц
Ч
Ш
Щ
Ъ
Ы
Ь
Э
Ю
Я

Па

паспортный контроль
[**pa**spartni kant**ro**l] passport
control

пассажир [pasa**J**eer] passenger

Пасха [**pa**sHa] Easter

паук [pa-**oo**k] spider

пахнуть [**pa**Hnoot] to smell

пачка [**pa**chka] packet; pack;
bundle

педаль f [pyed**a**l] pedal

пейзаж [pyayz**a**sh] landscape;
scenery

пелёнка [pyel**yo**nka] nappy,
diaper

пельменная [pyelm**ye**n-na-ya]
café selling ravioli

пеницилин [pyeneetsil**ee**n]
penicillin

пенсионер [pyensee-an**ye**r]
пенсионерка,
[pyensee-an**ye**rka] old-age
pensioner (man/woman)

пепельница [p**ye**pyelneetsa]
ashtray

пер. lane

первая помощь [p**ye**rva-ya
p**o**mash-ch] first aid

первый [p**ye**rvi] first

первый класс [p**ye**rvi klas] first
class

первый этаж [p**ye**rvi et**a**sh]
ground floor, (US) first floor

перевал [pyerev**a**l] pass
(mountain)

переводить/перевести
[pyerevad**ee**t/pyerevyest**ee**] to
translate; to interpret

переводчик [pyerev**o**tcheek]
translator; interpreter

переговорный пункт
[pyeryegav**o**rni p**oo**nkt]
communications centre

перед [p**ye**ryed] in front of; just
before

передняя часть [pyer**ye**dnya-ya
chast] front

переезд [pyeryeh-**ye**st] level
crossing

перейти [pyeryeh-eet**ee**] to
cross

перекрёсток [pyeryekr**yo**stak]
cross-roads; junction,
intersection

перелом [pyeryel**o**m] fracture

переодеться [pyeryeh-ad**ye**tsa]
to get changed

переполненный
[pyeryep**o**lnyen-ni] crowded

перерыв [pyeryer**iy**f] break;
interval

перерыв на обед с ... до ...
[pyeryer**iy**f na ab**ye**t s ... do ...]
closed for lunch from ... to ...

пересадка [pyeryes**a**tka] change;
transfer

пересесть [pyeryes**ye**st] to
change (trains etc)

пересылать/переслать
[pyeryesil**a**t/pyeryesl**a**t] to
forward

переулок [pyeryeh-**oo**lak] lane

переход [pyeryeh**o**t] transfer;
passage; crossing;
underpass, subway

переходить/перейти
[pyeryeh**a**d**ee**t/pyeryeh-eet**ee**] to
cross

переходник [pyeryeh**a**dn**ee**k]

adaptor

перманент [pyermanyent] perm

перчатки [pyerchatkee] gloves

песня [pyesnya] song

песок [pyesok] sand

петь [pyet] to sing

печатный материал [pyechatni matyeree-al] printed matter

печень m [pyechyen] liver

пешеход [pyeshenot] pedestrian

пешеходная зона [pyesheHodna-ya zona] pedestrian precinct

пешеходный переход [pyesheHodni pyeryeHot] pedestrian crossing

пешком [pyeshkom] on foot

пещера [pyesh-chyera] cave

пивной бар [peevnoy bar], пивнушка [peevnooshka] bar, beer cellar, pub

пилка для ногтей [peelka dlya naktyay] nailfile

писать/написать [peesat/ napeesat] to write

писчебумажный магазин [peesh-chyeboomajni magazeen] stationer's

письмо [peesmo] letter

питательный [peetatyelni] nutritious

пить/выпить [peet/viypeet] to drink

питьевая вода [peetyeva-ya vada] drinking water

пиццерия [peetseree-ya] pizzeria

пишущая машинка [peeshoosh-cha-ya mashiynka]

typewriter

пищевое отравление [peesh-chyevo-yeh atravlyenee-yeh] food poisoning

пл. square

плавание [plavanee-yeh] swimming

плавать запрещается [plavat zapryesh-cha-yetsa] no swimming

плавать/плыть [plavat/pliyt] to swim

плавки [plafkee] swimming trunks

плакат [plakat] poster

плакать [plakat] to cry

пластинка [plasteenka] record

пластмассовый [plasmas-savi] plastic

платите в кассу [plateetyeh f kas-soo] pay at the cash desk

платить/заплатить [plateet/ zaplateet] to pay

платный [platni] paid; to be paid for

платок [platok] headscarf

платформа [platforma] platform, (US) track

платье [platyeh] dress

плащ [plash-ch] raincoat

племянник [plyemyan-neek] nephew

племянница [plyemyan-neetsa] niece

плёнка [plyonka] film (for camera)

плечо [plyecho] shoulder

пломба [plomba] filling

плоский [ploskee] flat

плохо [ploHa] bad; badly
мне плохо [mnyeh ploHa] I feel
ill

плохой [plaHoy] bad

площадь f [plosh-chat] square

плыть [pliyt] to swim

плэйер [player] personal
stereo

пляж [plyash] beach

по [po] along; according to; on
по-английски [pa-angleeskee]
in English

поблагодарить [pablagadareet]
to thank

побриться [pabreetsa] to shave

повар [povar] cook

поверить [pavyereet] to believe

поворачивать/повернуть
[pavaracheevat/pavyernoot] to
turn

повредить [pavryedeet] to
damage

повторять/повторить
[pavtaryat/paftareet] to repeat

повязка [pavyaska] bandage

погладить [pagladeet] to iron;
to stroke

погода [pagoda] weather

погулять [pagoolyat] to go for a
walk

под [pot] below; under;
underneath

под. entrance number

подавленный [padavlyen-ni]
depressed

подарить [padareet] to give
(present)

подарок [padarak] present, gift

подбородок [padbarodak] chin

подвал [padval] basement

подвозить/подвезти
[padvazeet/padvyestee] to give
a lift to

поделиться [padyeleetsa] to
share

подержанный [padyerJan-ni]
secondhand

подмётка [padmyotka] sole

подниматься/подняться
[padneematsa/padnyatsa] to go
up

поднос [padnos] tray

подняться [padnyatsa] to go up

подобный [padobni] similar

подождать [padaJdat] to wait

подойти [paditee] to approach;
to arrive; to come

подписать [patpeesat] to sign

подпись f [potpees] signature

подросток [padrostak] teenager

подруга [padrooga] friend;
girlfriend

подтвердить [pat-vyerdeet] to
confirm

подумать [padoomat] to think

подушка [padooshka] pillow

подфарники [patfarneekee]
sidelights

подходить/подойти
[padHadeet/paditee] to
approach; to arrive; to come

подъезд [padyest] entrance

подъёмник [padyomneek]
ski-lift, chairlift

поезд [po-yest] train

поездка [pa-yestka] journey,
trip

пожалуйста [paJalsta] please

пожар [paJar] fire, blaze

пожарная команда [paJarna-ya kamanda] fire brigade

пожарный выход [paJarni viyнat] fire exit

пожелание: с наилучшими пожеланиями [s na-eeloochshimee paJelanee-yamee] best wishes

поживаете: как вы поживаете? [kak viy paJivayetyeh?] how are you?

позаботиться о [pazaboteetsa o] to take care of

позавчера [pazafchyera] the day before yesterday

позвать [pazvat] to call

позвонить [pazvaneet] to ring; to phone

поздно [pozna] late; it's late

поздравляю! [pazdravlya-yoo!] congratulations!

позже [poJ-Jeh] later on

познакомить [paznakomeet] to introduce

познакомиться [paznakomeetsa] to get to know, to become acquainted with, to meet

поймать [pImat] to catch

пока [paka] while

пока! [paka!] bye!

показывать/показать [pakazivat/pakazat] to show

покидать/покинуть [pakeedat/pakeenoot] to leave

по крайней мере [pa krInyay myeryeh] at least

покрасить [pakraseet] to paint

покупатель [pakoopatyel]

customer; buyer

покупать/купить [pakoopat/koopeet] to buy

покупки [pakoopkee] shopping идти за покупками [eet-tee za pakoopkamee] to go shopping

пол [pol] floor; sex

полдень m [poldyen] midday, noon

поле [polyeh] field

полезный [palyezni] useful

поликлиника [paleekleeneeka] surgery; medical centre

политика [paleeteeka] politics

политический [paleeteechyeskee] political

поллитра [pol-leetra] half a litre

полночь f [polnach] midnight

полный [polni] full

половина [palaveena] half половина второго [palaveena ftarova] half past one

положить [palaJeet] to put, to place

полотенце [palatyentseh] towel

получать/получить [paloochat/paloocheet] to receive

полчаса [polchasa] half an hour

поменять [pamyenyat] to change

померить [pamyereet] to try on

помнить/вспомнить [pomneet/fspomneet] to remember, to recall

я помню [ya pomnyoo] I remember

помогать/помочь [pamagat/pamoch] to help

помогите! [pamageeteeyeh!]
help!

помощь f [pomash-ch] help, aid,
assistance

помыть [pamiyt] to wash

помыть посуду [pamiyt
pasoodoo] to do the
washing-up

помыться [pamiytsa] to wash
(oneself)

понедельник [panyedyelneek]
Monday

понимать/понять [paneemat/
panyat] to understand

я не понимаю [ya nyeh
paneema-yoo] I don't
understand

понос [panos] diarrhoea

понять [panyat] to understand

поп-музыка [pop-moozika] pop
music

попробовать [paprobavat] to
taste; to try

порт [port] harbour, port

портфель m [partfyel] briefcase

порция [portsi-ya] portion

порядок [paryadak] order

у меня всё в порядке [oo
myenya fsyo f paryatkyeh]
fine, I'm OK, everything's OK

посадка [pasatka] landing;
boarding; arrival

посадочный талон [pasadachni
talon] boarding pass

посещать/посетить
[pasyesh-chat/pasyeteet] to
visit

послание [paslanee-yeh]
message

послать [paslat] to send

после [poslyeh] after

последний [paslyednee] last

послезавтра [poslyezaftra] the
day after tomorrow

послушать [paslooshat] to
listen (to)

посмотреть (на) [pasmatryet
(na)] to look (at); to watch

посольство [pasolstva] embassy

поставить [pastaveet] to put

поставить машину [pastaveet
mashiynoo] to park

постараться [pastaratsa] to try

постель f [pastyel] bed

постельное бельё [pastyelna-
yeh byelyo] bed linen

постирать [pasteerat] to do the
washing

посторонним вход воспрещён
[pastaroneem fнot
vaspryesh-chon] private, staff
only

посуда [pasooda] crockery

посылать/послать [pasilat/
paslat] to send

посылка [pasiylka] parcel

потерять [patyeryat] to lose

по техническим причинам [pa
tyeнneecheeskeem
preecheenam] for technical
reasons

потолок [patalok] ceiling

потом [patom] then;
afterwards

потому что [patamoo shta]
because

потребитель [patryebeeteyel]
consumer

потрясающий [patryasa-yoosh-chee] tremendous

похмелье [paнmyelyeh] hangover

похожий [paнoʃi] like, similar to

поцеловать [patselavat] to kiss

поцелуй [patseloo] kiss

почему? [pachyemoo?] why?

починить [pacheeneet] to mend, to repair

почки [pochkee] kidneys

почта [pochta] post office; mail

почта до востребования [pochta da-vastryebavanee-ya] poste restante, general delivery

почтальон [pachtalyon] postman, mailman

почти [pachtee] almost

почтовая бумага [pachtova-ya boomaga] writing paper

почтовый индекс [pachtovi eendeks] postcode, zip code

почтовый ящик [pachtovi yash-cheek] letterbox, mailbox

пояс [po-yas] belt

потерять [patyeryat] to lose

пр. avenue

правильный [praveelni] right, correct

правительство [praveetyelstva] government

православная церковь [pravaslavna-ya tserkaf] Russian Orthodox Church

правый [pravi] right

праздник [prazneek] public holiday

празднование [praznavanee-yeh] celebration

практичный [prakteechni] practical

прачечная [prachyechna-ya] laundry

прачечная-самообслуживания [prachyechna-ya-sama-apsloojivanee-ya] launderette

пребывание [pryebivanee-yeh] stay

предварительный заказ [pryedvareetyelni zakas] reservation

предварительный заказ билетов [pryedvareetyelni zakas beelyetaf] seat reservation

предлагать/предложить [pryedlagat/pryedlaJeet] to offer, to suggest

предложение [pryedlaJenee-yeh] offer, proposal

предложить [pryedlaJeet] to offer, to suggest

предохранитель m [pryedaнraneetyel] fuse

предпочитать [pryetpacheetat] to prefer

председатель m [pryedsyedatyel] chairman

представитель m [pryetstaveetyel] representative; agent

презерватив [pryezyervateef] condom

прекрасный [pryekrasni] beautiful; fine; excellent

прелестный [pryel**ye**sni] pretty

преподаватель m [pryepadav**a**tyel] teacher; lecturer

Прибалтика [preeb**a**lteeka] Baltic States

прибыль f [pr**ee**bil] profit

прибытие [preeb**i**ytee-yeh] arrival

привет [preev**ye**t] hello, hi

прививка [preev**ee**fka] vaccination

привлекательный [preevlyek**a**tyelni] attractive

привычка [preev**i**ychka] habit

привязной ремень [preevyazn**oy** ryem**yen**] seatbelt

приглашать/пригласить [preeglash**a**t/preeglas**ee**t] to invite

приглашение [preeglash**e**nee-yeh] invitation

пригород [pr**ee**garat] suburbs

пригородный поезд [pr**ee**garadni p**o**-yest] local train, suburban train

пригородная касса [pr**ee**garadna-ya k**a**s-sa] ticket office for suburban trains

приготовить [preegat**o**veet] to cook; to prepare

приезд [pree-**ye**st] arrival

приезжать/приехать [pree-yezd**a**t/pree-**ye**Hat] to arrive (by transport)

приём посылок [pree-**yo**m pas**i**ylak] parcels counter

приехать [pree-**ye**Hat] to arrive (by transport)

прийти [preet**ee**] to come, to arrive (on foot)

прикурить: у вас есть прикурить? [oo vas yest preekoor**ee**t?] have you got a light?

прилёт [preel**yo**t] arrival

пример [preem**ye**r] example

примерно [preem**ye**rna] approximately

принадлежать [preenadlyeJ**at**] to belong

принимать/принять [preeneem**at**/preen**ya**t] to accept, to take

принтер [pr**ee**nter] printer

приносить/принести [preenas**ee**t/preenyest**ee**] to bring

принять [preen**ya**t] to accept, to take

природа [preer**o**da] nature

пристегните ремни [preestyegn**ee**tyeh ryemn**ee**] fasten seat belts

приходить/прийти [preeHad**ee**t/preet**ee**] to come, to arrive (on foot)

причал [preech**a**l] quay

причина [preech**ee**na] cause; reason

приятного аппетита! [pree-**ya**tnava apyet**ee**ta!] enjoy your meal!

приятный [pree-**ya**tni] pleasant, nice

пробка [pr**o**pka] plug; traffic jam

проблема [prablyema] problem

пробовать/попробовать [probavat/paprobovat] to taste; to try

проверять/проверить [pravyeryat/pravyereet] to check

прогноз погоды [prognos pagodi] weather forecast

программа [program-ma] programme

прогулка [pragoolka] walk

продавать/продать [pradavat/pradat] to sell

продаётся [prada-yotsa] for sale

продажа [pradaJa] sale; marketing

продажа билетов [pradaJa beelyetaf] tickets on sale

проданный [pradan-ni] sold

продать [pradat] to sell

продукция [pradooktsi-ya] product

проездной билет [pra-yeznoy beelyet] monthly season ticket

проживание с двухразовым питанием [praJivanee-yeh zdvooH-razavim peetanee-yem] half board

проживание с трёхразовым питанием [praJivanee-yeh stryoH-razavim peetanee-yem] full board

производство [pra-eezvotstva] production

произнести [pra-eeznyestee] to pronounce

произносить/произнести

[pra-eeznaseet/pra-eeznyestee] to pronounce

прокат [prakat] rental, hire

прокат автомобилей [prakat aftamabeelyay] car rental

прокол [prakol] puncture

промышленность f [pramiyshlyen-nast] industry

пропуск [propoosk] pass; hotel card

проснуться [prasnootsa] to wake up

проспект [praspyekt] brochure; avenue

простите [prasteetyeh] excuse me, sorry

простите? [prasteetyeh?] pardon?, pardon me?

простой [prastoy] simple

простыня [prastinya] sheet

просьба [prosba] request

просьба не ... [prosba nyeh ...] please do not ...

протестант [pratyestant] Protestant

против [proteef] against

противозачаточное средство [prateevazachatachna-yeh sryetstva] contraceptive

прохладный [praHladni] cool

процент [pratsent] per cent

прочитать [pracheetat] to read

прошлый [proshli] last

в прошлом году [fproshlam gadoo] last year

на прошлой неделе [na proshli nyedyelyeh] last week

проявлять/проявить [pra-yavlyat/pra-yaveet] to develop

пруд [proot] pond

прыгать/прыгнуть [priygat/ priygnoot] to jump

прыщик [priysh-cheek] spot, pimple

прямо [pryama] straight ahead

прямой [pryamoy] direct; straight

прямой номер [pryamoy nomyer] direct dialling

прямой рейс [pryamoy ryays] direct flight

птица [pteetsa] bird; poultry

публика [poobleeka] audience; public

пуговица [poogaveetsa] button

пункт [poonkt] point; station; place, spot; centre

пункт скорой помощи [poonkt skori pomash-chee] first-aid post

пустой [poostoy] empty

путеводитель m [pootyevadeetyel] guidebook

путешествовать [pootyeshestvavat] to travel

путь m [poot] path; way

пчела [pchyela] bee

пылесос [pilyesos] vacuum cleaner

пьеса [pyesa] play (theatre)

пьяный [pyani] drunk

пятка [pyatka] heel (of foot)

пятнадцатый [pyatnatsati] fifteenth

пятнадцать [pyatnatsat] fifteen

пятница [pyatneetsa] Friday

пятно [pyatno] stain

пятый [pyati] fifth

пять [pyat] five

пятьдесят [pyadyesyat] fifty

пятьсот [pyatsot] five hundred

Р

р. rouble

работа [rabota] job; work

работает с ... до ... [rabota-yet s ... do ...] open from ... to ...

работать [rabotat] to work

это не работает [eta nyeh rabota-yet] it's not working

рад [rat] glad

радио [radee-o] radio

раз [ras] time (occasion)

один раз [adeen ras] once

разбудить [razboodeet] to wake up

разве? [razvyeh?] really?

разведён [razvyedyon], разведена [razvyedyena] divorced (man/woman)

развилка [razveelka] junction; fork (in road)

разговаривать [razgavareevat] to talk

разговаривать с водителем запрещается [razgavareevat svadeetyelyem zapryesh-cha-yetsa] do not speak to the driver

разговор [razgavor] conversation

раздевалка [razdyevalka] changing room

размен [razmyen] change

размер [razmyer] size

разный [razni] various,

different
разочарованный
[razacharovan-ni] disappointed
разрешается [razryesha-yetsa] it
is allowed
разрешать/разрешить
[razryeshat/razryeshiyt] to let,
to allow
разрешение [razryeshenee-yeh]
permission; licence
разрешить [razryeshiyt] to let,
to allow
разумный [razoomni] sensible
район [rion] district
раковина [rakaveena] sink
ракушка [rakooshka] shell
рана [rana] injury
раненый [ranyeni] injured
рано [rana] early
раскладушка [raskladooshka]
campbed
распаковать (чемодан)
[raspakavat (chyemadan)] to
unpack
расписание [raspeesanee-yeh]
timetable, (US) schedule
распродажа [raspradaJa] sale
рассказ [raskas] story
рассказать [raskazat] to tell
расслабиться [ras-slabeetsa] to
relax
расстояние [ras-sta-yanee-yeh]
distance
расстройство желудка
[rastroystva Jelootka]
indigestion
растение [rastyenee-yeh] plant
расчёска [raschoska] comb
ребёнок [ryebyonak] child;

baby
ребро [ryebro] rib
ревматизм [ryevmateezm]
rheumatism
ревнивый [ryevneevi] jealous
регистратура [ryegeestratoora]
reception
регистрация [ryegeestratsi-ya]
check-in; registration
регистрация багажа
[ryegeestratsi-ya bagaJa]
check-in
регулировщик
[ryegooleerovsh-cheek] traffic
warden
регулярный рейс [ryegoolyarni
ryays] scheduled flight
редкий [ryetkee] rare
резать [ryezat] to cut
резина [ryezeena] rubber
резиночка [ryezeenachka]
rubber band
рейс [ryays] flight
река [ryeka] river
реклама [ryeklama]
advertisement; advertising
рекламировать [ryeklameeravat]
to advertise
рекомендовать
[ryekamyendavat] to
recommend
религия [ryeleeegee-ya] religion
ремень вентилятора [ryemyen
vyenteelyatara] fan belt
ремесленные изделия
[ryemyeslyen-ni-yeh eezdyelee-
ya] crafts
ремонт [ryemont] repair
ремонт обуви [ryemont oboovee]

shoe repairs
ремонт сумок [ryemont soomak] bag repairs
ресторан [ryestaran] restaurant
рецепт [ryetsept] prescription; recipe
решать/решить [ryeshat/ ryeshiyt] to decide
решение [ryeshyenee-yeh] decision
Рига [reega] Riga
родина [rodeena] native country; home(land)
родители [radeetyelee] parents
родиться [radeetsa] to be born
родственники [rotstvyen-neekee] relatives
Рождество [raJdyestvo] Christmas
с Рождеством! [s raJdyestvom!] merry Christmas!
роза [roza] rose
розетка [razyetka] socket
розовый [rozavi] pink
рок-музыка [rok-moozika] rock music
роман [raman] novel
Россия [ras-see-ya] Russia
рот [rot] mouth
рубашка [roobashka] shirt
рубль m [roobl] rouble
руины [roo-eeni] ruins
рука [rooka] arm; hand
руками не трогать [rookamee nyeh trogat] do not touch
руль m [rool] steering wheel

русская [rooska-ya] Russian
русские [rooskee-yeh] the Russians
русский [rooskee] Russian
русский язык [rooskee yaziyk] Russian (language)
Русь [roos] Russia (historical)
ручей [roochyay] stream
ручка [roochka] handle; pen
ручная кладь [roochna-ya klat] hand luggage, hand baggage
ручной тормоз [roochnoy tormas] handbrake
рыба [riyba] fish
рыбная ловля [riybna-ya lovlya] fishing
рыбная ловля запрещена [riybna-ya lovlya zapryesh-chyena] no fishing
рыбный магазин [riybni magazeen] fishmonger's
рыжий [riyJi] red-headed
рынок [riynak] market
рюкзак [ryoogzak] rucksack
рюмка [ryoomka] wine glass
ряд [ryat] row
рядом (с) [ryadam (s)] next to

С

с [s] with
с нарочным [s narachnim] special delivery
сад [sat] garden
садиться/сесть [sadeetsa/syest] to sit down; to get in
салфетка [salfyetka] napkin
самовар [samavar] samovar

самолёт [samalyot] plane
самолётом [samalyotam] by
air
самообслуживание
[sama-apslooJivanee-yeh]
self-service
самый [sami] the most
санитарный день [saneetarni
dyen] closed for cleaning
Санкт Петербург [sankt
pyetyerboork] St Petersburg
сапог [sapok] boot
сауна [sa-oona] sauna
свадьба [svadba] wedding
свежий [svyeJ] fresh
свёкор [svyokar] father-in-law
(husband's father)
свекровь [svyekrof]
mother-in-law (husband's
mother)
свёрток [svyortak] package
свет [svyet] light
светло- [svyetla-] light (colour)
светофор [svyetafor] traffic
lights
свеча [svyecha] candle
свеча зажигания [svyecha
zaJiganee-ya] sparkplug
свинья [sveenya] pig
свитер [sveeter] sweater,
jumper
свободно [svabodna] free;
vacant; fluent
свободный [svabodni] free;
vacant; fluent
свободных мест нет [svabodniH
myest nyet] no vacancies
своё [sva-yo], свои [sva-ee],
свой [svoy], своя [sva-ya] my;

your; his; its; her; our; their;
mine; yours; hers; ours;
theirs
свояченица [sva-yachyeneetsa]
sister-in-law (wife's sister)
связываться/связаться (с)
[svyazivatsa/svyazatsa (s)] to
get in touch with
святой [svyatoy] holy; saint
священник [svyash-chyen-neek]
priest
сгореть [zgaryet] to burn
сделать [zdyelat] to do; to
make
сделать пересадку [zdyelat
pyeryesatkoo] to change (trains
etc)
себе [syebyeh], себя [syebya]
myself; yourself; himself;
herself; itself; ourselves;
yourselves; themselves
север [syevyer] north
к северу от [k syevyeroo at]
north of
Северная Ирландия
[syevyerna-ya eerlandee-ya]
Northern Ireland
сегодня [syevodnya] today
сегодня вечером [syevodnya
vyechyeram] this evening,
tonight
сегодня днём [syevodnya dnyom]
this afternoon
сегодня утром [syevodnya
ootram] this morning
седьмой [syedmoy] seventh
сейчас [syaychas] now, at the
moment
секретарша f [syekryetarsha]

secretary

секретарь m [syekryetar] secretary

секс [seks] sex

секунда [syekoonda] second

семнадцатый [syemnatsati] seventeenth

семнадцать [syemnatsat] seventeen

семь [syem] seven

семьдесят [syemdyesyat] seventy

семьсот [syemsot] seven hundred

семья [syemya] family

сенная лихорадка [syen-na-ya leeHaratka] hayfever

сентябрь m [syentyabr] September

сердечный приступ [syerdyechni preestoop] heart attack

сердитый [syerdeeti] angry

сердце [syertseh] heart

серебро [syeryebro] silver

середина [syeryedeena] middle

серый [syeri] grey

серьги [syergee] earrings

серьёзный [syeryozni] serious

сестра [syestra] sister

сесть [syest] to sit down; to get in

Сибирь f [seebeer] Siberia

сигара [seegara] cigar

сигарета [seegaryeta] cigarette

сильный [seelni] strong

синий [seenee] blue

синяк [seenyak] bruise

скажите, пожалуйста ... [skaJeetyeh, paJalsta ...] can you tell me ...?

сказать [skazat] to say; to speak

скала [skala] cliff; rock

скандальный [skandalni] shocking

скатерть f [skatyert] tablecloth

сквозняк [skvaznyak] draught

скидка [skeetka] discount

складная детская коляска [skladna-ya dyetska-ya kalyaska] pushchair, (US) stroller

склон [sklon] slope

сковорода [skavarada] frying pan

скользкий [skolskee] slippery

сколько? [skolka?] how much?; how many?

сколько вам лет? [skolka vam lyet?] how old are you?

сколько это стоит? [skolka eta sto-eet?] how much is it?

скорая помощь [skora-ya pomash-ch] ambulance; first aid

скорее [skaryeh-yeh] rather

скорее! [skaryeh-yeh!] quickly!

скоро [skora] soon

скорость f [skorast] speed; gear

скрывать/скрыть [skrivat/skriyt] to hide

скрыть [skriyt] to hide

скучный [skooshni] boring

слабительное [slabeetyelna-yeh] laxative

слабый [slabi] weak

сладкий [slatkee] sweet (to taste)

слайд [slit] slide (photographic)

слева [slyeva] on the left

следовать [slyedavat] to follow

следующая станция ... [slyedoo-yoosh-cha-ya stantsi-ya ...] next station ...

следующий [slyedoo-yoosh-chee] next; following

в следующем году [f slyedoo-yoosh-chyem gadoo] next year

на следующей неделе [na slyedoo-yoosh-chay nyedyelyeh] next week

следующий день [slyedoo-yoosh-chee dyen] the next day

слепой [slyepoy] blind

слишком ... [sleeshkam ...] too ...

слишком много [sleeshkam mnoga] too much

не слишком много [nyeh sleeshkam mnoga] not too much

словарь m [slavar] dictionary

слово [slova] word

сложный [sloJni] complicated

сломанный [sloman-ni] broken

сломать [slamat] to break

сломаться [slamatsa] to break down

служащий [slooJash-chee] employee

служба [slooJba] service; employment; job; work; duty

служба размещения [slooJba razmyesh-chyenee-ya] reception desk

служебный вход [slooJebni fHot]

staff entrance

случай [sloochee] chance

случайно [sloochIna] by chance

случаться/случиться [sloochatsa/sloocheetsa] to happen

слушать/послушать [slooshat/paslooshat] to listen (to)

слышать/услышать [slIyshat/oosliyshat] to hear

смерть f [smyert] death

сметь [smyet] to dare

смешать [smyeshat] to mix

смеяться/засмеяться [smyeh-yatsa/zasmyeh-yatsa] to laugh

смотреть/посмотреть (на) [smatryet/pasmatryet (na)] to look (at); to watch

смочь [smoch] can, to be able to

вы сможете ...? [viy smoJetyeh ...?] will you be able to ...?

он/она сможет [on/ana smoJet] he/she will be able to

смутно [smootna] vaguely

сначала [snachala] first; at first

снег [snyek] snow

СНГ [es-en-geh] CIS

снова [snova] again; once again

сноха [snaHa] daughter-in-law

собака [sabaka] dog

соблюдайте тишину [sablyoodItyeh teeshinoo] please be quiet

собой [saboy] (by) myself; (by) yourself; (by) himself;

(by) herself; (by) itself; (by) ourselves; (by) yourselves; (by) themselves

с собой [s sab**oy**] to take away, (US) to go

соболь m [s**o**bal] sable

собор [sab**o**r] cathedral

собрание [sab**ra**nee-yeh] meeting

собственный [s**o**pstvyen-ni] own; proper; personal

Советский Союз [sav**ye**tskee sa-**yoos**] Soviet Union

современный [savryem**ye**n-ni] modern

согласен: я согласен/согласна [ya sagl**a**syen/sagl**a**sna] I agree (said by man/woman)

согласованность расписания [saglas**o**van-nast raspees**a**nee-ya] connection

Соединённые Штаты Америки [sayedeen**yo**n-ni-yeh sht**a**ti am**ye**reekee] United States

сожаление: к сожалению [k saJal**ye**nee-yoo] unfortunately

соки-воды [s**o**kee-v**o**di] fruit juices and mineral water

солгать [salg**a**t] to lie, to tell a lie

солёный [sal**yo**ni] salty; savoury; pickled

солнечный [s**o**lnyechni] sunny

солнечный ожог [s**o**lnyechni aJ**o**k] sunburn

солнечный свет [s**o**lnyechni svyet] sunshine

солнечный удар [s**o**lnyechni

oodar] sunstroke

солнце [s**o**ntseh] sun

сон [son] dream; sleep

сопровождать [sapravaJd**a**t] to accompany

сорок [s**o**rak] forty

сосед [sas**ye**t], соседка [sas**ye**tka] neighbour (man/woman)

сохранять/сохранить [saHran**ya**t/saHran**ee**t] to keep

социализм [satsi-al**ee**zm] socialism

Сочельник [sach**ye**lneek] Christmas Eve

спальное место [sp**a**lna-yeh m**ye**sta] couchette

спальный вагон [sp**a**lni vag**o**n] sleeping car

спальный мешок [sp**a**lni mysh**o**k] sleeping bag

спальня [sp**a**lnya] bedroom

спасатель m [spas**a**tel] lifeguard

спасательный пояс [spas**a**telni po-**ya**s] lifebelt

спасибо [spas**ee**ba] thank you

спасибо большое [spas**ee**ba balsh**o**-yeh] thank you very much

спать [spat] to sleep

специальность f [spyetsi-**a**lnast] speciality

спешить [spyesh**iy**t] to hurry

СПИД [speed] AIDS

спина [speen**a**] back (of body)

список [sp**ee**sak] list

спичка [sp**ee**chka] match

спокойной ночи [spak**oy**nay n**o**chee] good night

спорт [sport] sport

спортивное оборудование [sparteevna-yeh abaroodavanee-yeh] sports equipment

спортивный центр [sparteevni tsentr] sports centre

справа [sprava] on the right

справедливый [spravyedleevi] fair, just

справка [sprafka] information

справочная [spravachna-ya] enquiries; directory enquiries

справочное бюро [spravachna-yeh byooro] information office

справочный стол [spravachni stol] information desk

спрашивать/спросить [sprashivat/spraseet] to ask

спускаться/спуститься [spooskatsa/spoosteetsa] to go down

спущенная шина [spoosh-chyen-na-ya shiyna] flat tyre

среда [sryeda] Wednesday

среди [sryedee] among

среднего размера [sryednyeva razmyera] medium-sized

средство от насекомых [sryetstva at nasyekomiн] insect repellent

средство против загара [sryetstva proteev zagara] sunblock

срок [srok] period

срочно [srochna] urgent; urgently

срочный [srochni] urgent

СССР [es-es-es-er] USSR

ставить/поставить [staveet/pastaveet] to put

стадион [stadee-on] stadium

стакан [stakan] glass

становиться/стать [stanaveetsa/stat] to become

станция [stantsi-ya] station (underground, bus etc)

станция техобслуживания [stantsi-ya tyeнap-slooJivanee-ya] garage (for repairs), service station

стараться/постараться [staratsa/pastaratsa] to try

старше [starsheh] older

старый [stari] old

стать [stat] to become

стекло [styeklo] glass (material)

стена [styena] wall

стиральная машина [steeralna-ya mashiyna] washing machine

стиральный порошок [steeralni parashok] washing powder

стирать/постирать [steerat/pasteerat] to do the washing

сто [sto] hundred

стоимость [sto-eemast] charge, cost

стоимость международной отправки [sto-eemast myeJdoonarodnay atprafkee] overseas postage

стоить [sto-eet] to cost

стол [stol] table

столкновение [stalknavyenee-yeh] crash

столовая [stalova-ya] dining room; canteen

столовые приборы [stalovi-yeh preebori] cutlery

стоп-кран [stop-kran] emergency cord

сторона [starana] side

сто тысяч [sto tiysyach] hundred thousand

стоянка [sta-yanka] car park, parking lot

стоянка такси [sta-yanka taksee] taxi rank

стоять [sta-yat] to stand

страна [strana] country

страница [straneetsa] page

странный [stran-ni] strange

страх [straH] fear

страхование [straHavanee-yeh] insurance

стрижка [streeshka] haircut

стройный [stroyni] shapely

студент [stoodyent], студентка [stoodyentka] student (male/ female)

стул [stool] chair

стыдно: мне стыдно [mnyeh stiydna] I'm ashamed

стюард [styoo-art] steward

стюардесса [styoo-ardesa] stewardess

суббота [soob-bota] Saturday

сувенир [soovyeneer] souvenir

сумасшедший [soomashetshi] mad; madman

сумка [soomka] bag

сумочка [soomachka] handbag, (US) purse

сутки [sootkee] 24 hours, day and night

сухой [sooHoy] dry

сушить [sooshiyt] to dry

схема [sHyema] diagram; network map

сцепление [stseplyenee-yeh] clutch

счастливо оставаться! [sh-chasleeva astavatsa!] good night!; enjoy your stay!

счастливого пути! [sh-chasleevava pootee!] have a good trip!

счастливый [sh-chasleevi] happy

счастье [sh-chastyeh] happiness

к счастью [k sh-chastyoo] fortunately

счёт [sh-chot] bill, (US) check

США [seh-sheh-a] USA

сшить [s-shit] to sew

съесть [syest] to eat

сыграть [sigrat] to play

сын [siyn] son

сырой [siroy] damp; raw

сюрприз [syoorprees] surprise

Т

T trolleybus or tram stop

та [ta] that; that one

табак [tabak] tobacco

таблетка [tablyetka] pill, tablet

так [tak] so; this way; like this

так! [tak!] well!

так же красиво, как ... [tak Jeh kraseeva, kak ...] as beautiful as ...

так как [tak kak] as; since

так себе [tak syeb**yeh**] so-so
также [t**a**gjeh] also
такси [taks**ee**] taxi
таксофон [taks**a**fon] public
  phone
талия [t**a**lee-ya] waist
талкучка [talk**oo**chka] flea
  market
Таллин [t**a**l-leen] Tallin
талон [tal**o**n] ticket
тальк [talk] talcum powder
там [tam] there
  там внизу [tam vneez**oo**]
  down there
таможенная декларация
  [tam**o**Jen-na-ya dyeklar**a**tsi-ya]
  Customs declaration form
таможенный контроль
  [tam**o**Jeni kantr**o**l] Customs
  inspection
таможня [tam**o**Jnya] Customs
тампон [tamp**o**n] tampon
танцевать [tantsev**a**t] dance
тапочки [t**a**pachkee] slippers
таракан [tarak**a**n] cockroach
тарелка [tar**ye**lka] plate
тариф [tar**ee**f] charge, tariff
Ташкент [tashk**ye**nt]
  Tashkent
Тбилиси [tbeel**ee**see] Tbilisi
твёрдый [tv**yo**rdi] hard
твоего [tva-yev**o**] (of) your; (of)
  yours
твоей [tva-**yay**] your; yours; of
  your; of yours; to your; to
  yours; by your; by yours
твоему [tva-yem**oo**] (to) your;
  (to) yours
твоё [tva-**yo**] your; yours

твоём [tva-y**o**m] your; yours
твои [tva-**ee**] your; yours
твоим [tva-**ee**m] (by) your;
  (by) yours; (to) your; (to)
  yours
твоими [tva-**ee**mee] (by) your;
  (by) yours
твоих [tva-**ee**н] (of) your; (of)
  yours
твой [tvoy] your; yours
твою [tva-**yoo**] your; yours
твоя [tva-**ya**] your; yours
те [t**ye**h] those
театр [t**ye**h-atr] theatre
театральная касса
  [t**ye**h-atr**a**lna-ya k**a**s-sa] box
  office
тебе [tyeb**ye**h] you; to you
тебя [tyeb**ya**] you; of you
  у тебя [oo tyeb**ya**] you
  have
телевизор [tyelyev**ee**zar]
  television, TV set
телеграмма [tyelyegr**a**m-ma]
  telegram
тележка [tyel**ye**shka] trolley
телекс [t**ye**lyeks] telex
телефон [tyelyef**o**n] telephone
телефон-автомат
  [tyelyef**o**n-aftam**a**t] payphone
телефонная будка
  [tyelyef**o**n-na-ya b**oo**tka] phone
  box
телефонный код [tyelyef**o**n-ni
  kot] dialling code
телефонный справочник
  [tyelyef**o**n-ni spr**a**vachneek]
  telephone directory
тело [t**ye**la] body

тем [tyem] (by) that; (by) that
one; (to) those

теми [**tye**mee] (by) those

тёмный [**tyo**mni] dark

температура [tyempyerat**oo**ra]
temperature

тени для век [**tye**nee dlya vyek]
eye shadow

теннис [**tye**n-nees] tennis

тень f [tyen] shadow; shade
в тени [f tyen**ee**] in the shade

тепло [tyepl**o**] warm; it's warm

тёплый [**tyo**pli] warm

термометр [tyerm**o**myetr]
thermometer

термос [**te**rmas] Thermos®
flask

терпеть [tyerp**ye**t] to bear, to
stand

терять/потерять [tyery**a**t/
patyery**a**t] to lose

тесный [**tye**sni] tight; cramped

тесть m [tyest] father-in-law
(wife's father)

тётя [**tyo**tya] aunt

тех [tyeH] those; of those

течь f [tyech] leak

течь [tyech] to flow; to stream;
to leak

тёща [**tyo**sh-cha] mother-in-law
(wife's mother)

тихий [t**ee**Hee] quiet

тише [t**ee**sheh] quieter

тише! [t**ee**sheh!] quiet!

тишина [teesh**i**na] silence

ткань f [tkan] material

то [to] that; that one

тобой [tab**oy**] (by) you

тогда [tagd**a**] then

того [tav**o**] (of) that; (of) that
one

тоже [t**o**Jeh] too; also
я тоже [ya t**o**Jeh] me too

той [toy] that; that one; of that;
of that one; to that; to that
one

толкать/толкнуть [talk**a**t/
talkn**oo**t] to push

толкнуть [talkn**oo**t] to push

толпа [talp**a**] crowd

толстый [t**o**lsti] fat (adj)

только [t**o**lka] only; just

только по будним дням [t**o**lka
pab**oo**dneem dnyam] weekdays
only

том [tom] that; that one

тому [tam**oo**] (to) that; (to)
that one

тональный крем [tan**a**lni kryem]
foundation cream

тонкий [t**o**nkee] thin

тонуть/утонуть [tan**oo**t/
ootan**oo**t] to drown

торговый центр [targ**o**vi tsentr]
shopping centre

тормоза [tarmaz**a**] brakes

тормозить/затормозить
[tarmaz**ee**t/zatarmaz**ee**t] to
brake

тот [tot] that; that one

тот же самый [tot Jeh s**a**mi] the
same

тощий [t**o**sh-chee] skinny

трава [trav**a**] grass; herb; weed

традиционный [tradeetsi-**o**n-ni]
traditional

традиция [trad**ee**tsi-ya]
tradition

транзитная посадка [tranzeetna-ya pasatka] intermediate stop

тратить [trateet] to spend

требовать [tryebavat] to demand

тревога [tryevoga] alarm

третий [tryetee] third

три [tree] three

тридцатый [treetsati] thirtieth

тридцать [treetsat] thirty

тринадцатый [treenatsati] thirteenth

тринадцать [treenatsat] thirteen

триста [treesta] three hundred

трогать/тронуть [trogat/tronoot] to touch

тройка [troyka] troika

тронуть [tronoot] to touch

тропинка [trapeenka] path

тротуар [tratoo-ar] pavement, sidewalk

трубка [troopka] pipe (to smoke)

трубопровод [troobapravot] pipe; pipeline

трудный [troodni] difficult

трусики [trooseekee] pants, panties

трусы [troosiy] underpants

ту [too] that; that one

туалет [too-alyet] toilet, rest room

туалетная бумага [too-alyetna-ya boomaga] toilet paper

туалеты [too-alyeti] toilets, rest rooms

туман [tooman] fog

туннель m [toon-nel] tunnel

тургруппа [toorgroop-pa] tour group

турист [tooreest] tourist

туристическая поездка [tooreesteechyeska-ya payeztka] package tour

Турция [toortsi-ya] Turkey

туфли [tooflee] shoes

тушь для ресниц f [toosh dlya ryesneets] mascara

ты [tiy] you

тысяча [tiysyacha] thousand

тюрьма [tyoorma] prison

тяжёлый [tyajoli] heavy

тянуть [tyanoot] to pull

У

у [oo] at; by; near; with

у них [oo neeH] they have

у вас [oo vas] you have

у тебя [oo tyebya] you have

у неё [oo nyeh-yo] she has; it has

у нас [oo nas] we have

у него [oo nyevo] he has; it has

у меня [oo myenya] I have

у вас есть ...? [oo vas yest ...?] have you got ...?

у меня нет ... [oo myenya nyet ...] I don't have ...

убивать/убить [oobeevat/oobeet] to kill

убирать/убрать [oobeerat/oobrat] to take away; to clean

убить [oobeet] to kill

убрать [oobrat] to take away; to clean

уверенный [oov**ye**ryen-ni] sure

увидеть [oov**ee**dyet] to see

увлажняющий крем [oovlaɅn**ya**-yoosh-chee kryem] moisturizer

увлекательный [oovlyek**a**tyelni] exciting

угол [**oo**gal] corner

удар [**oo**dar] blow; stroke

ударять/ударить [ood**a**ryat/ ood**a**reet] to hit

удача [ood**a**cha] luck; success

удивительный [oodeev**ee**tyelni] surprising

удлинитель [oodleen**ee**tyel] extension lead

удобный [ood**o**bni] comfortable

удостоверение [oodasta-vyer**ye**nee-yeh] certificate

уезжать/уехать [ooyezɅat/ oo**ye**Ʌat] to leave

ужалить [ooɅ**a**leet] to sting

ужас [**oo**Ʌas], ужасно [ooɅ**a**sna] it's awful, it's ghastly

ужасный [ooɅ**a**sni] awful, terrible, ghastly

уже [ooɅ**eh**] already

ужин [**oo**Ʌin] dinner; supper

ужинать [**oo**Ʌinat] to have dinner

узкий [**oo**skee] narrow

узнавать/узнать [oozn**a**vat/ oozn**a**t] to recognize

уйти [ooyt**ee**] to go away

указатель поворота m [ookaz**a**tyel pavar**o**ta] indicator

укладывать/уложить вещи [ookl**a**divat/oolaɅ**ee**t v**ye**sh-chee] to pack

укол [ook**o**l] injection

Украина [ookra-**ee**na] Ukraine

украсть [ookr**a**st] to steal

укус [ook**oo**s] bite

ул., улица [**oo**leetsa] street на улице [na **oo**leetsyeh] outside; in the street

уличное движение [**oo**leechna-yeh dveeɅ**e**nee-yeh] traffic

уложить вещи [oolaɅ**ee**t v**ye**sh-chee] to pack

уложить волосы феном [oolaɅ**ee**t v**o**lasi f**ye**nam] to blow-dry

улучшить [ool**oo**tshit] to improve

улыбаться/улыбнуться [oolib**a**tsa/oolibn**oo**tsa] to smile

улыбка [ool**i**ypka] smile

улыбнуться [ooliybn**oo**tsa] to smile

умелый [oom**ye**li] skilful

умирать/умереть [oomeer**a**t/ oomyer**ye**t] to die

умный [**oo**mni] clever, intelligent

умывальник [oomiv**a**lneek] washbasin

универмаг [ooneevyerm**a**k] department store

универсам [ooneevyers**a**m] supermarket

университет [ooneevyerseet**ye**t] university

упасть [oop**a**st] to fall

упасть в обморок [oop**a**st v **o**bmarak] to faint

управляющий [oopravl**ya**-

yoosh-chee] manager

уровень масла [**oo**ravyen m**a**sla]
oil level

уродливый [**oo**r**o**dleevi] ugly

урок [**oo**r**o**k] lesson

уронить [**oo**ran**ee**t] to drop

услышать [**oo**sl**i**yshat] to hear

успех [**oo**sp**ye**н] success
желаю успеха! [Je**l**ay**oo**
oosp**ye**на!] good luck!

успокойтесь ! [**oo**spak**oy**tyes!]
calm down!

усталый [**oo**st**a**li] tired

устройство [**oo**str**oy**stva] device

усы [**oo**s**iy**] moustache

утонуть [**oo**tan**oo**t] to drown

утро [**oo**tra] morning
утра [**oo**tr**a**] in the morning;
a.m.
в пять часов утра [f pyat
chas**of** ootr**a**] at 5 a.m.

утюг [**oo**ty**oo**k] iron (for clothes)

ухо [**oo**на] ear

уходить/уйти [**oo**наd**ee**t/ooy**tee**]
to go away
уходите! [**oo**наd**ee**tyeh!] go
away!

учёт [**oo**ch**o**t] stocktaking

учитель m [**oo**ch**ee**tyel],
учительница
[**oo**ch**ee**tyelneetsa] teacher

учиться [**oo**ch**ee**tsa] to learn; to
study

Уэльс [**oo**-**e**ls] Wales

уэльский [**oo**-**e**lskee] Welsh

Ф

факс [faks] fax

факсимильный аппарат
[fakseem**ee**lni ap**a**rat] fax
machine

фамилия [fam**ee**lee-ya]
surname

фары [f**a**ri] headlights

февраль m [fyevr**a**l] February

фейерверк [fyay-yerv**ye**rk]
fireworks

фен [fyen] hairdryer

ферма [f**ye**rma] farm

Финляндия [feenl**ya**ndee-ya]
Finland

фиолетовый [fee-al**ye**tavi]
purple

фирма [f**ee**rma] firm, company

флаг [flak] flag

фонарик [fan**a**reek] torch

фонтан [fant**a**n] fountain

фотоаппарат [fata-ap**a**rat]
camera

фотограф [fat**o**graf]
photographer

фотографировать
[fatagraf**ee**ravat] to take
photos

фотография [fatagr**a**fee-ya]
photograph

Франция [fr**a**ntsi-ya] France

французский [frants**oo**skee]
French

французский язык
[frants**oo**skee yaz**i**yk] French
(language)

фрукты [fr**oo**kti] fruit

фунт [foont] pound

фуражка [foorashka] cap
фургон [foorgon] van
футбол [foodbol] football
футболка [foodbolka] T-shirt
футбольное поле [foodbolna-yeh polyeh] football pitch

X

халат [Halat] dressing gown
химчистка [Heemcheestka] dry-cleaner
хлеб [Hlyep] bread
хлопок [Hlopak] cotton
ходить [Hadeet] to go (on foot), to walk; to suit
хозяин [Hazya-een] owner; host
хозяйственный магазин [Hazyıstvyen-ni magazeen] hardware store
хоккей [Hakyay] hockey
холм [Holm] hill
холодильник [Haladeelneek] fridge
холодный [Halodni] cold
холостяк [Halastyak] bachelor
хороший [Haroshi] good
хорошо [Harosho] well
хорошо! [Harosho!] good!
мне хорошо [mnyeh Harosho] I'm well
хотеть [Hatyet] to want
я хотел/хотела [ya Hatyel/Hatyela] I wanted (said by man/woman)
я хотел/хотела бы ... [ya Hatyel/Hatyela bi ...] I would like ... (said by man/woman)
хотим [Hateem] we want

хотите [Hateetyeh] you want
хотя [Hatya] although
хотят [Hatyat] they want
хочет [Hochyet] he wants; she wants; it wants
хочется: мне хочется ... [mnyeh Hochyetsa ...] I feel like ...
хочешь [Hochyesh] you want
хочу [Hachoo] I want
храбрый [Hrabri] brave
храните в сухом/прохладном/тёмном месте [Hraneetyeh f sooHom/praHladnam/tyomnam myestyeh] keep in a cool/dark/dry place
хранить [Hraneet] to keep; to preserve
хрустящий картофель [Hroostyash-chee kartofyel] crisps, (US) chips
художник [Hoodoɹneek] artist, painter
худой [Hoodoy] thin
худший [Hootshi] worst
хуже [Hooɹeh] worse

Ц

царь m [tsar] tsar
цвет [tsvyet] colour
цветная плёнка [tsvyetna-ya plyonka] colour film
цветок [tsvyetok] flower
цветочный магазин [tsvyetochni magazeen] florist's, flower shop
цветы [tsvyetiy] flowers
целовать/поцеловать [tselavat/patselavat] to kiss

целый [tseli] whole
цена [tsena] price
центр [tsentr] centre
центр города [tsentr gorada] city centre
центральное отопление [tsentralna-yeh ataplyenee-yeh] central heating
цепочка [tsepochka] chain
церковь f [tserkav] church

Ч

чаевые [cha-yeviyeh] tip
чайник [chIneek] kettle; teapot
чартерный рейс [charterni ryays] charter flight
час [chas] hour; one o'clock
в ... часа [f ... chasa] at ... o'clock
в ... часов [f ... chasof] at ... o'clock
часто [chasta] often
частый [chasti] often
часть f [chast] part
часы [chasiy] watch; clock; hours
часы приёма [chasiy pree-yoma] visiting hours
часы работы [chasiy raboti] opening hours, opening times
чашка [chashka] cup
чаще [chash-chyeh] more often
чего [chyevo] what; of what
чек [chyek] cheque, (US) check
чековая книжка [chyekava-ya kneeshka] cheque/check book
человек [chyelavyek] person

челюсть f [chyelyoost] jaw
чем [chyem] than; what; by what
чём [chyom] what
чемодан [chyemadan] suitcase
чему [chyemoo] what; to what
через [chyeryes] through; across; in
через три дня [chyeryes tree dnya] in three days
чёрно-белый [chorna-byeli] black and white
Чёрное море [chorna-yeh moryeh] Black Sea
чёрный [chorni] black
честный [chyesni] honest
четверг [chyetvyerk] Thursday
четвёртый [chetvyorti] fourth
четверть f [chyetvyert] quarter
четверть часа [chyetvyert chasa] quarter of an hour
четверть второго [chyetvyert ftarova] quarter past one
без четверти два [byes chyetvyertee dva] quarter to two
четыре [chetiyryeh] four
четыреста [chyetiyryesta] four hundred
четырнадцатый [chetiyrnatsati] fourteenth
четырнадцать [chetiyrnatsat] fourteen
Чешская республика [chyeshska-ya ryespoobleeka] Czech Republic
чинить/починить [cheeneet/pacheeneet] to mend
число [cheeslo] date; number

чистить [cheesteet] to clean
чистый [cheesti] clean; pure
читать/прочитать [cheetat/ pracheetat] to read
что [shto] what; that
что-нибудь [shto-neeboot] anything
что-то [shto-ta] something
чувство [choostva] feeling
чувствовать [choostvavat] to feel
чувствовать себя [choostvavat syebya] to feel
чулки [choolkee] stockings
чуть [choot] hardly, scarcely; a little
чьё: чьё это? [cho eta?] whose is this?

Ш

шампунь m [shampoon] shampoo
шапка [shapka] hat (with flaps)
шариковая ручка [shareekava-ya roochka] ballpoint pen
шарф [sharf] scarf (neck)
шашлычная [shashliychna-ya] café selling kebabs
швейцар [shvyaytsar] porter; doorman
Швейцария [shvyaytsaree-ya] Switzerland
Швеция [shvyetsi-ya] Sweden
шевелиться/шевельнуться [shevyeleetsa/shevyelnootsa] to move; to stir
шезлонг [shezlonk] deckchair

шёл [shol] went; was going
шёлковый [sholkavi] silk
шерсть f [sherst] wool
шестнадцатый [shesnatsati] sixteenth
шестнадцать [shesnatsat] sixteen
шестой [shestoy] sixth
шесть [shest] six
шестьдесят [shesdyesyat] sixty
шестьсот [shes-sot] six hundred
шея [sheh-ya] neck
шина [shiyna] tyre
широкий [shirokee] wide
шить/сшить [shit/s-shit] to sew
шкаф [shkaf] cupboard; wardrobe, closet
школа [shkola] school
шла [shla] went; was going
шли [shlee] were going
шло [shlo] went; was going
шляпа [shlyapa] hat
шнурки [shnoorkee] shoelaces
шоколад [shakalat] chocolate
шорты [shorti] shorts
шоссе [shas-seh] highway
Шотландия [shatlandee-ya] Scotland
шотландский [shatlandskee] Scottish
штепсельная вилка [shtepsyelna-ya veelka] plug (electric)
штопор [shtopar] corkscrew
штраф [shtraf] fine
шум [shoom] noise
шумный [shoomni] noisy

шурин [shooreen]
brother-in-law (wife's brother)
шутка [shootka] joke

Щ

щётка [sh-chotka] brush

Э

экипаж [ekeepash] crew
эластичный [elasteechni]
elastic
электрический
[elyektreechyeskee] electric
электричество
[elyektreechyestva] electricity
электричка [elyektreechka]
suburban train
электронная почта
[elyektron-na-ya pochta]
electronic mail
Эстония [estonee-ya] Estonia
эт. floor
эта [eta] it (is); that; this; this
one
этаж [etash] floor; storey
первый этаж [pyervi etash]
ground floor, (US) first floor
эти [etee] these; those
этим [eteem] (by) this; (by)
this one; (to) these
этими [eteemee] (by) these
этих [eteeH] these; of these
это [eta] it (is); that; this (one)
этого [etava] (of) this; (of) this
one
этой [etI] this; this one; of this;
of this one; to this; to this

one; by this; by this one
этом [etam] this; this one
этому [etamoo] (to) this; (to)
this one
этот [etat] it (is); that; this;
this one
эту [etoo] this; this one

Ю

юбка [yoopka] skirt
ювелирные изделия
[yoovyeleerni-yeh eezdyelee-ya]
jewellery
ювелирный магазин
[yoovyeleerni magazeen]
jeweller's shop
юг [yook] south
к югу от [k yoogoo at] south of
Южная Африка [yooJna-ya
afreeka] South Africa
южный [yooJni] southern
юмор [yoomar] humour

Я

я [ya] I
явиться на регистрацию
[yaveetsa na ryegeestratsi-yoo] to
check in
яд [yat] poison
язык [yaziyk] tongue; language
Ялта [yalta] Yalta
январь m [yanvar] January
ярлык [yarliyk] label
ярмарка [yarmarka] fair;
market
ярус [yaroos] circle; tier
ясный [yasni] clear; obvious

Menu Reader:

Food

ESSENTIAL TERMS

bread хлеб [Hlyep]
butter масло [masla]
cup чашка [chashka]
dessert десерт [dyesyert]
fish рыба [riyba]
fork вилка [veelka]
glass стакан [stakan]
knife нож [nosh]
main course основное блюдо [asnavno-yeh blyooda]
meat мясо [myasa]
menu меню [myenyoo]
pepper перец [pyerets]
plate тарелка [taryelka]
salad салат [salat]
salt соль f [sol]
set menu комплексный обед [komplyeksni abyet]
soup суп [soop]
spoon ложка [loshka]
starter закуска [zakooska]
table стол [stol]

another ..., please ещё одно ..., пожалуйста [yesh-cho ... peeva, paJalsta]
excuse me! простите! [prasteetyeh!]
could I have the bill, please? счёт, пожалуйста [sh-chot, paJalsta]

абрикос [abreekos] apricot

азу [azoo] small pieces of meat in a savoury sauce

ананас [ananas] pineapple

антрекот [antryekot] entrecote steak

апельсин [apyelseen] orange

апельсиновое варенье [apyelseenava-yeh varyenyeh] marmalade

арахис [araHees] peanuts

арбуз [arboos] water melon

ассорти мясное [asartee myasno-yeh] assorted meats

ассорти рыбное [asartee riybna-yeh] assorted fish

баклажан [baklaJan] aubergine

банан [banan] banana

баранина [baraneena] mutton, lamb

баранина на вертеле [baraneena na vyertyelyeh] mutton grilled on a skewer

баранки [barankee] ring-shaped rolls

бараньи котлеты [baranee katlyeti] lamb chops

батон [baton] baguette

бекон [byekon] bacon

белый хлеб [byeli Hlyep] white bread

беф строганов [byef-stroganaf] beef Stroganoff

битки [beetkee] rissoles; hamburgers

битки из баранины [beetkee eez baranini] lamb meatballs

бифштекс [beefshteks] steak

бифштекс натуральный [beefshteks natooralni] fried or grilled steak

блинчики [bleencheekee] pancakes

блинчики с вареньем [bleencheekee svaryenyem] pancakes with jam

блины [bleeniy] buckwheat pancakes, blini

блины с икрой [bleeniy sikroy] blini with caviar

блины со сметаной [bleeniy sa smyetanı] blini with sour cream

блюда из птицы [blyooda ees pteetsi] poultry dishes

блюдо [blyooda] dish, course

бородинский хлеб [baradeenskee Hlyep] dark rye bread

борщ [borsh-ch] beef, beetroot and cabbage soup

брынза [briynza] sheep's cheese, feta

брюссельская капуста [bryoos-syelska-ya kapoosta] Brussels sprouts

бублик [boobleek] type of bagel

буженина с гарниром [booJeneena zgarneeram] cold boiled pork with vegetables

булки [boolkee] rolls

булочка [boolachka] roll

бульон [boolyon] clear meat soup, bouillon

бульон с пирожками [boolyon speerashkamee] clear meat

soup served with small
meat pies

бульон с фрикадельками
[bool**yon** sfreekad**e**lkamee]
clear soup with meatballs

бутерброд [booterb**r**ot]
sandwich

бутерброд с мясом [booterb**r**ot
sm**ya**sam] meat sandwich

бутерброд с сыром [booterb**r**ot
s-s**iy**ram] cheese sandwich

буханка [boo**н**anka] loaf

ванильный [van**ee**lni] vanilla

вареники [var**ye**neekee] curd
or fruit dumplings

варёный [var**yo**ni] boiled

варенье [var**ye**nyeh] jam,
preserve

ватрушка [vatr**oo**shka]
cheesecake

вермишель [vyermeesh**e**l]
vermicelli

вегетарианский [vyegyetaree-
anskee] vegetarian

ветчина [vyetch**ee**na] ham

взбитые сливки [vzb**ee**ti-yeh
sl**ee**fkee] whipped cream

винегрет [veenyegr**ye**t] Russian
vegetable salad: beetroot,
potatoes, onions, peas,
carrots and pickled
cucumbers in mayonnaise
or oil

виноград [veenagr**a**t] grapes

вишня [v**ee**shnya] sour
cherries

галушка [gal**oo**shka] Ukrainian
dumpling

гамбургер [g**a**mboorgyer]
hamburger

гарнир [garn**ee**r] vegetables

говядина [gav**ya**deena] beef

говядина отварная с хреном
[gav**ya**deena atvarna-ya
s**н**r**ye**nam] boiled beef with
horseradish

говядина тушёная [gav**ya**deena
toosh**o**na-ya] stewed beef

голубцы [gal**oo**ptsiy] cabbage
leaves stuffed with meat and
rice

горох [gar**o**н] peas

горошек [gar**o**shek] peas

горчица [garch**ee**tsa] mustard

горячие закуски [gar**ya**chee-yeh
zak**oo**skee] hot starters, hot
appetizers

горячий [gar**ya**chee] hot

грейпфрут [gr**a**ypfroot]
grapefruit

гренки [gr**ye**nkee] croutons

гренок [gr**ye**nak] toast

грецкие орехи [gr**ye**tskee-yeh
ar**ye**нee] walnut

гречка [gr**ye**chka] buckwheat

гречневая каша [gr**ye**chnyeva-
ya k**a**sha] buckwheat
porridge

грибы [greeb**iy**] mushrooms

грибы в сметане [greeb**iy**
fsmyet**a**nyeh] mushrooms in
sour cream

грибы маринованные [greeb**iy**
mareen**o**vani-yeh] marinated
mushrooms

груша [gr**oo**sha] pear

гуляш из говядины [gool**ya**sh

eez gav**ya**deeni] beef goulash

гусь [goos] goose

десерт [dyes**yert**] dessert

джем [djem] jam

дичь [deech] game

домашний [dam**a**shnee] home-made

домашняя птица [dam**a**shnya-ya pt**ee**tsa] poultry

дыня [d**i**ynya] melon

еда [yed**a**] food; meal

ежевика [yeJev**ee**ka] blackberries

жареная рыба [J**a**ryena-ya r**i**yba] fried fish

жареный [J**a**ryeni] grilled; fried; roast

жареный картофель [J**a**ryeni kart**o**fyel] fried potatoes

жареный на вертеле [J**a**ryeni na v**yer**tyel-yeh] grilled on a skewer

желе [Jel**yeh**] jelly

жир [Jiyr] lard

жульен [Jool**yen**] mushrooms or meat cooked with onions and sour cream

завтрак [z**a**ftrak] breakfast

закуска [zak**oo**ska] snack; starter, appetizer

закуски [zak**oo**skee] starters, appetizers

заливная рыба [zaleevn**a**-ya r**i**yba] fish in aspic

заливной [zaleevn**oy**] in aspic

замороженные продукты [zamar**o**Jen-ni-yeh prad**oo**kti]

frozen food

запеканка [zapyek**a**nka] baked pudding; shepherd's pie

запечённый [zapyech**o**nni] baked

зелёный горошек [zyel**yo**ni gar**o**shek] green peas

зелёный лук [zyel**yo**ni look] spring onions

зелёный салат [zyel**yo**ni sal**a**t] green salad

земляника [zyemlyan**ee**ka] wild strawberries

зразы [zr**a**zi] meat cutlets stuffed with rice, buckwheat or mashed potatoes

изделия из теста [eezd**ye**lee-ya ees t**ye**sta] pastry dishes

изюм [eez**yoo**m] sultanas; raisins

икра [eekr**a**] caviar

икра баклажанная [eekr**a** baklaJ**a**nna-ya] mashed fried aubergines with onions and tomatoes

икра зернистая [eekr**a** zyern**ee**sta-ya] fresh caviar

икра кетовая [eekr**a** k**ye**tova-ya] red caviar

индейка [eend**ya**yka] turkey

инжир [eenJ**iy**r] figs

кабачки [kabachk**ee**] courgettes

камбала [k**a**mbala] plaice

капуста [kap**oo**sta] cabbage

карп [karp] carp

карп с грибами [karp zgreeb**a**mee] carp with

mushrooms
картофель [kartofyel] potatoes
картофельное пюре
[kartofyelna-yeh pyooreh]
mashed potatoes
картофель с ветчиной и
шпиком [kartofyel
zvyetcheenoy ee shpeekam]
potatoes with ham and
bacon fat
картофель фри [kartofyel free]
chips, French fries
каша [kasha] porridge
каштан [kashtan] chestnut
кебаб [kebap] kebab
кекс [kyeks] fruit cake
кета [kyeta] Siberian salmon
кетчуп [kyetchoop] ketchup
кильки [keelkee] sprats
кисель [keesyel] thin fruit jelly
кисель из клубники [keesyel
ees kloobneekee] strawberry
jelly
кисель из чёрной смородины
[keesyel ees chornı smarodeeni]
blackcurrant jelly
кислая капуста [keesla-ya
kapoosta] sauerkraut
кислые щи [keesli-yeh sh-chee]
sauerkraut soup
клубника [kloobneeka]
strawberries
клюква [klyookva] cranberries
колбаса [kalbasa] salami
sausage
комплексный обед
[komplyeksni abyet] set menu
компот [kampot] stewed fruit
in a light syrup; compote

компот из груш [kampot eez
groosh] stewed pears
компот из сухофруктов
[kampot ees sooнa-frooktaf]
stewed dried fruit
консервы [kansyervi] tinned
foods
конфета [kanfyeta] sweet,
candy
копчёная колбаса [kapchona-ya
kalbasa] smoked sausage
копчёная сёмга [kapchona-ya
syomga] smoked salmon
копчёные свиные рёбрышки
[kapchoni-yeh sveeniy-yeh
ryobrishkee] smoked pork
ribs
копчёный [kapchoni] smoked
коржики [korjikee] shortbread
корица [kareetsa] cinnamon
котлета [katlyeta] cutlet;
burger; rissole
котлеты по-киевски [katlyeti
pa-kee-yefskee] chicken Kiev
котлеты с грибами [katlyeti
zgreebamee] steak with
mushrooms
кофейный [kafyayni] coffee-
flavoured; coffee
краб [krap] crab
крабовые палочки [krabavi-yeh
palachkee] crab sticks
красная икра [krasna-ya eekra]
red caviar
красная смородина [krasna-ya
smarodeena] redcurrants
креветки [kryevyetkee] prawns
крем [kryem] butter cream
кровь: с кровью [s krovyoo]

rare

кролик [kroleek] rabbit

кукуруза [kookoorooza] sweet corn

кулебяка [koolyebyaka] pie with meat, fish or vegetables

курица [kooreetsa] chicken

лапша [lapsha] noodles

лесные орехи [lyesniy-yeh aryeHee] hazelnuts

лимон [leemon] lemon

ломтик [lomteek] slice

лососина [lasaseena] smoked salmon

лосось [lasos] salmon

лук [look] onions

майонез [mI-anes] mayonnaise

макаронные изделия [makaron-ni-yeh eezdyelee-ya] pasta

макароны [makaroni] macaroni

малина [maleena] raspberries

мандарин [mandareen] mandarin; tangerine

манная каша [man-na-ya kasha] semolina

маргарин [margareen] margarine

маслины [masleeni] olives

масло [masla] butter; oil

мёд [myot] honey

медовый [myedovi] honey

меню [myenyoo] menu

мидии [meedee-ee] mussels

миндаль [meendal] almonds

моллюски [mal-lyooskee]

shellfish

молоко [malako] milk

молочный [malochni] milk; dairy

молочный кисель [malochni keesyel] milk jelly

морковь [markof] carrots

мороженое [maroJena-yeh] ice cream

мороженое малиновое [maroJena-yeh maleenava-yeh] raspberry ice cream

мороженое 'пломбир' [maroJena-yeh plambeer] ice cream

мороженое клубничное [maroJena-yeh kloobneechna-yeh] strawberry ice cream

мороженое молочное [maroJena-yeh malochna-yeh] dairy ice cream

мороженое молочное с ванилином [maroJena-yeh malochna-yeh svaneeleenam] vanilla dairy ice cream

мороженое шоколадное [maroJena-yeh shakaladna-yeh] chocolate ice cream

морская капуста [marska-ya kapoosta] sea kale

морские продукты [marskee-yeh pradookti] seafood

мука [mooka] flour

мясной [myasnoy] meat

мясной бульон [myasnoy boolyon] clear meat soup

мясо [myasa] meat

на вертеле [na vyertyelyeh] on a skewer

на вынос [na **vi**ynas] to take away, to go

национальные русские блюда [natsi-an**a**lni-yeh r**oo**skee-yeh bl**yoo**da) Russian national dishes

начинка [nach**ee**nka] filling

обед [ab**ye**t] lunch

овощи [**o**vash-chee] vegetables

овощной [avash-chn**oy**] vegetable

овощной суп [avash-chn**oy** soop] vegetable soup

огурец [agoor**ye**ts] cucumber

огурцы со сметаной [agoorts**iy** sa smyet**a**nl] cucumber with sour cream

окорок [**o**karak] gammon

окрошка [akr**o**shka] cold soup made with kvas, vegetables and meat

оладьи [al**a**dee] thick pancakes

оливки [al**ee**fkee] olives

омар [am**a**r] lobster

омлет [aml**ye**t] omelette

омлет натуральный [aml**ye**t nat**oo**ralni] plain omelette

омлет с ветчиной [aml**ye**t svyetcheen**oy**] ham omelette

орехи [ar**ye**Hee] nuts

осётр запечённый в сметане [as**yo**tr zapyech**o**ni fsmyet**a**nyeh] sturgeon baked in sour cream

осетрина заливная [asyetr**ee**na zaleevn**a**-ya] sturgeon in aspic

осетрина под белым соусом

[asyetr**ee**na pat b**ye**lim so-oosam] sturgeon in white sauce

осетрина с гарниром [asyetr**ee**na zgarn**ee**ram] sturgeon with vegetables

осетрина с пикантным соусом [asyetr**ee**na speek**a**ntnim so-oosam] sturgeon in piquant sauce

основное блюдо [asnavn**o**-yeh bl**yoo**da] main course

отбивная котлета [atbeevn**a**-ya katl**ye**ta] chop

отварная рыба [atvarn**a**-ya r**iy**ba] poached fish

отварной [atvarn**oy**] boiled; poached

отварной цыплёнок [atvarn**oy** tsiply**o**nak] boiled chicken

палтус [**pa**ltoos] halibut

панированный [paneer**o**vanni] in breadcrumbs

панированный цыплёнок [paneer**o**vanni tsiply**o**nak] chicken in breadcrumbs

паштет [pasht**ye**t] pâté; pie

пельмени [pyelm**ye**nee] type of ravioli

первое блюдо [p**ye**rva-yeh bl**yoo**da] first course

перец [p**ye**rets] pepper

персик [p**ye**rseek] peach

петрушка [pyetr**oo**shka] parsley

печёнка [pyech**o**nka] liver

печёный [pyech**o**ni] baked

печенье [pyech**ye**nyeh] biscuit,

cookie; pastry

печень трески в масле
[p**y**echyen tr**y**eskee vm**a**sl-yeh]
cod liver in oil

пирог [peer**o**k] pie; tart; cake

пирог с повидлом [peer**o**k
spav**ee**dlam] jam tart

пирог с мясом [peer**o**k
sm**ya**sam] meat pie

пирог с яблоками [peer**o**k
s**ya**blakamee] apple pie

пирожки [peerashk**ee**] pies

пирожки с капустой
[peerashk**ee** skap**oo**sti]
cabbage pies

пирожки с мясом [peerashk**ee**
sm**ya**sam] meat pies

пирожки с творогом
[peerashk**ee** stv**o**ragam]
cottage cheese pies

пирожное [peeroJna-yeh]
pastries; cake; pastry

пицца [p**ee**tsa] pizza

плавленый сыр [pl**a**vlyeni siyr]
processed cheese

плов [plof] pilaf

повидло [pav**ee**dla] jam

под белым соусом [pat b**ye**lim
s**o**-oosam] in white sauce

поджаренный [padJ**a**ryen-ni]
grilled; fried

поджаренный хлеб [padJ**a**ryen-
ni Hlyep] toast

под майонезом [pad mɪ-
an**e**zam] in mayonnaise

подсолнечное масло
[pats**o**lnyechna-yeh m**a**sla]
sunflower oil

пожарские котлеты [paJ**a**rskee-

yeh katl**ye**ti] minced chicken
patties

помидор [pameed**o**r] tomato

пончики [p**o**ncheekee]
doughnuts

порция [p**o**rtsi-ya] portion

почки [p**o**chkee] kidneys

приправа к салату [preepr**a**va k
sal**a**too] salad dressing

простокваша [prastakv**a**sha]
natural set yoghurt

пряник [pr**ya**neek]
gingerbread

пряность [pr**ya**nast] spice

птица [pt**ee**tsa] poultry

рагу из баранины [rag**oo** eez
bar**a**neeni] lamb ragout

рагу из говядины [rag**oo** eez
gav**ya**deeni] beef ragout

рак [rak] crayfish

рассол [ras-s**o**l] pickle

рассольник [ras-s**o**lneek] meat
or fish soup with pickled
cucumbers

ржаной хлеб [rJan**o**y Hlyep] rye
bread

рис [rees] rice

ромштекс с луком [r**o**mshteks
sl**oo**kam] rump steak with
onions

ростбиф с гарниром [r**o**stbeef
zgarn**ee**ram] roast beef with
vegetables

рубленое мясо [r**oo**blyena-yeh
m**ya**sa] minced meat

рубленые котлеты [r**oo**blyeni-
yeh katl**ye**ti] rissoles

рулет [rool**ye**t] meat and

potato roll; swiss roll

рулет из рубленой телятины
[rool**y**et eez **r**oo**b**lyenı
tyel**ya**teeni] minced veal roll

русская кухня [**r**ooska-ya
k**oo**Hnya] Russian cuisine

рыба [**r**iyba] fish

рыбные блюда [**r**iybni-yeh
bl**yoo**da] fish dishes

рыбный [**r**iybni] fish

ряженка [**rya**Jenka] fermented
baked milk, similar to thick
yoghurt

салат [sal**a**t] lettuce; salad

салат зелёный [sal**a**t zyel**yo**ni]
green salad

салат из картофеля [sal**a**t ees
kart**o**fyelya] potato salad

салат из лука [sal**a**t eez l**oo**ka]
spring onion salad

салат из огурцов [sal**a**t eez
agoorts**o**f] cucumber salad

салат из помидоров [sal**a**t ees
pameed**o**raf] tomato salad

салат из помидоров с
брынзой [sal**a**t ees
pameed**o**raf zbr**i**ynzı] tomato
salad with sheep's cheese

салат из редиски [sal**a**t eez
ryed**ee**skee] radish salad

салат из яблок [sal**a**t eez
yablak] apple salad

салат мясной [sal**a**t myasn**oy**]
meat salad

салат с крабами [sal**a**t
skr**a**bamee] crab salad

салат столичный [sal**a**t
stal**ee**chni] potato salad with

meat, carrots, peas and
mayonnaise

сало [s**a**la] salted pork fat,
sliced and eaten with rye
bread (Ukrainian)

самообслуживание [sama-
apsl**oo**Jivanee-yeh] self-service

сандвич [s**a**ndveech] sandwich

сардельки [sard**e**lkee] thick
frankfurters

сардины [sard**ee**ni] sardines

сардины в масле [sard**ee**ni
vm**a**slyeh] sardines in oil

сахар [s**a**Har] sugar

свежий [sv**ye**Ji] fresh

свёкла [sv**yo**kla] beetroot

свинина [sveen**ee**na] pork

свинина жареная с гарниром
[sveen**ee**na J**a**ryena-ya
zgarn**ee**ram] fried pork with
vegetables

свинина с квашеной капустой
[sveen**ee**na skv**a**shenı kap**oo**stı]
pork with sauerkraut

свиной [sveen**oy**] pork

свиные отбивные [sveen**iy**-yeh
atbeevn**iy**-yeh] pork chops

с гарниром [zgarn**ee**ram] with
vegetables

селёдка малосольная
[syel**yo**tka malas**o**lna-ya]
slightly salted herring

сельдь [syeld] herring

сёмга [s**yo**mga] salmon

скумбрия горячего копчения
[sk**oo**mbree-ya gar**ya**chyeva
kapch**ye**nee-ya] smoked
mackerel

скумбрия запечённая

[sk**oo**mbree-ya zapyech**o**na-ya]
baked mackerel

сладкий [sl**a**tkee] sweet

сладкое [sl**a**tka-yeh] dessert,
sweet course

слива [sl**ee**va] plum

сливки [sl**ee**fkee] cream

сливочное масло [sl**ee**vachna-
yeh m**a**sla] butter

с майонезом [smɪ-an**e**zam] with
mayonnaise

сметана [smyet**a**na] sour
cream

солёное печенье [sal**yo**na-yeh
pyech**ye**nyeh] savoury
biscuits

солёные огурцы [sal**yo**ni-yeh
ag**oo**rts**iy**] pickled cucumbers

солёные помидоры [sal**yo**ni-
yeh pameed**o**ri] pickled
tomatoes

солёный [sal**yo**ni] salty;
savoury; salted; pickled

соль [sol] salt

солянка [sal**ya**nka] spicy soup
made from fish or meat and
vegetables; stewed meat and
cabbage with spices

сосиски [sas**ee**skee]
frankfurters

соус [s**o**-oos] sauce

спаржа [sp**a**rJa] asparagus

с рисом [s r**ee**sam] with rice

стерлядь [st**ye**rlyat] small
sturgeon

студень [st**oo**dyen] meat jelly;
galantine; aspic

судак [s**oo**dak] pike-perch

судак в белом вине [s**oo**dak

vb**ye**lam veen-**yeh**] pike-perch
in white wine

судак жареный в тесте [s**oo**dak
Jar**ye**ni fty**e**styeh] pike-perch
fried in batter

суп [soop] soup

суп из свежих грибов [soop ees
sv**ye**Jih greeb**o**f] fresh
mushroom soup

суп картофельный [soop
kart**o**fyelni] potato soup

суп-лапша с курицей [soop
l**a**psha sk**oo**reetsay] chicken
noodle soup

суп мясной [soop myasn**oy**]
meat soup

суп с грибами [soop
zgreeb**a**mee] mushroom soup

суп томатный [soop tam**a**tni]
tomato soup

с хреном [sHr**ye**nam] with
horseradish sauce

сыр [siyr] cheese

сырник [s**iy**rneek] small
cheesecake; cottage cheese
pancake or fritter

сырой [sir**oy**] raw

творог [tvar**o**k] cottage cheese

телятина [tyel**ya**teena] veal

телячьи отбивные [tyel**ya**chee
atbeevn**iy**-yeh] veal chops

тесто [t**ye**sta] pastry; dough

тефтели с рисом [tyeft**ye**lee
sr**ee**sam] meatballs with rice

тмин [tmeen] thyme

томатный соус [tam**a**tni s**o**-oos]
tomato sauce

торт [tort] cake, gateau

травы [travi] herbs

треска [tryeska] cod

тунец [toonyets] tuna fish

тушёный [tooshoni] stewed

укроп [ookrop] dill

уксус [ooksoos] vinegar

устрицы [oostreetsi] oysters

утка [ootka] duck

уха [ooнa] fish soup

фаршированная рыба
[farshirovan-na-ya riyba]
stuffed fish

фаршированные помидоры
[farshirovan-ni-yeh pameedori]
stuffed tomatoes

фаршированный [farshirovan-
ni] stuffed

фасоль [fasol] French beans;
haricot beans

филе [filyeh] fillet

фирменные блюда [feermyen-
ni-yeh blooda] speciality
dishes

фисташки [feestashkee]
pistachio nuts

форель [faryel] trout

фрикадельки [freekadyelkee]
meatballs

фрикадельки из телятины в
соусе [freekadyelkee ees
tyelyateeni vso-oosyeh] veal
meatballs in gravy

фруктовое мороженое
[frooktova-yeh maroJena-yeh]
fruit ice cream

фрукты [frookti] fruit

харчо [Harcho] Georgian thick,
spicy mutton soup

хлеб [Hlyep] bread

холодной [Halodni] cold

холодные закуски [Halodni-yeh
zakooskee] cold starters,
cold appetizers

хорошо прожаренный
[Harasho praJaryen-ni] well-
done

хрен [Hryen] horseradish

хрустящий картофель
[Hroostyash-chee kartofyel]
crisps, (US) chips

цветная капуста [tsvyetna-ya
kapoosta] cauliflower

цыплёнок [tsiplyonak] chicken

цыплёнок в тесте [tsiplyonak
ftyestyeh] chicken in pastry

цыплёнок по-охотничьи
[tsiplyonak pa-aнotneechee]
chicken chasseur

цыплёнок 'табака' [tsiplyonak
tabaka] Georgian chicken
with garlic, grilled or fried

цыплёнок фрикасе [tsiplyonak
freekaseh] chicken fricassee

чахохбили [chaнoнbeelee]
Georgian-style chicken
casserole

черешня [cheryeshnya] sweet
cherries

чёрная смородина [chorna-ya
smarodeena] blackcurrants

черника [chyerneeka]
bilberries

чёрный перец [chorni pyeryets]
black pepper

чёрный хлеб [chorni Hlyep]

black bread, rye bread
чеснок [chyesn**o**k] garlic
чечевица [chyechyev**ee**tsa]
  lentils

шашлык [shashl**iy**k] kebab
шашлык из баранины
  [shashl**iy**k eez bar**a**neeni] lamb
  kebab
шашлык из свинины с рисом
  [shashl**iy**k ees sveen**ee**ni
  sr**ee**sam] pork kebab with
  rice
шницель [shn**ee**tsel] schnitzel
шницель с яичницей
  глазуньей [shn**ee**tsel sya-
  eeshneetsay glaz**oo**nyay]
  schnitzel with fried egg
шоколад [shakal**a**t] chocolate
шпинат [shpeen**a**t] spinach
шпроты [shpr**o**ti] sprats

щи [sh-chee] cabbage soup
щука [sh-ch**oo**ka] pike

эскалоп [eskal**o**p] escalope
эскимо [eskeem**o**] choc-ice

яблоко [y**a**blaka] apple
яблочный пирог [y**a**blachni
  peer**o**k] apple pie
язык [yaz**iy**k] tongue
яичница [ya-**ee**shneetsa] fried
  egg; omelette
яичница болтунья [ya-
  eeshneetsa balt**oo**nya]
  scrambled eggs
яичница глазунья [ya-
  eeshneetsa glaz**oo**nya] fried
  eggs
яйцо [y**iy**tso] egg

яйцо вкрутую [y**iy**tso fkroot**oo**-
  yoo] hard-boiled egg
яйцо всмятку [y**iy**tso fsm**ya**tkoo]
  soft-boiled egg
яйцо под майонезом [y**iy**tso pad
  mi-an**e**zam] egg mayonnaise

А
Б
В
Г
Д
Е
Ё
Ж
З
И
Й
К
Л
М
Н
О
П
Р
С
Т
У
Ф
Х
Ц
Ч
Ш
Щ
Ъ
Ы
Ь
Э
Ю
Я

Menu Reader:

Drink

ESSENTIAL TERMS

beer пиво [p**ee**va]

bottle бутылка [boot**i**ylka]

brandy коньяк [kan**ya**k]

coffee кофе m [k**o**fyeh]

cup чашка [ch**a**shka]

fruit juice фруктовый сок [fr**oo**kt**o**vi sok]

gin джин [djin]

gin and tonic джин с тоником [djin st**o**neekam]

glass стакан [st**a**k**a**n]

  (wine glass) бокал [b**a**k**a**l]

milk молоко [m**a**lak**o**]

mineral water минеральная вода [meenyer**a**lna-ya v**a**d**a**]

red wine красное вино [kr**a**sna-yeh veen**o**]

soda (water) газированная вода [gazeer**o**van-na-ya v**a**d**a**]

soft drink безалкогольный напиток [byezalkag**o**lni nap**ee**tak]

sugar сахар [s**a**Har]

tea чай m [chī]

tonic (water) тоник [t**o**neek]

vodka водка [v**o**tka]

water вода [v**a**d**a**]

whisky виски [v**ee**skee]

white wine белое вино [b**y**ela-yeh veen**o**]

wine вино [veen**o**]

wine list карта вин [k**a**rta veen]

another beer please ещё одно пиво, пожалуйста [yesh-ch**o** adn**o** p**ee**va, paЈ**a**lsta]

a cup of tea, please чашку чая, пожалуйста [ch**a**shkoo ch**a**-ya, paЈ**a**lsta]

a glass of ... стакан ... [st**a**k**a**n]

абрикосовый сок [abrekosavi sok] apricot juice

Акашени [akashenee] Georgian red wine

апельсиновый сок [apyelseenavi sok] orange juice

аперитив [apyereeteef] aperitif

Арарат® [ararat] brandy from Armenia

армянский коньяк [armyanskee kanyak] Armenian brandy

бальзам [balzam] alcoholic herbal drink flavoured with honey and fruit

безалкогольный напиток [byezalkagolni napeetak] soft drink

безо льда [byezalda] without ice

без сахара [byes saHara] without sugar

белое вино [byela-yeh veeno] white wine

Белый Аист® [byeli a-eest] brand of cognac

Боржоми® [barJomee] brand of mineral water

брют [bryoott] dry, brut

вермут [vyermoot] vermouth

вино [veeno] wine

виноградный сок [veenagradni sok] grape juice

виски [veeskee] whisky

вишнёвый сок [veeshnyovi sok] cherry juice

вода [vada] water

водка [votka] vodka

водка Зубровка® [votka zoobrofka] bison grass vodka

водка Лимонная® [votka leemon-na-ya] lemon vodka

водка Московская® [votka maskofska-ya] brand of vodka

водка Охотничья® [votka aHotneechya] hunter's vodka flavoured with juniper berries, ginger and cloves

водка Перцовка® [votka pyertsovka] pepper vodka

водка Старка® [votka starka] apple and pear-leaf vodka

водка Столичная® [votka staleechna-ya votka] brand of vodka

газированная вода [gazeerovan-na-ya vada] fizzy water

газированный [gazeerovan-ni] fizzy

горилка [gareelka] Ukrainian vodka

Гурджани [goordJanee] Georgian dry white wine

грузинское вино [groozeenska-yeh veeno] Georgian wine

джин [djin] gin

джин с тоником [djin stoneekom] gin and tonic

заварка [zavarka] strong leaf tea brew to which boiling water is added

игристое вино [eegreesta-yeh veeno] sparkling wine

А Ь Б В Г Д Е Ё Ж З И Й К Л М Н О П Р С Т У Ф Х Ц Ч Ш Щ Ъ Ы Ь Э Ю Я

какао [kaka-o] cocoa

карта вин [karta veen] wine list

квас [kvas] kvas – non-alcoholic drink made from fermented bread and water

кефир [kyefeer] sour yoghurt drink

Киндзмараули [kindzmara-oolee] Georgian red wine

кисель [keesyel] thickened fruit juice drink

клюквенный морс [klyookvyen-ni mors] cranberry drink

Кока-Кола® [koka-kola] Coca-Cola®

коктейль [kaktayl] cocktail

компот [kampot] fruit syrup drink with pieces of fresh or dried fruit

коньяк [kanyak] brandy

кофе [kofyeh] coffee

кофе по-турецки [kofyeh pa-tooryetskee] Turkish coffee

кофе с молоком [kofyeh smalakom] coffee with milk

красное вино [krasna-yeh veeno] red wine

креплёное вино [kryeplyona-yeh veeno] fortified wine

кумыс [koomiys] fermented drink made from mare's milk

лёд [lyot] ice; ice cubes

ликёр [leekyor] liqueur

лимон [leemon] lemon

лимонад [leemanat] lemonade

Массандра [mas-sandra] Crimean fortified wine

минеральная вода [meenyeralna-ya vada] mineral water

молоко [malako] milk

Московское® [maskofska-yeh] brand of bottled light ale

Мукузани [mookoozanee] Georgian red wine

напитки [napeetkee] drinks

напиток [napeetak] drink

Нарзан® [narzan] brand of mineral water

настойка [nastoyka] liqueur made from berries or other fruit

пиво [peeva] beer

пиво Балтика® [peeva balteeka] brand of bottled beer

пиво Жигулёвское пиво® [peeva Jigoolyofska-yeh] brand of bottled beer

пиво Очаковское® [peeva achakofska-yeh] brand of bottled beer

пиво Тверское [peeva tvyersko-yeh] dark beer

полусладкий [palooslatkee] medium-sweet

полусладкое вино [palooslatka-yeh veeno] medium-sweet wine

полусухое вино [poloosooно-yeh veeno] medium-dry wine

полусухой [poloosooноy] medium-dry

Пепси® [pepsee] Pepsi®

портвейн [portvyayn] port-style drink

растворимый кофе [rastvareemi kofyeh] instant coffee

ром [rom] rum

Саперави [sapyeravi] Georgian red wine

сахар [saHar] sugar

светлое пиво [svyetla-yeh peeva] lager

сладкий [slatkee] sweet

сладкое вино [slatka-yeh veeno] dessert wine

сливки [sleefkee] cream

с молоком [smalakom] with milk

сок [sok] juice

со льдом [saldom] with ice

с сахаром [s-saHaram] with sugar

столовое вино [stalova-yeh veeno] table wine

сухой [sooHoy] dry

томатный сок [tamatni sok] tomato juice

травяной чай [travyanoy chI] herbal tea

Фанта® Fanta®

Цинандали [tsinandalee] Georgian dry white wine

чай [chI] tea

чай с лимоном [chI sleemonam] lemon tea

чёрный кофе [chorni kofyeh] black coffee

шампанское [shampanska-yeh] champagne

яблочный сок [yablachni sok] apple juice

А Б В Г Д Е Ё Ж З И Й К Л М Н О П Р С Т У Ф Х Ц Ч Ш Щ Ъ Ы Ь Э Ю Я

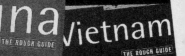

yoosh-chee] manager

уровень масла [**oo**ravyen m**a**sla] oil level

уродливый [oor**o**dleevi] ugly

урок [**oo**rok] lesson

уронить [ooran**ee**t] to drop

услышать [oosl**i**yshat] to hear

успех [oosp**ye**н] success

желаю успеха! [jel**a**yoo oospy**e**нa!] good luck!

успокойтесь! [oospak**oy**tyes!] calm down!

усталый [oost**a**li] tired

устройство [oostr**oy**stva] device

усы [oos**iy**] moustache

утонуть [ootan**oo**t] to drown

утро [**oo**tra] morning

утра [**oo**tra] in the morning; a.m.

в пять часов утра [f pyat chas**o**f o**o**tra] at 5 a.m.

утюг [ooty**oo**k] iron (for clothes)

ухо [**oo**нa] ear

уходить/уйти [ooнad**ee**t/ooyt**ee**] to go away

уходите! [ooнad**ee**tyeh!] go away!

учёт [ooch**o**t] stocktaking

учитель m [ooch**ee**tyel], учительница [oocheet**ye**lneetsa] teacher

учиться [ooch**ee**tsa] to learn; to study

Уэльс [oo-**e**ls] Wales

уэльский [oo-**e**lskee] Welsh

Ф

факс [faks] fax

факсимильный аппарат [fakseem**ee**lni apar**a**t] fax machine

фамилия [fam**ee**lee-ya] surname

фары [f**a**ri] headlights

февраль m [fyevr**a**l] February

фейерверк [fyay-yerv**ye**rk] fireworks

фен [fyen] hairdryer

ферма [f**ye**rma] farm

Финляндия [feenl**ya**ndee-ya] Finland

фиолетовый [fee-aly**e**tavi] purple

фирма [f**ee**rma] firm, company

флаг [flak] flag

фонарик [fan**a**reek] torch

фонтан [fant**a**n] fountain

фотоаппарат [fata-apar**a**t] camera

фотограф [fat**o**graf] photographer

фотографировать [fatagraf**ee**ravat] to take photos

фотография [fatagr**a**fee-ya] photograph

Франция [fr**a**ntsi-ya] France

французский [frants**oo**skee] French

французский язык [frants**oo**skee yaz**i**yk] French (language)

фрукты [fr**oo**kti] fruit

фунт [foont] pound

фуражка [foorashka] cap
фургон [foorgon] van
футбол [foodbol] football
футболка [foodbolka] T-shirt
футбольное поле [foodbolna-yeh polyeh] football pitch

X

халат [Halat] dressing gown
химчистка [Heemcheestka] dry-cleaner
хлеб [Hlyep] bread
хлопок [Hlopak] cotton
ходить [Hadeet] to go (on foot), to walk; to suit
хозяин [Hazya-een] owner; host
хозяйственный магазин [Hazylstvyen-ni magazeen] hardware store
хоккей [Hakyay] hockey
холм [Holm] hill
холодильник [Haladeelneek] fridge
холодный [Halodni] cold
холостяк [Halastyak] bachelor
хороший [Haroshi] good
хорошо [Harasho] well
  хорошо! [Harasho!] good!
  мне хорошо [mnyeh Harasho] I'm well
хотеть [Hatyet] to want
  я хотел/хотела [ya Hatyel/ Hatyela] I wanted (said by man/ woman)
  я хотел/хотела бы ... [ya Hatyel/Hatyela bi ...] I would like ... (said by man/woman)
хотим [Hateem] we want

хотите [Hateetyeh] you want
хотя [Hatya] although
хотят [Hatyat] they want
хочет [Hochyet] he wants; she wants; it wants
хочется: мне хочется ... [mnyeh Hochyetsa ...] I feel like ...
хочешь [Hochyesh] you want
хочу [Hachoo] I want
храбрый [Hrabri] brave
храните в сухом/прохладном/ тёмном месте [Hraneetyeh f sooHom/praHladnam/tyomnam myestyeh] keep in a cool/ dark/dry place
хранить [Hraneet] to keep; to preserve
хрустящий картофель [Hroostyash-chee kartofyel] crisps, (US) chips
художник [Hoodojneek] artist, painter
худой [Hoodoy] thin
худший [Hootshi] worst
хуже [Hoojeh] worse

Ц

царь m [tsar] tsar
цвет [tsvyet] colour
цветная плёнка [tsvyetna-ya plyonka] colour film
цветок [tsvyetok] flower
цветочный магазин [tsvyetochni magazeen] florist's, flower shop
цветы [tsvyetiy] flowers
целовать/поцеловать [tselavat/ patselavat] to kiss